D1241704

REPRINTS OF ECONOMIC CLASSICS

THE

THEORY OF POLITICAL ECONOMY

Also Published in

Reprints of Economic Classics

By W. STANLEY JEVONS

THE COAL QUESTION 1906

INVESTIGATIONS IN CURRENCY & FINANCE 1884

METHODS OF SOCIAL REFORM 1883

THE PRINCIPLES OF ECONOMICS 1905

THE THEORY

OF

POLITICAL ECONOMY

BY

W. STANLEY JEVONS

LL.D. (Edin.), M.A. (Lond.), F.R.S.

WITH PREFACE AND NOTES AND AN EXTENSION OF THE
BIBLIOGRAPHY OF MATHEMATICAL ECONOMIC WRITINGS

BY

H. STANLEY JEVONS, M.A., B.Sc., F.S.S.

PROFESSOR OF ECONOMICS AND POLITICAL SCIENCE IN THE UNIVERSITY COLLEGE
OF SOUTH WALES AND MONMOUTHSHIRE

FIFTH EDITION

REPRINTS OF ECONOMIC CLASSICS

Augustus M. Kelley, Bookseller
New York 1965

First Edition, 1871.
Second Edition, 1879.
Third Edition, 1888.
Fourth Edition, 1911.

Fifth edition 1957 by arrangement with H. Stanley Jevons.
Reprinted 1965.

Library of Congress Catalogue Card Number
65 - 18334

PRINTED IN THE UNITED STATES OF AMERICA
by SENTRY PRESS, NEW YORK, N. Y. 10019

PREFACE TO THE FIFTH EDITION

In writing the Preface to the fourth edition of the *Theory
of Political Economy* I ventured to predict that it would
be the last. That edition was in fact exhausted a few years
ago; but Messrs. Macmillan were unable to see their way
to reprint the book. I was glad therefore to have an offer
from the representative of an American firm to bring out
a new edition, for there is a continuing demand for the
Theory, which has found a place amongst the economic
classics of the nineteenth century.

Its appeal lies not merely in the Author's clarity and
freshness of diction, but in its combination of two previously
separate schools of thought — those favoring respectively
the psychological and the mathematical methods in economics. It is still a matter of controversy whether economics
should be regarded as a calculus of pleasure and pain or,
more correctly, of positive and negative feeling, or whether
it should be treated as the science of preferences in the
satisfaction of human wants. For myself, I believe that
those who refuse or neglect to study the psychological basis
of economics as one branch of the science of human behavior
are less likely than those who do so to arrive at sound conclusions tending in their applications to maximise human
happiness.

In the preface to the fourth edition I explained that it
had been my intention to continue my father's bibliography

of mathematico-economic writings by drawing up a bibliography of all books and articles of that kind published from 1880 to 1910; but that as the work was still very far from complete I had decided that the new edition should be issued without it. It was my intention that it should be published later as an independent volume.

Unfortunately, no sooner was the fourth edition published than I became deeply interested in housing reform in the mining valleys of South Wales, and in a few months had resigned from the chair of Economics and Political Science at Cardiff to devote my whole time to housing reform. In 1914, soon after the outbreak of war, I was appointed to the newly established research chair in economics in the University of Allahabad. From 1911 on, therefore, only spasmodic progress was made with the bibliography; and finally I gave up all hope of completing it, though I still have most of the cards.

The purpose of the intended bibliography has been partially served by the publication of *A Select Bibliography of Modern Economic Theory*, 1870 to 1929, edited by H. E. Batson, in the series of bibliographies issued by the London School of Economics. Mention may also be made of the bibliography of mathematico-economic writings prepared by Professor Irving Fisher and published first as an appendix to his article entitled *Cournot and Mathematical Economics* (*Quarterly Journal of Economics, January*, 1898), and later in his edition of Cournot's *Researches into the Mathematical Principles of the Theory of Wealth* (Economic Classics Series, 1927). Professor Fisher's bibliography is classified and annotated; and is probably an almost complete list of all published writings on economics of a mathematical character up to 1897. He did not add entries for the later years when reprinting the bibliography in 1927, for, as he wrote in the preface, the mathematical method was now so widely recognised as applicable to economics that the number of publications to be included in the bibliography would have been greatly increased and there was also less need to emphasize its importance.

In preparing the third edition of the *Theory*, my mother, with the assistance of Mr. Foxwell and others, continued the bibliography to 1888 and added a few titles which my father had not discovered. These later are shown in square brackets. When editing the fourth edition I omitted all titles dated after 1879 as it was my intention to include them in the separate bibliography mentioned above. As this omission may seem to have detracted somewhat from the value of the fourth edition, the part of the bibliography omitted from it is now restored, so that it appears exactly as in the third edition, except for the correction of a few printer's errors.

I close this preface with the hope that looking back to the development of the marginal theory in the nineteenth century will prove as stimulating to students of economics in the United States as in Britain, now that the *Theory of Political Economy* is once more available. I shall not venture to prophesy again as to whether this will be the last edition.

PREFACE TO THE FIRST EDITION

(1871)

THE contents of the following pages can hardly meet with ready acceptance among those who regard the Science of Political Economy as having already acquired a nearly perfect form. I believe it is generally supposed that Adam Smith laid the foundations of this science; that Malthus, Anderson, and Senior added important doctrines; that Ricardo systematised the whole; and, finally, that Mr. J. S. Mill filled in the details and completely expounded this branch of knowledge. Mr. Mill appears to have had a similar notion; for he distinctly asserts that there was nothing in the Laws of Value which remained for himself or any future writer to clear up. Doubtless it is difficult to help feeling that opinions adopted and confirmed by such eminent men have much weight of probability in their favour. Yet, in the other sciences this weight of authority has not been allowed to restrict the free examination of new opinions and theories; and it has often been ultimately proved that authority was on the wrong side.

There are many portions of Economical doctrine which appear to me as scientific in form as they are consonant with facts. I would especially mention the Theories of Population and Rent, the latter a theory of a distinctly mathematical character, which seems to give a clue to the correct mode of treating the whole science. Had Mr. Mill contented himself with asserting the unquestionable truth of the Laws of Supply and Demand, I should have agreed with him. As founded upon facts, those laws cannot be shaken by any theory; but it does not therefore follow that our conception of Value is perfect and final. Other generally accepted doctrines have always appeared to me purely delusive, especially the so-called Wage Fund Theory. This theory pretends to give a solution of the main problem of the science—to determine the wages of labour; yet, on close examination, its conclusion is found to be a mere truism, namely, that the average rate of wages is found by dividing the whole amount appropriated to the payment of wages by the number of those between whom it is divided. Some other supposed conclusions of the science are of a less harmless character, as, for instance, those regarding the advantage of exchange (see the section on "The Gain by Exchange," p. 142).

In this work I have attempted to treat Economy as a Calculus of Pleasure and Pain, and have sketched out, almost irrespective of previous opinions, the form which the science, as it seems to me, must ultimately take. I have long thought that as it deals throughout with quantities, it must be a mathematical science in matter if not in language. I have endeavoured to arrive at accurate quantitative notions concerning Utility, Value, Labour, Capital, etc., and I have often been surprised to find how clearly some of the most difficult notions, especially that most puzzling of notions *Value*, admit of mathematical analysis and expression. The Theory of Economy thus treated presents a close analogy to the science of Statical Mechanics, and the Laws of Exchange are found to resemble the Laws of Equilibrium of a lever as determined by the principle of virtual velocities. The nature of Wealth and Value is explained by the consideration of indefinitely small amounts of pleasure and pain, just as the Theory of Statics is made to rest upon the equality of indefinitely small amounts of energy. But I believe that dynamical branches of the Science of Economy may remain to be developed, on the consideration of which I have not at all entered.

Mathematical readers may perhaps think that I have explained some elementary notions, that of the Degree of Utility for instance, with unnecessary prolixity. But it is to the neglect of Economists to obtain clear and accurate notions of quantity and degree of utility that I venture to attribute the present difficulties and imperfections of the science;

and I have purposely dwelt upon the point at full length. Other readers will perhaps think that the occasional introduction of mathematical symbols obscures instead of illustrating the subject. But I must request all readers to remember that, as Mathematicians and Political Economists have hitherto been two nearly distinct classes of persons, there is no slight difficulty in preparing a mathematical work on Economy with which both classes of readers may not have some grounds of complaint.

It is very likely that I have fallen into errors of more or less importance, which I shall be glad to have pointed out ; and I may say that the cardinal difficulty of the whole theory is alluded to in the section of Chapter IV. upon the "Ratio of Exchange," beginning at p. 91 (that on "the Law of Indifference," p. 90 of this edition). So able a mathematician as my friend Professor Barker, of Owens College, has had the kindness to examine some of the proof sheets carefully ; but he is not, therefore, to be held responsible for the correctness of any part of the work.

My enumeration of the previous attempts to apply mathematical language to Political Economy does not pretend to completeness even as regards English writers ; and I find that I forgot to mention a remarkable pamphlet " On Currency " published anonymously in 1840 (London, Charles Knight and Co.) in which a mathematical analysis of the operations of the Money Market is attempted.   The method of treatment is not unlike that adopted by Dr. Whewell, to whose Memoirs a reference is made; but finite or occasionally infinitesimal differences are introduced. On the success of this anonymous theory I have not formed an opinion; but the subject is one which must some day be solved by mathematical analysis. Garnier, in his treatise on Political Economy, mentions several continental mathematicians who have written on the subject of Political Economy; but I have not been able to discover even the titles of their Memoirs.

PREFACE TO THE SECOND EDITION

(1879)

IN preparing this second edition certain new sections have been added, the most important of which are those treating of the *dimensions of economic quantities* (pp. 61-69, 83-84, 178-179, 233-235). The subject, of course, is one which lies at the basis of all clear thought about economic science. It cannot be surprising that many debates end in logomachy, when it is still uncertain how many meanings the word *value* has, or what kind of a quantity *utility* itself is. Imagine the mental state of astronomers if they could not agree among themselves whether *Right Ascension* was the name of a heavenly body, or a force or an angular magnitude. Yet this would not be worse than failing to ascertain clearly whether by value we mean a numerical ratio, or a mental state, or a mass of commodity. John Stuart Mill tells us explicitly [1] that " The value of a thing means the quantity of some other thing, or

[1] *Principles of Political Economy*, book iii. chap. vi. sec. i. 1. This definition occurs at the beginning of a carefully prepared summary of the principles of the theory of value.

of things in general, which it exchanges for." It might of course be explained that Mill did not intend what he said; but as the statement stands it makes value into a thing, and is just as philosophic as if one were to say, "Right Ascension means the planet Mars, or planets in general."

These sections upon the dimensions of economic quantities have caused me great perplexity, especially as regards the relation between utility and time (pp. 64-69). The theory of capital and interest also involves some subtleties. I hope that my solutions of the questions raised will be found generally correct; but where they do not settle a question, they may sometimes suggest one which other writers may answer. A correspondent, Captain Charles Christie, R.E., to whom I have shown these sections after they were printed, objects reasonably enough that commodity should not have been represented by M, or Mass, but by some symbol, for instance Q, which would include quantity of space or time or force, in fact almost any kind of quantity. Services often involve time, or force exerted, or space passed over, as well as mass. In this objection I quite concur, and I must therefore request the reader either to interpret M with a wider meaning than is given to it in p. 64, or else mentally to substitute another symbol.

In treating the dimensions of interest, I point out the curious fact that so profound a mathematician as the late Dean Peacock went quite astray upon the subject (pp. 250-253). Other new sections are those in which I introduce the idea of negative and approximately zero value, showing that negative value may be brought under the forms of the equations of exchange without any important modification. Readers of Mr. Macleod's works are of course familiar with the idea of negative value ; but it was desirable for me to show how important it really is, and how naturally it falls in with the principles of the theory. I may also draw attention to the section (pp. 102-106) in which I illustrate the mathematical character of the equations of exchange by drawing an exact analogy between them and the equations applying to the equilibrium of the lever.

Two or three correspondents, especially Herr Harald Westergaard of Copenhagen, have pointed out that a little manipulation of the symbols, in accordance with the simple rules of the differential calculus, would often give results which I have laboriously argued out. The whole question is one of maxima and minima, the mathematical conditions of which are familiar to mathematicians. But, even if 1 were capable of presenting the subject in the concise symbolic style satisfactory to the taste of a practised mathematician, I should prefer in an essay of this kind to attain my results by a course of argument which is not only fundamentally true, but is clear and convincing to many readers who, like myself, are not skilful and professional mathematicians. In short, I do not write for mathematicians, nor as a mathematician, but as an economist wishing to convince

other economists that their science can only be satisfactorily treated on an explicitly mathematical basis.
When mathematicians recognise the subject as one
with which they may usefully deal, I shall gladly
resign it into their hands. I have expressed a feeling
in more than one place that the whole theory might
probably have been put in a more general form by
treating labour as a negative utility, and thus bringing
it under the ordinary equations of exchange. But
the fact is there is endless occupation for an economist
in developing and improving his science, and I have
found it requisite to reissue this essay, as the biblio-
poles say, " with all faults." I have, however,
carefully revised every page of the book, and have
reason to hope that little or no real error remains in
the doctrines stated. The faults are in the form
rather than the matter.

Among minor alterations, I may mention the
substitution for the name Political Economy of the
single convenient term *Economics*. I cannot help
thinking that it would be well to discard, as quickly
as possible, the old troublesome double-worded name
of our Science. Several authors have tried to introduce totally new names, such as Plutology, Chrematistics, Catallactics, etc. But why do we need anything better than Economics? This term, besides
being more familiar and closely related to the old
term, is perfectly analogous in form to *Mathematics*,
Ethics, *Æsthetics*, and the names of various other
branches of knowledge, and it has moreover the

authority of usage from the time of Aristotle. Mr.
Macleod is, so far as I know, the re-introducer of the
name in recent years, but it appears to have been
adopted also by Mr. Alfred Marshall at Cambridge.
It is thus to be hoped that *Economics* will become
the recognised name of a science, which nearly a
century ago was known to the French Economists
as *la science économique.* Though employing the
new name in the text, it was obviously undesirable
to alter the title-page of the book.

When publishing a new edition of this work,
eight years after its first appearance, it seems natural
that I should make some remarks upon the changes
of opinion about economic science which have taken
place in the interval. A remarkable discussion has
been lately going on in the reviews and journals concerning the logical method of the science, touching
even the question whether there exists any such
science at all. Attention was drawn to the matter
by Mr. T. E. Cliffe Leslie's remarkable article[1] " On
the Philosophical Method of Political Economy," in
which he endeavours to dissipate altogether the deductive science of Ricardo. Mr. W. T. Thornton's
writings have a somewhat similar tendency. The
question has been further stirred up by the admirable
criticism to which it was subjected in the masterly
address of Professor J. K. Ingram, at the last meeting

---

[1] *Hermathena*, No. iv., 1876, pp. 1-32. Republished in Mr.
Leslie's collected *Essays in Political and Moral Philosophy*, Dublin,
1879, pp. 216-242.

of the British Association. This Address has been reprinted in several publications [1] in England, and has been translated into the chief languages of Western Europe. It is evident, then, that a spirit of very active criticism is spreading, which can hardly fail to overcome in the end the prestige of the false old doctrines. But what is to be put in place of them? At the best it must be allowed that the fall of the old orthodox creed will leave a chaos of diverse opinions. Many would be glad if the supposed science collapsed altogether, and became a matter of history, like astrology, alchemy, and the occult sciences generally. Mr. Cliffe Leslie would not go quite so far as this, but would reconstruct the science in a purely inductive or empirical manner. Either it would then be a congeries of miscellaneous disconnected facts, or else it must fall in as one branch of Mr. Spencer's Sociology. In any case, I hold that *there must arise a science of the development of economic forms and relations.*

But as regards the fate of the deductive method, I disagree altogether with my friend Mr. Leslie; he is in favour of simple deletion; I am for thorough reform and reconstruction. As I have previously explained,[2] the present chaotic state of Economics

---

[1] *Journal of the London Statistical Society*, December 1878, vol. xli. pp. 602-629. *Journal of the Statistical and Social Inquiry Society of Ireland*, August 1878, vol. vii. Appendix. Also as a separate publication, Longmans, London, 1878.

[2] "The Future of Political Economy," *Fortnightly Review*, November 1876, vol. viii., N.S., pp. 617-631. Translated in the *Journal des Économistes*, March 1877, 3me Série, vol. xlv., p. 325.

arises from the confusing together of several branches
of knowledge.   Subdivision is the remedy.   We
must distinguish the empirical element from the
abstract theory, from the applied theory, and from
the more detailed art of finance and administration.
Thus will arise various sciences, such as commercial
statistics, the mathematical theory of economics,
systematic and descriptive economics, economic sociology, and fiscal science.   There may even be a kind
of cross subdivision of the sciences; that is to say,
there will be division into branches as regards the
subject, and division according to the manner of
treating the branch of the subject.   The manner may
be theoretical, empirical, historical, or practical; the
subject may be capital and labour, currency, banking, taxation, land tenure, etc.—not to speak of the
more fundamental division of the science as it treats
of consumption, production, exchange, and distribution of wealth.   In fact, the whole subject is so
extensive, intricate, and diverse, that it is absurd to
suppose it can be treated in any single book or in
any single manner.   It is no more one science than
statics, dynamics, the theory of heat, optics, magneto-
electricity, telegraphy, navigation, and photographic
chemistry are one science.   But as all the physical
sciences have their basis more or less obviously in the
general principles of mechanics, so all branches and
divisions of economic science must be pervaded by
certain general principles.   It is to the investigation
of such principles—to the tracing out of the mechanics

of self-interest and utility, that this essay has been devoted. The establishment of such a theory is a necessary preliminary to any definite drafting of the superstructure of the aggregate science.

Turning now to the theory itself, the question is not so much whether the theory given in this volume is true, but whether there is really any novelty in it. The exclusive importance attributed in England to the Ricardian School of Economists, has prevented almost all English readers from learning the existence of a series of French, as well as a few English, German, or Italian economists, who had from time to time treated the science in a more or less strictly mathematical manner. In the first edition (pp. 14-18), I gave a brief account of such writings of the kind as I was then acquainted with; it is from the works there mentioned, if from any, that I derived the idea of investigating Economics mathematically. To Lardner's *Railway Economy* I was probably most indebted, having been well acquainted with that work since the year 1857. Lardner's book has always struck me as containing a very able investigation, the scientific value of which has not been sufficiently estimated; and in chapter xiii. (pp. 286-296, etc.) we find the Laws of Supply and Demand treated mathematically and illustrated graphically.

In the preface to the first edition (p. xi),[1] I remarked that in his treatise on Political Economy, M. Joseph Garnier mentioned several continental

[1] See p. ix of this edition.

mathematicians who had written on the subject of
Economics, and I added that I had not been able to
discover even the titles of their memoirs. This, however, must have been the result of careless reading
or faulty memory, for it will be found that Garnier
himself[1] mentions the titles of several books and
memoirs. The fact is that, writing as I did then at a
distance from any large library, I made no attempt to
acquaint myself with the literature of the subject,
little thinking that it was so copious and in some
cases so excellent as is now found to be the case.
With the progress of years, however, my knowledge
of the literature of political economy has been much
widened, and the hints of friends and correspondents
have made me aware of the existence of many remarkable works which more or less anticipate the views
stated in this book. While preparing this new
edition, it occurred to me to attempt the discovery of
all existing writings of the kind. With this view I
drew up a chronological list of all the mathematico-
economic works known to me, already about seventy
in number, which list, by the kindness of the editor,
Mr. Giffen, was printed in the *Journal of the London
Statistical Society* for June 1878 (vol. xli. pp. 398-
401), separate copies being forwarded to the leading
economists, with a request for additions and corrections. My friend, M. Léon Walras, Rector of the
Academy of Lausanne, after himself making considerable additions to the list, communicated it to

---

[1] *Traité d'Économie Politique*, 5ᵐᵉ éd., Paris, 1863, pp. 700-2.

the *Journal des Économistes* (December 1878), to the editor of which we are much indebted for its publication. Copies of the list were also sent to German and Italian economical journals. For the completion of the bibliographical list I am under obligations to Professor W. B. Hodgson, Professor Adamson, Mr. W. H. Brewer, M.A., H.M. Inspector of Schools, the Baron d'Aulnis de Bourouill, Professor of Political Economy at Utrecht, M. N. G. Pierson of Amsterdam, M. Vissering of Leiden, Professor Luigi Cossa of Pavia, and others.

All reasonable exertions have thus been made to render complete and exhaustive the list of mathematico-economic works and papers, which is now printed in the first [now fifth] Appendix to this book (pp. 322-339). It is hardly likely that many additions can be made to the earlier parts of the lists, but I shall be much obliged to any readers who can suggest corrections or additions. I shall also be glad to be informed of any new publications suitable for insertion in the list. On the other hand, it is possible that some of the books mentioned in the list ought not to be there. I have not been able in all cases to examine the publications myself, so that some works inserted at the suggestion of correspondents may have been named under misconception of the precise purpose of the list. Economic works, for instance, containing numerical illustrations and statistical facts numerically expressed, however abundantly, have not been intentionally included, unless there was also mathe-

matical method in the reasoning. Without this
condition the whole literature of numerical commercial statistics would have been imported into
my list. In other cases only a small portion of a
book named can be called mathematico-economic;
but this fact is generally noted by the quotation of
the chapters or pages in question. The tendency,
however, has been to include rather than to exclude,
so that the reader might have before him the whole
field of literature requiring investigation.

To avoid misapprehension it may be well to
explain that the ground for inserting any publication or part of a publication in this list, is its containing *an explicit recognition of the mathematical
character of economics, or the advantage to be attained
by its symbolical treatment.* I contend that all economic writers must be mathematical so far as they
are scientific at all, because they treat of economic
quantities, and the relations of such quantities,
and all quantities and relations of quantities come
within the scope of the mathematics. Even those
who have most strongly and clearly protested against
the recognition of their own method, continually
betray in their language the quantitative character
of their reasonings. What, for instance, can be more
clearly mathematical in matter than the following
quotation from Cairnes's chief work:[1]—"We can
have no difficulty in seeing how cost in its principal

---

[1] *Some Leading Principles of Political Economy Newly Expounded,*
pt. 1, chap. iii. p. 97.

elements is to be computed. In the case of labour, the cost of producing a given commodity will be represented by the number of average labourers employed in its production—regard at the same time being had to the severity of the work and the degree of risk it involves—multiplied by the duration of their labours. In that of abstinence, the principle is analogous : the sacrifice will be measured by the quantity of wealth abstained from, taken in connection with the risk incurred, and multiplied by the duration of the abstinence." Here we deal with computation, multiplication, degree of severity, degree of risk, quantity of wealth, duration, etc., all essentially mathematical things, ideas, or operations. Although my esteemed friend and predecessor has in his preliminary chapter expressly abjured my doctrines, he has unconsciously adopted the mathematical method in all but appearance.

We might easily go further back, and discover that even the father of the science, as he is often considered, is thoroughly mathematical. In the fifth chapter of the First Book of the *Wealth of Nations*, for instance, we find Adam Smith continually arguing about " quantities of labour," " measures of value," " measures of hardship," " proportion," " equality," etc. ; the whole of the ideas in fact are mathematical. The same might be said of almost any other passages from the scientific parts of the treatise, as distinguished from the historical parts. In the first chapter of the Second Book (29th paragraph), we read—" The produce of land, mines, and fisheries, when their natural fertility is equal, is in proportion to the extent and proper application of the capitals employed about them. When the capitals are equal, and equally well applied, it is in proportion to their natural fertility." Now every use of the word *equal* or *equality* implies the existence of a mathematical equation ; an equation is simply an equality ; and every use of the word proportion implies a ratio expressible in the form of an equation.

I hold, then, that to argue mathematically, whether correctly or incorrectly, constitutes no real differentia as regards writers on the theory of economics. But it is one thing to argue and another thing to understand and to recognise explicitly the method of the argument. As there are so many who talk prose without knowing it, or, again, who syllogise without having the least idea what a syllogism is, so economists have long been mathematicians without being aware of the fact. The unfortunate result is that they have generally been bad mathematicians, and their works must fall. Hence the explicit recognition of the mathematical character of the science was an almost necessary condition of any real improvement of the theory. It does not follow, of course, that to be explicitly mathematical is to ensure the attainment of truth, and in such writings as those of Canard and Whewell, we find plenty of symbols and equations with no result of value, owing to the fact that they simply translated into symbols the doctrines obtained, and erroneously obtained, without their use.   Such writers misunderstood and inverted altogether the function of mathematical symbols, which is to guide our thoughts in the slippery and complicated processes of reasoning. Ordinary language can usually express the first axioms of a science, and often also the matured results ; but only in the most lame, obscure, and tedious way can it lead us through the mazes of inference.

The bibliographical list, of which I am speaking, is no doubt a very heterogeneous one, and may readily be decomposed into several distinct classes of economic works.   In a first class may be placed the writings of those economists who have not at all attempted mathematical treatment in an express or systematic manner, but who have only incidentally acknowledged its value by introducing symbolic or graphical statements.   Among such writers may be mentioned especially Rau (1868), Hagen (1844), J. S. Mill (1848), and Courcelle-Seneuil (1867).   Many readers may be surprised to hear that John Stuart Mill has used mathematical symbols ; but, on turning to Book III., chapters xvii. and xviii., of the *Principles of Political Economy*, those difficult and tedious chapters in which Mill leads the reader through the Theory of International Trade and International Values, by means of yards of linen and cloth, the reader will find that Mill at last yields, and expresses himself concisely and clearly [1] by means of equations between m, n, p, and q.   His mathematics

[1] Book iii. chap. xviii. sec. 7.

are very crude; still there is some approach to a correct mathematical treatment, and the result is that these chapters, however tedious and difficult, will probably be found the truest and most enduring parts of the whole treatise.

A second class of economists contains those who have abundantly employed mathematical apparatus, but, misunderstanding its true use, or being otherwise diverted from a true theory, have built upon the sand. Misfortunes of this kind are not confined to the science of economics, and in the most exact branches of physical science, such as mechanics, molecular physics, astronomy, etc., it would be possible to adduce almost innumerable mathematical treatises, which must be pronounced nonsense. In the same category must be placed the mathematical writings of such economists as Canard (1801), Whewell (1829, 1831, and 1850), Esmenard du Mazet (1849 and 1851), and perhaps Du Mesnil-Marigny (1860).

The third class forms an antithesis with the second, for it contains those authors who, without any parade of mathematical language or method, have nevertheless carefully attempted to reach precision in their treatment of quantitative ideas, and have thus been led to a more or less complete comprehension of the true theory of utility and wealth. Among such writers Francis Hutcheson, the Irish founder of the great Scotch School, and the predecessor of Adam Smith at Glasgow, probably stands first. His employment of mathematical symbols [1] seems rather crude and premature, but the precision of his ideas about the estimation of quantities of good and evil is beyond praise. He thoroughly anticipates the foundations of Bentham's moral system, showing that the Moment of Good or Evil is, in a compound proportion of the Duration and Intenseness, affected also by the Hazard or uncertainty of our existence.[2] As to Bentham's ideas, they are adopted as the starting-point of the theory given in this work, and are quoted at the beginning of chapter ii. (pp. 28-9). Bentham has repeated his statement as to the mode of measuring happiness in several different works and pamphlets, as for instance in that remarkable one called " A Table of the Springs of Action " (London, 1817, p. 3); and also in the " Codification Proposal, addressed by Jeremy Bentham to all Nations professing Liberal Opinions " (London, 1822, pp. 7-11). He here speaks explicitly of the application of *arithmetic* to questions of utility, meaning no doubt the application of mathematical methods. He even describes (p. 11) the four circumstances governing the value of a pleasure or pain as the *dimensions* of its value, though he is incorrect in treating *propinquity* and *certainty* as dimensions.

It is worthy of notice that Destutt de Tracy, one of the most philosophic of all economists, has in a few words recognised the true method of treatment,

---

[1] 1720. Hutcheson. *An Inquiry,* 1729, etc., pp. 186-198.

[2] 1728. Hutcheson. *An Essay,* etc., pp. 34-43, and elsewhere.

though he has not followed up his own idea. Referring to the circumstances which, in his opinion, render
all economic and moral calculations very delicate, he
says,[1] " On ne peut guère employer dans ces matières
que des considérations tirées de la théorie des limites."
So well known an English economist as Malthus has
also shown in a few lines his complete appreciation of
the mathematical nature of economic questions. In
one of his excellent pamphlets[2] he remarks, " Many
of the questions, both in morals and politics, seem to
be of the nature of the problems *de maximis et
minimis* in Fluxions; in which there is always a
point where a certain effect is the greatest, while on
either side of this point it gradually diminishes."
But I have not thought it desirable to swell the
bibliographical list by including all the works in
which there are to be found brief or casual remarks
of the kind.

I may here remark that all the writings of Mr.
Henry Dunning Macleod exhibit a strong tendency
to mathematical treatment. Some of his works or
papers in which this mathematical spirit is most
strongly manifested have been placed in the list. It
is not my business to criticise his ingenious views, or

---

[1] *Élémens d'Ideologie*, ive et v^e Parties. *Traité de la Volonté et
de ses effets*, Paris, 1815, 8vo, p. 499. Edition of 1826, p. 335.
American Edition, *A Treatise on Political Economy, translated from the
unpublished French original.* Georgetown, D.C., 1817, p. xiii.

[2] *Observations on the Effects of the Corn Laws, and of a rise or fall in
the price of Corn on the Agriculture and General Wealth of the Country.*
London, 1814, p. 30 ; 3rd ed., 1815, p. 32.

to determine how far he really has created a mathematical system.   While I certainly differ from him on many important points, I am bound to acknowledge the assistance which I derive from the use of several of his works.

In the fourth and most important class of mathematico-economic writers must be placed those who have consciously and avowedly attempted to frame a mathematical theory of the subject, and have, if my judgment is correct, succeeded in reaching a true view of the Science.   In this class certain distinguished French philosophers take precedence and priority.   One might perhaps go back with propriety to Condillac's work, *Le Commerce et le Gouvernement*, first published in the year 1776, the same year in which the *Wealth of Nations* appeared.   In the first few chapters of this charming philosophic work we meet perhaps the earliest distinct statement of the true connection between value and utility.   The book, however, is not included in the list because there is no explicit attempt at mathematical treatment.   It is the French engineer Dupuit who must probably be credited with the earliest perfect comprehension of the theory of utility.   In attempting to frame a precise measure of the utility of public works, he observed that the utility of a commodity not only varies immensely from one individual to another, but that it is also widely different for the same person according to circumstances.   He says, " nous verrions que l'utilité du morceau de pain peut croître pour le même individu depuis zéro jusqu'au chiffre de sa fortune entière" (1849, Dupuit, *De l'influence des Péages*, etc., p. 185). He establishes, in fact, a theory of the *gradation of utility*, beautifully and perfectly expounded by means of geometrical diagrams, and this theory is undoubtedly coincident in essence with that contained in this book. He does not, however, follow his ideas out in an algebraic form. Dupuit's theory was the subject of some controversy in the pages of the *Annales des Ponts et Chaussées*, but did not receive much attention elsewhere, and I am not aware that any English economist ever knew anything about these remarkable memoirs.

The earlier treatise of Cournot, his admirable *Recherches sur les principes mathématiques de la théorie des richesses* (Paris, 1838), resembles Dupuit's memoirs in being, until within the last few years, quite unknown to English economists. In other respects Cournot's method is contrasted to Dupuit's. Cournot did not frame any ultimate theory of the ground and nature of utility and value, but, taking the palpable facts known concerning the relations of price, production and consumption of commodities, he investigated these relations analytically and diagraphically with a power and felicity which leaves little to be desired. This work must occupy a remarkable position in the history of the subject. It is strange that it should have remained for me among Englishmen to discover its value. Some years since (1875) Mr. Todhunter wrote to me

as follows : " I have sometimes wondered whether
there is anything of importance in a book published
many years since by M. A. A. Cournot, entitled
*Recherches sur les principes mathématiques de la
théorie des richesses.* I never saw it, and when I
have mentioned the title, I never found any person
who had read the book. Yet Cournot was eminent
for mathematics and metaphysics, and so there may
be some merit in this book." I procured a copy of
the work as far back as 1872, but have only recently
studied it with sufficient care to form any definite
opinion upon its value. Even now I have by no
means mastered all parts of it, my mathematical
power being insufficient to enable me to follow
Cournot in all parts of his analysis. My impression
is that the first chapter of the work is not remarkable ; that the second chapter contains an important
anticipation of discussions concerning the proper
method of treating prices, including an anticipation
(p. 21) of my logarithmic method of ascertaining
variations in the value of gold ; that the third
chapter, treating of the conditions of the foreign
exchanges, is highly ingenious if not particularly
useful ; but that by far the most important part of
the book commences with the fourth chapter upon
the " Loi du débit." The remainder of the book, in
fact, contains a wonderful analysis of the laws of
supply and demand, and of the relations of prices,
production, consumption, expenses and profits.
Cournot starts from the assumption that the débit or

demand for a commodity is a function of the price, or $D = F(p)$; and then, after laying down empirically a few conditions of this function, he proceeds to work out with surprising power the consequences which follow from those conditions. Even apart from its economic importance, this investigation, so far as I can venture to judge it, presents a beautiful example of mathematical reasoning, in which knowledge is apparently evolved out of ignorance. In reality the method consists in assuming certain simple conditions of the functions as conformable to experience, and then disclosing by symbolic inference the implicit results of these conditions. But I am quite convinced that the investigation is of high economic importance, and that, when the parts of political economy to which the theory relates come to be adequately treated, as they never have yet been, the treatment must be based upon the analysis of Cournot, or at least must follow his general method. It should be added that his investigation has little relation to the contents of this work, because Cournot does not recede to any theory of utility, but commences with the phenomenal laws of supply and demand.

Discouraged apparently by the small amount of attention paid to his mathematical treatise, Cournot in a later year (1863) produced a more popular non-symbolic work on Economics; but this later work does not compare favourably in interest and importance with his first treatise.

English economists can hardly be blamed for their

ignorance of Cournot's economic works when we find French writers equally bad. Thus the authors of Guillaumin's excellent *Dictionnaire de l'Économie Politique*, which is on the whole the best work of reference in the literature of the science, ignore Cournot and his works altogether, and so likewise does Sandelin in his copious *Répertoire Général d'Économie Politique*. M. Joseph Garnier in his otherwise admirable text-book[1] mixes up Cournot with far inferior mathematicians, saying: "Dans ces derniers temps M. Esmenard du Mazet, et M. du Mesnil-Marigny ont aussi fait abus, ce nous semble, des formules algébriques; les Recherches sur les Principes Mathématiques des Richesses de M. Cournot, ne nous ont fourni aucun moyen d'élucidation." Mac-Culloch of course knows nothing of Cournot. Mr. H. D. Macleod has the merit at least of mentioning Cournot's work, but he misspells the name of the author, and gives only the title of the book, which he had probably never seen.

We now come to a truly remarkable discovery in the history of this branch of literature. Some years since my friend Professor Adamson had noticed in one of Kautz's works on Political Economy[2] a brief reference to a book said to contain a theory of pleasure and pain, written by a German author named Hermann Heinrich Gossen. Although he had advertised for it, Professor Adamson was unable to

[1] *Traité d'Économie Politique*, cinquième édition, p. 701.
[2] *Theorie und Geschichte der National-Oekonomik*, 1858, vol. i. p. 9.

obtain a sight of this book until August 1878, when he fortunately discovered it in a German bookseller's catalogue, and succeeded in purchasing it. The book was published at Brunswick in 1854; it consists of 278 well-filled pages, and is entitled, *Entwickelung der Gesetze des menschlichen Verkehrs, und der daraus fliessenden Regeln für menschliches Handeln*, which may be translated—"Development of the laws of Human Commerce, and of the consequent Rules of Human Action." I will describe the contents of this remarkable volume as they are reported to me by Professor Adamson.

Gossen evidently held the highest possible opinion of the importance of his own theory, for he commences by claiming honours in economic science equal to those of Copernicus in astronomy. He then at once insists that mathematical treatment, being the only sound one, must be applied throughout; but, out of consideration for the reader, the higher analysis will be explicitly introduced only when it is requisite to determine maxima and minima. The treatise then opens with the consideration of Economics as the theory of pleasure and pain, that is as the theory of the procedure by which the individual and the aggregate of individuals constituting society, may realise the maximum of pleasure with the minimum of painful effort. The natural law of pleasure is then clearly stated, somewhat as follows: *Increase of the same kind of consumption yields pleasure continuously diminishing*

up to the point of satiety.   This law he illustrates
geometrically, and then proceeds to investigate the
conditions under which the total pleasure from one
or more objects may be raised to a maximum.

The term *Werth* is next introduced, which may,
Professor Adamson thinks, be rendered with strict
accuracy as *utility*, and Gossen points out that the
quantity of utility, material or immaterial, is measured
by the quantity of pleasure which it affords.   He
classifies useful objects as : (1) those which possess
pleasure-giving powers in themselves ; (2) those which
only possess such powers when in combination with
other objects ; (3) those which only serve as means
towards the production of pleasure-giving objects.
He is careful to point out that there is no such thing
as absolute utility, utility being purely a relation
between a thing and a person.   He next proceeds to
give the derivative laws of utility somewhat in the
following manner :—That separate portions of the
same pleasure-giving object have very different degrees
of utility, and that in general for each person only
a limited number of such portions has utility ; any
addition beyond this limit is useless, but the point of
uselessness is only reached after the utility has gone
through all the stages or degrees of intensity.   Hence
he draws the practical conclusion that each person
should so distribute his resources as to render the
final increments of each pleasure-giving commodity
of equal utility for him.

In the next place Gossen deals with labour,

starting from the proposition that the utility of any product must be estimated after deduction of the pains of labour required to produce it. He describes the variation of the pain of labour much as I have done, exhibiting it graphically, and inferring that we must carry on labour to the point at which the utility of the product equals the pain of production. In treating the theory of exchange he shows how barter gives rise to an immense increase of utility, and he infers that exchange will proceed up to the point at which the utilities of the portions next to be given and received are equal. A complicated geometrical representation of the theory of exchange is given. The theory of rent is investigated in a most general manner, and the work concludes with somewhat vague social speculations, which, in Professor Adamson's opinion, are of inferior merit compared with the earlier portions of the treatise.

From this statement it is quite apparent that Gossen has completely anticipated me as regards the general principles and method of the theory of Economics. So far as I can gather, his treatment of the fundamental theory is even more general and thorough than what I was able to scheme out. In discussing the book, I lie under the serious difficulty of not being able to read it ; but, judging from what Professor Adamson has written or read to me, and from an examination of the diagrams and symbolic parts of the work, I should infer that Gossen has been unfortunate in the development of his theory.

Instead of dealing, as Cournot and myself have done, with undetermined functions, and introducing the least possible amount of assumption, Gossen assumed, for the sake of simplicity, that economic functions follow a linear law, so that his curves of utility are generally taken as straight lines. This assumption enables him to work out a great quantity of precise formulas and tabular results, which fill many pages of the book. But, inasmuch as the functions of economic science are seldom or never really linear, and usually diverge very far from the straight line, I think that the symbolic and geometric illustrations and developments introduced by Gossen must for the most part be put down among the many products of misplaced ingenuity. I may add, in my own behalf, that he does not seem really to reach the equations of exchange as established in this book; that the theory of capital and interest is wanting; and that there is a total absence of any resemblance between the working out of the matter, except such as arises from a common basis of truth.

The coincidence, however, between the essential ideas of Gossen's system and my own is so striking, that I desire to state distinctly, in the first place, that I never saw nor so much as heard any hint of the existence of Gossen's book before August 1878, and to explain, in the second place, how it was that I did not do so. My unfortunate want of linguistic power has prevented me, in spite of many attempts, from ever becoming familiar enough with German to

read a German book. I once managed to spell out
with assistance part of the logical lecture notes of
Kant; but that is my sole achievement in German
literature. Now this work of Gossen has remained
unknown even to most of the great readers of
Germany. Professor Adamson remarks that the
work seems to have attracted no attention in
Germany. The eminent and learned economist of
Amsterdam, Professor N. G. Pierson, writes to me:
" Gossen's book is totally unknown to me. Roscher
does not mention it in his very laborious *History of
Political Economy in Germany.* I never saw it
quoted; but I will try to get it. It is very curious
that such a remarkable work has remained totally
unknown even to a man like Professor Roscher, who
has read everything." Mr. Cliffe Leslie, also, who
has made the German Economists his special study,
informs me that he was quite unaware of the existence of the book.[1] Under such circumstances it
would have been far more probable that I should
discover the theory of pleasure and pain, than that
I should discover Gossen's book, and I have carefully
pointed out, both in the first edition and in this,
certain passages of Bentham, Senior, Jennings, and
other authors, from which my system was, more or
less consciously, developed. I cannot claim to be

---

[1] A copy of Gossen's book will be found in the Library of the
British Museum (Press mark 8408. cc. 16). It was not acquired by
that institution until May 24, 1865, as shown by the date stamped
upon the copy.

totally indifferent to the rights of priority ; and from the year 1862, when my theory was first published in brief outline, I have often pleased myself with the thought that it was at once a novel and an important theory.   From what I have now stated in this preface it is evident that novelty can no longer be attributed to the leading features of the theory.   Much is clearly due to Dupuit, and of the rest a great share must be assigned to Gossen.   Regret may easily be swallowed up in satisfaction if I succeed eventually in making that understood and valued which has been so sadly neglected.

Almost nothing is known to me concerning Gossen ; it is uncertain whether he is living or not. On the title-page he describes himself as " königlich preussischem Regierungs - Assessor ausser Dienst," which may be translated " Royal Prussian Government Assessor, retired " ; but the tone of his remarks here and there seems to indicate that he was a disappointed if not an injured man.   The reception of his one work can have lent no relief to these feelings ; rather it must much have deepened them.   The book seems to have contained his one cherished theory ; for I can find under the name of Gossen no trace of any other publication or scientific memoir whatever.   The history of these forgotten works is, indeed, a strange and discouraging one ; but the day must come when the eyes of those who cannot see will be opened.   Then will due honour be given to all who like Cournot and Gossen have laboured in a thankless field of human knowledge, and have met with the neglect or ridicule they might well have expected. Not indeed that such men do really work for the sake of honour; they bring forth a theory as the tree brings forth its fruit.

It remains for me to refer to the mathematico-economic writings of M. Léon Walras, the Rector of the Academy of Lausanne. It is curious that Lausanne, already distinguished by the early work of Isnard (1781), should recently have furnished such important additions to the science as the Memoirs of Walras. For important they are, not only because they complete and prove that which was before published elsewhere in the works described above, but because they contain a third or fourth independent discovery of the principles of the theory. If we are to trace out "the filiation of ideas" by which M. Walras was led to his theory, we should naturally look back to the work of his father, Auguste Walras, published at Paris in 1831, and entitled *De la nature de la richesse, et de l'origine de la valeur*. In this work we find, it is true, no distinct recognition of the mathematical method, but the analysis of value is often acute and philosophic. The principal point of the work moreover is true, that value depends upon *rarity*—"La valeur," says Auguste Walras, "dérive de la rareté." Now it is precisely upon this idea of the degree of rarity of commodities that Léon Walras bases his system. The fact that some four or more independent writers such as Dupuit, Gossen, Walras, and myself should in such different ways have reached substantially the same views of the fundamental ideas of economic science, cannot but lend great probability, not to say approximate certainty, to those views.   I am glad to hear that M. Walras intends to bring out a new edition of his Mathematico-Economic Memoirs, to which the attention of my readers is invited.   The titles of his publications will be found in the Appendix I. [V. of this edition].

The works of Von Thünen and of several other German economists contain mathematical investigations of much interest and importance.   A considerable number of such works will be found noted in the list, which, however, is especially defective as regards German literature.   I regret that I am not able to treat this branch of the subject in an adequate manner.

My bibliographical list shows that in recent years, that is to say since the year 1873, there has been a great increase in the number of mathematico-economic writings.   The names of Fontaneau, Walras, Avigdor, Lefèvre, Petersen, Boccardo, recur time after time.   In such periodicals as the *Journal des Actuaires français*, or the *National-Oekonomisk Tidsskrift*—a journal so creditable to the energy and talent of the Danish Economic School—the mathematical theory of Economics is treated as one of established interest and truth, with which readers would naturally be acquainted.   In England we have absolutely no periodical in which such discussions could be conducted. The reader will not fail to remark that it is into the hands of French, Italian, Danish, or Dutch writers that this most important subject is rapidly passing. They will develop that science which only excites ridicule and incredulity among the followers of Mill and Ricardo. There are just a few English mathematicians, such as Fleeming Jenkin, George Darwin, Alfred Marshall, or H. D. Macleod, and one or two Americans like Professor Simon Newcomb, who venture to write upon the obnoxious subject of mathematico-economic science. I ought to add, however, that at Cambridge (England) the mathematical treatment of Economics is becoming gradually recognised owing to the former influence of Mr. Alfred Marshall, now the Principal of University College, Bristol, whose ingenious mathematico-economic problems, expounded *more geometrico*, have just been privately printed at Cambridge.

If we overlook Hutcheson, who did not expressly write on Economics, the earliest mathematico-economic author seems to be the Italian Ceva, whose works have just been brought to notice in the *Giornale degli Economisti* (see 1878, Nicolini). Ceva wrote in the early part of the eighteenth century, but I have as yet no further information about him. The next author in the list is the celebrated Beccaria, who printed a very small, but distinctly mathematical, tract on Taxation as early as 1765. Italians were

thus first in the field. The earliest English work of
the kind yet discovered is an anonymous *Essay on
the Theory of Money*, published in London in 1771,
five years before the era of the *Wealth of Nations*.
Though crude and absurd in some parts, it is not
devoid of interest and ability, and contains a distinct
and partially valid attempt to establish a mathematical theory of currency. This remarkable Essay
is, so far as I know, wholly forgotten and almost lost
in England. Neither MacCulloch nor any other
English economist known to me, mentions the work.
I discovered its existence a few months ago by acci-
dentally finding a copy on a bookseller's stall. But
it shames an Englishman to learn that English
works thus unknown in their own country are known
abroad, and I owe to Professor Luigi Cossa, of the
University of Pavia, the information that the Essay
was written by Major-General Henry Lloyd, an author
of some merit in other branches of literature. Signor
Cossa's excellent *Guido alla studio di Economia
Politica*, a concise but judiciously written text-book,
is well qualified to open our eyes as to the insular
narrowness of our economic learning. It is a book
of a kind much needed by our students of Economics, and I wish that it could be published in
an English dress.

From this bibliographical survey emerges the
wholly unexpected result, that the mathematical
treatment of Economics is coeval with the science
itself. The notion that there is any novelty or

originality in the application of mathematical methods or symbols must be dismissed altogether. While there have been political economists there has always been a certain number who with various success have struck into the unpopular but right path. The unfortunate and discouraging aspect of the matter is the complete oblivion into which this part of the literature of Economics has always fallen, oblivion so complete that each mathematico-economic writer has been obliged to begin almost *de novo*. It is with the purpose of preventing for the future as far as I can such ignorance of previous exertions, that I have spent so much pains upon this list of books.

I should add that in arranging the list I have followed, very imperfectly, the excellent example set by Professor Mansfield Merriman, of the Sheffield Scientific School of Yale College, in his " List of Writings relating to the Method of Least Squares." [1] Such bibliographies are of immense utility, and I hope that the time is nearly come when each student of a special branch of science or literature will feel bound to work out its bibliography, unless, of course, the task shall have been already accomplished. The reader will see that, in Appendix II. [IV. of this edition], I have taken the liberty of working out also a part of the bibliography of my own writings.

Looking now to the eventual results of the theory, I must beg the reader to bear in mind that this book was never put forward as containing a systematic

---

[1] *Transactions of the Connecticut Academy*, 1877, vol. iv. pp. 151-232.

view of Economics.   It treats only of the theory, and
is but an elementary sketch of elementary principles.
The working out of a complete system based on these
lines must be a matter of time and labour, and I
know not when, if ever, I shall be able to attempt it.
In the last chapter, I have, however, indicated the
manner in which the theory of wages will be affected.
This chapter is reprinted almost as it was written in
1871 ; since then the wage-fund theory has been
abandoned by most English Economists, owing to the
attacks of Mr. Cliffe Leslie, Mr. Shadwell, Professor
Cairnes, Professor Francis Walker, and some others.
Quite recently more extensive reading and more
careful cogitation have led to a certain change in my
ideas concerning the superstructure of Economics—in
this wise :

Firstly, I am convinced that the doctrine of
wages, which I adopted in 1871, under the impression that it was somewhat novel, is not really novel
at all, except to those whose view is bounded by the
maze of the Ricardian Economics.   The true doctrine
may be more or less clearly traced through the
writings of a succession of great French Economists,
from Condillac, Baudeau, and Le Trosne, through
J.-B. Say, Destutt de Tracy, Storch, and others, down
to Bastiat and Courcelle-Seneuil.   The conclusion to
which I am ever more clearly coming is that the only
hope of attaining a true system of Economics is to
fling aside, once and for ever, the mazy and preposter-
ous assumptions of the Ricardian School.   Our English

Economists have been living in a fool's paradise. The truth is with the French School, and the sooner we recognise the fact, the better it will be for all the world, except perhaps the few writers who are too far committed to the old erroneous doctrines to allow of renunciation.

Although, as I have said, the true theory of wages is not new as regards the French School, it is new, or at any rate renewed, as regards our English Schools of Economics. One of the first to treat the subject from the right point of view was Mr. Cliffe Leslie, in an article first published in *Fraser's Magazine* for July 1868, and subsequently reprinted in a collection of Essays.[1] Some years afterwards Mr. J. L. Shadwell independently worked out the same theory of wages which he has fully expounded in his admirable *System of Political Economy*.[2] In Hearn's *Plutology*, however, as pointed out in the text of this book (pp. 271-273), we find the same general idea that wages are the share of the produce which the laws of supply and demand enable the labourer to secure. It is probable that like ideas might be traced in other works were this the place to attempt a history of the subject.

Secondly, I feel sure that when, casting ourselves free from the Wage-Fund Theory, the Cost of Production doctrine of Value, the Natural Rate of

---

[1] "Land Systems and Industrial Economy of Ireland, England, and Continental Countries." London, 1870. Appendix, pp. 357-379.

[2] London, 1877, Trübner.

Wages, and other misleading or false Ricardian doctrines, we begin to trace out clearly and simply the
results of a correct theory, it will not be difficult to
arrive at a true doctrine of wages.   This will probably
be reached somewhat in the following way:—We must
regard labour, land, knowledge, and capital as conjoint
conditions of the whole produce, not as causes each of
a certain portion of the produce.   Thus in an elementary state of society, when each labourer owns all
the three or four requisites of production, there would
really be no such thing as wages, rent, or interest at
all.   Distribution does not arise even in idea, and the
produce is simply the aggregate effect of the aggregate
conditions.   It is only when separate owners of the
elements of production join their properties, and
traffic with each other, that distribution begins, and
then it is entirely subject to the principles of value
and the laws of supply and demand.   Each labourer
must be regarded, like each landowner and each
capitalist, as bringing into the common stock one
part of the component elements, bargaining for the
best share of the produce which the conditions of
the market allow him to claim successfully.   In
theory the labourer has a monopoly of labour of each
particular kind, as much as the landowner of land,
and the capitalist of other requisite articles.   Property is only another name for monopoly.   But when
different persons own property of exactly the same
kind, they become subject to the important Law of
Indifference, as I have called it (pp. 90-93), namely,

that in the same open market, at any one moment, there cannot be two prices for the same kind of article. Thus *monopoly is limited by competition*, and no owner, whether of labour, land, or capital, can, theoretically speaking, obtain a larger share of produce for it than what other owners of exactly the same kind of property are willing to accept.

So far there may seem to be nothing novel in this view; it is hardly more than will be found stated in a good many economic works. But as soon as we begin to follow out this simple view, the consequences are rather startling. We are forced, for instance, to admit that rates of wages are governed by the same formal laws as rents. This view is not new to the readers of Storch, who in the third book of his excellent *Cours d'Economie Politique* has a chapter [1] "De la Rente des talens et des qualités morales." But it is a very new doctrine to one whose economic horizon is formed by Mill and Fawcett, Ricardo and Adam Smith. Even Storch has not followed out the doctrine thoroughly; for he applies the idea of rent only to cases of *eminent* talent. It must be evident, however, that talent and capacity of all kinds are only a question of degree, so that, according to the Law of Continuity, the same principle must apply to all labourers.

A still more startling result is that, so far as cost of production regulates the values of commodities, wages must enter into the calculation on exactly the

[1] Chap. v. vol. i. p. 304.

same footing as rent.   Now it is a prime point of the Ricardian doctrines that rent does not enter into cost of production.   As J. S. Mill says,[1] " Rent, therefore, forms no part of the cost of production which determines the value of agricultural produce."   And again,[2] " Rent is not an element in the cost of production of the commodity which yields it ; except in the cases," etc.   Rent in fact is represented as the effect not the cause of high value ; wages on the contrary are treated as the cause, not the effect.   But if rent and wages be really phenomena subject to the same formal laws, this opposite relation to value must involve error. The way out of the difficulty is furnished by the second sentence of the paragraph from which the last quotation was taken.   Mill goes on to say : " But when land capable of yielding rent in agriculture is applied to some other purpose, the rent which it would have yielded is an element in the cost of production of the commodity which it is employed to produce."   Here Mill edges in as an exceptional case that which proves to be the rule, reminding one of other exceptional cases described as " Some peculiar cases of value" (see p. 197 below), which I have shown to include almost all commodities.

Now Mill allows that when land capable of yielding rent in agriculture is applied to some other purpose, the rent which would have been produced

---

[1] *Principles of Political Economy*, book iii. chap. v. sec. 2, paragraph 3.

[2] *Ibid.* book iii. chap. vi. sec. 1, article 9.

in agriculture is an element in the cost of production
of other commodities. But wherefore this distinction
between agriculture and other branches of industry?
Why does not the same principle apply between two
different modes of agricultural employment? If land
which has been yielding £2 per acre rent as pasture
be ploughed up and used for raising wheat, must not
the £2 per acre be debited against the expenses of the
production of wheat? Suppose that somebody introduced the beetroot culture into England with a view
to making sugar; this new branch of industry could
not be said to pay unless it yielded, besides all other
expenses, the full rents of the lands turned from other
kinds of culture. But if this be conceded, the same
principle must apply generally; a potato-field should
pay as well as a clover-field, and a clover-field as a
turnip-field; and so on. The market prices of the
produce must adjust themselves so that this shall in
the long run be possible. The rotation of crops, no
doubt, introduces complication into the matter, but
does not modify the general reasoning. The principle
which emerges is that *each portion of land should
be applied to that culture or use which yields the
largest total of utility, as measured by the value
of the produce*; if otherwise applied there will
be loss. Thus the rent of land is determined by
the excess of produce in the most profitable
employment.

But when the matter is fully thought out, it will
be seen that exactly the same principle applies to

wages. A man who can earn six shillings a day in one employment will not turn to another kind of work unless he expects to get six shillings a day or more from it. There is no such thing as absolute cost of labour; it is all matter of comparison. Every one gets the most which he can for his exertions; some can get little or nothing, because they have not sufficient strength, knowledge, or ingenuity; others get much, because they have, comparatively speaking, a monopoly of certain powers. Each seeks the work in which his peculiar faculties are most productive of utility, as measured by what other people are willing to pay for the produce. Thus wages are clearly the effect not the cause of the value of the produce. But when labour is turned from one employment to another, the wages it would otherwise have yielded must be debited to the expenses of the new product. Thus the parallelism between the theories of rent and wages is seen to be perfect in theory, however different it may appear to be in the details of application. Precisely the same view may be applied, *mutatis mutandis*, to the rent yielded by fixed capital, and to the interest of free capital. In the last case, the Law of Indifference peculiarly applies, because free capital, loanable for a certain interval, is equally available for all branches of industry; hence, at any moment and place, the interest of such capital must be the same in all branches of trade.

I ought to say that Mill, as pointed out to me by Professor Adamson, has a remarkable section at the end of chapter v. of Book III. of the *Principles*, in which he explains that all inequalities, artificial or natural, give rise to extra gains of the nature of Rent. This section is a very satisfactory one inasmuch as it tends to support the view on which I am now insisting, a view, however, which, when properly followed out, will overthrow many of the principal doctrines of the Ricardo-Mill Economics. Those who have studied Mill's philosophic character as long and minutely as I have done, will not for a moment suppose that the occurrence of this section in Mill's book tends to establish its consistency with other portions of the same treatise.

But of course I cannot follow out the discussion of this matter in a mere preface. The results to be expected are partly indicated in my *Primer of Political Economy*, but in that little treatise my remarks upon the Origin of Rent (p. 94), as originally printed in the first edition, were erroneous, and the section altogether needs to be rewritten. When at length a true system of Economics comes to be established, it will be seen that that able but wrong-headed man, David Ricardo, shunted the car of Economic science on to a wrong line—a line, however, on which it was further urged towards confusion by his equally able and wrong-headed admirer, John Stuart Mill. There were Economists, such as Malthus and Senior, who had a far better comprehension of the true doctrines (though not free from the Ricardian errors), but they were driven out of the field by the unity and influence of the Ricardo-

Mill school. It will be a work of labour to pick up the fragments of a shattered science and to start anew, but it is a work from which they must not shrink who wish to see any advance of Economic Science.

THE CHESTNUTS,
HAMPSTEAD HEATH, N.W.
May, 1879.

PREFACE TO THE THIRD EDITION

(1888)

THE present edition of the *Theory of Political Economy* is an exact reprint of the second edition, with the exception of the first Appendix containing the bibliographical list of mathematico-economic books. I desired to add to that list several books which it had been my husband's intention to include in the next edition, and when I consulted my friend, Mr. H. S. Foxwell, he advised me to continue it up to the present date. I am greatly indebted to the kindness of those friends who have enabled me to accomplish this; and amongst others my thanks are especially due to the Rev. P. H. Wicksteed, Professor F. Y. Edgeworth, and Professor Harald Westergaard of Copenhagen, for the trouble they have taken in revising proofs for me, as well as in supplying me with the titles of those books which ought to be included. We have endeavoured to follow the rules which Mr. Jevons has laid down in the preface to the second edition, and though the list is probably not complete, I hope that no work of importance has been omitted.

A few books published during my husband's lifetime, but which were, I believe, unknown to him, are now included, but I have enclosed them within brackets. I have also marked the place at which the additional list prepared by himself ends.

HARRIET A. JEVONS.

August, 1888.

PREFACE TO THE FOURTH EDITION

In preparing a new edition of this work, I had to keep in mind two facts: first, that it is still read by a large number of students for the sake of its exposition of some of the fundamental principles of economics which are not as yet more adequately treated in any other book in the English language; and secondly, that it is already in some sense a classic. An occasional alteration of the text, and some explanation of difficult passages, seemed desirable for the assistance of the student; but the interest of the book as the first important English attempt to develop a system of economics from a basis of psychological facts, and by the mathematical method, prescribed a faithful reprint of the text as the author himself left it. I have adhered so far to the latter course, that, with the exception of a few slight changes of punctuation, designed more readily to exhibit the sense, there are practically no alterations of the text. The very few which I have permitted myself are such as were needed to correct obvious slips, save one (p. 263, line 1) which was indicated by the author himself in his copy of the second edition. On the other hand, wherever a short footnote could render the author's meaning clearer, or could correct one of the few slight errors which I have discovered, I have not hesitated to insert it, always distinguishing the new footnotes with the mark—[Ed.].

The appendixes I have felt at liberty to treat more freely than the text, and they now embrace three new ones. The first appendix is an attempt to elucidate my father's treatment of the theory of interest, the truth and originality of which have not, I think, been widely enough appreciated, owing to the perplexity caused by his omission to make his assumptions clear and to interpret his result in concrete terms. I can only hope that my view of his meaning will be endorsed by others who may look into his statement of the theory once more.

In Appendix II. I have printed a fragment of MS. on Capital and Interest which I found amongst my father's notes intended for his *Principles of Economics.* Somehow it escaped publication in the volume devoted to the fragments of the Principles, but it seemed to me sufficiently original and complete to be worth preserving in permanent form.

Appendix III. is inserted for its historic interest, being a reprint of the author's first statement of his newly devised mathematical theory of economics. He read this paper at the meeting of the British Association at Cambridge in 1862, and an abstract of it was printed in the Report of the Association for that year. The paper was afterwards printed in full in the *Journal of the Statistical Society* for 1866 ; but both publications failed to attract attention. According to one of my father's MS. notes, which I have been lucky enough to discover, the publication of the *Theory of Political Economy* might have been delayed considerably later than 1871 had it not been for the appearance in 1868 and 1870 of articles by Professor Fleeming Jenkin (see Appendix V.) which are distinctly mathematical in method and contain a number of very ingenious geometrical diagrams illustrating the laws of supply and demand. My father in this note mentions that Professor Jenkin had opened a correspondence with him on the subject of the mathematical treatment of economics and the use of curves, and that this was followed by the publication of the latter's " Graphic Representation of the Laws of Supply and Demand," and concludes: " Partly in consequence of this I was led to write and publish the *Theory* in 1871."

Appendix IV. contains the author's bibliography of his own writings on economic subjects, which has been amplified and brought up to date to include recent new editions of his works.

The fifth Appendix contains Professor Jevons's own list of mathematico-economic writings, with the addition of a few books unknown to him which are enclosed in square brackets. It will be noticed that it has been enlarged by valuable notes on the contents of many of the books. The MS. of these notes in my father's hand I found in a box with letters and other notes referring to the mathematical treatment of economics. Whether they were prepared merely for his own use in writing the preface to the second edition ; or whether, having intended to publish them with his bibliography in the second edition, he rejected them as too lengthy ; or whether he was waiting to complete his notes for a third edition, or some separate publication, I do not know. They are evidence of the enthusiasm and labour which he devoted to the subject, and can hardly fail to be of use to future students to whom access to the original papers may often be difficult.

It was my intention to continue my father's work by drawing up a bibliography of all books, articles, and published writings of any kind which have appeared from 1880 to 1910 inclusive, so far as I was able to discover them, to form a sixth appendix. Living as I do without access to any good library, the work proceeded slowly ; and the decision to produce a classified bibliography, which entailed reading a good part of many papers, further retarded matters. Mathematical works on economics have happily become so numerous that a mere list of them without indication of their contents would be of little use.

For convenience in searching periodicals, I adopted the rule of including all papers dealing with economic theory by the graphic or symbolic methods, and those only ; but a few other books and articles not employing any mathematical mode of expression were to be included on the ground that their subject matter is dealt with in a manner amply recognising the quantitative character of the science. Although several hundreds of card entries have been made and classified, the work is still very far from complete. As there seems little prospect of my being able to give time to its completion in the near future, I have at last reluctantly decided to issue this edition without this general bibliography.

Probably this is a wise decision from several points of view. It will not only allow of its being published later as an independent book in a handy form, but I believe that by the co-operation of other economists, which I intend soon to seek, a bibliography might ultimately emerge which might be of the greatest service to the progress of this science.

If a dedication were not somewhat out of place in a volume which is only a new edition by another than the author, I should like by such a sign to associate my mother closely with the reissue of this book. She watched with lively interest and sympathy the issue of the first two editions; the third she herself prepared. I remember as a child reading the proofs aloud to her, and she followed with eager interest my preparation of this fourth edition. The book is so much hers that I wish she could have lived to have the satisfaction of seeing the issue of what is probably the final edition.

CONTENTS

CHAPTER I

INTRODUCTION

CHAPTER II

THEORY OF PLEASURE AND PAIN

CHAPTER III

THEORY OF UTILITY

CHAPTER IV

THEORY OF EXCHANGE

CHAPTER V

THEORY OF LABOUR

CHAPTER VI

THEORY OF RENT

CHAPTER VII

THEORY OF CAPITAL

CHAPTER VIII

CONCLUDING REMARKS

APPENDIX I

APPENDIX II

APPENDIX III

APPENDIX IV

APPENDIX V

APPENDIX VI

CHAPTER I

INTRODUCTION

THE science of Political Economy rests upon a few notions of an apparently simple character. Utility, wealth, value, commodity, labour, land, capital, are the elements of the subject; and whoever has a thorough comprehension of their nature must possess or be soon able to acquire a knowledge of the whole science. As almost every economic writer has remarked, it is in treating the simple elements that we require the most care and precision, since the least error of conception must vitiate all our deductions. Accordingly, I have devoted the following pages to an investigation of the conditions and relations of the above-named notions.

Repeated reflection and inquiry have led me to the somewhat novel opinion, that *value depends entirely upon utility*. Prevailing opinions make labour rather than utility the origin of value; and there are even those who distinctly assert that labour is the *cause* of value. I show, on the contrary, that we have only to trace out carefully the natural laws of the variation of utility, as depending upon the quantity of commodity in our possession, in order to arrive at a satisfactory theory of exchange, of which the ordinary laws of supply and demand are a necessary consequence. This theory is in harmony with facts; and, whenever there is any apparent reason for the belief that labour is the cause of value, we obtain an explanation of the reason. Labour is found often to determine value, but only in an indirect manner, by varying the degree of utility of the commodity through an increase or limitation of the supply.

These views are not put forward in a hasty or ill-considered manner. All the chief points of the theory were sketched out ten years ago; but they were then published only in the form of a brief paper communicated to the Statistical or Economic Section of the British Association at the Cambridge Meeting, which took place in the year 1862. A still briefer abstract of that paper was inserted in the Report of the Meeting,[1] and the paper itself was not printed until June 1866.[2] Since writing that paper, I have, over and over again, questioned the truth of my own notions, but without ever finding any reason to doubt their substantial correctness.

[1] *Reports of Sections*, p. 158.
[2] *Journal of the Statistical Society*, vol. xxix. p. 282.

Mathematical Character of the Science

It is clear that Economics, if it is to be a science at all, must be a mathematical science. There exists much prejudice against attempts to introduce the methods and language of mathematics into any branch of the moral sciences. Many persons seem to think that the physical sciences form the proper sphere of mathematical method, and that the moral sciences demand some other method,—I know not what. My theory of Economics, however, is purely mathematical in character. Nay, believing that the quantities with which we deal must be subject to continuous variation, I do not hesitate to use the appropriate branch of mathematical science, involving though it does the fearless consideration of infinitely small quantities. The theory consists in applying the differential calculus to the familiar notions of wealth, utility, value, demand, supply, capital, interest, labour, and all the other quantitative notions belonging to the daily operations of industry. As the complete theory of almost every other science involves the use of that calculus, so we cannot have a true theory of Economics without its aid.

To me it seems that *our science must be mathematical, simply because it deals with quantities.* Wherever the things treated are capable of being *greater or less*, there the laws and relations must be mathematical in nature. The ordinary laws of supply and demand treat entirely of quantities of commodity demanded or supplied, and express the manner in which the quantities vary in connection with the price. In consequence of this fact the laws *are* mathematical. Economists cannot alter their nature by denying them the name; they might as well try to alter red light by calling it blue. Whether the mathematical laws of Economics are stated in words, or in the usual symbols, x, y, z, p, q, etc., is an accident, or a matter of mere convenience. If we had no regard to trouble and prolixity, the most complicated mathematical problems might be stated in ordinary language, and their solution might be traced out by words. In fact, some distinguished mathematicians have shown a liking for getting rid of their symbols, and expressing their arguments and results in language as nearly as possible approximating to that in common use. In his *Système du Monde*, Laplace attempted to describe the truths of physical astronomy in common language; and Thomson and Tait interweave their great *Treatise on Natural Philosophy* with an interpretation in ordinary words, supposed to be within the comprehension of general readers.[1]

---

[1] The large-type or non-symbolic portion of the Treatise has been reprinted in a separate volume, under the title *Elements of Natural Philosophy*, by Professors Sir W. Thomson and P. G. Tait. Part I. Oxford, Clarendon Press, 1873. But the authors appear to me to be inaccurate in describing this work, in the preface, as *non-mathematical*. It is comparatively *non-symbolic*, but equally mathematical with the complete Treatise.

These attempts, however distinguished and ingenious their authors, soon disclose the inherent defects of the grammar and dictionary for expressing complicated relations. The symbols of mathematical books are not different in nature from language; they form a perfected system of language, adapted to the notions and relations which we need to express. They do not constitute the mode of reasoning they embody; they merely facilitate its exhibition and comprehension. If, then, in Economics, we have to deal with quantities and complicated relations of quantities, we must reason mathematically; we do not render the science less mathematical by avoiding the symbols of algebra, —we merely refuse to employ, in a very imperfect science, much needing every kind of assistance, that apparatus of appropriate signs which is found indispensable in other sciences.

Confusion between Mathematical and Exact Sciences

Many persons entertain a prejudice against mathematical language, arising out of a confusion between the ideas of a mathematical science and an exact science. They think that we must not pretend to calculate unless we have the precise data which will enable us to obtain a precise answer to our calculations; but, in reality, there is no such thing as an exact science, except in a comparative sense. Astronomy is more exact than other sciences, because the position of a planet or star admits of close measurement; but, if we examine the methods of physical astronomy, we find that they are all approximate. Every solution involves hypotheses which are not really true : as, for instance, that the earth is a smooth, homogeneous spheroid. Even the apparently simpler problems in statics or dynamics are only hypothetical approximations to the truth.[1]

We can calculate the effect of a crowbar, provided it be perfectly inflexible and have a perfectly hard fulcrum,—which is never the case.[2] The data are almost wholly deficient for the complete solution of any one problem in natural science. Had physicists waited until their data were perfectly precise before they brought in the aid of mathematics, we should have still been in the age of science which terminated at the time of Galileo.

When we examine the less precise physical sciences, we find that physicists are, of all men, most bold in developing their mathematical theories in advance of their data. Let any one who doubts this examine Airy's " Theory of the Tides," as given in the *Encyclopædia Metropolitana* ; he will there find a wonderfully complex mathematical theory which is confessed by its author to be incapable of exact or even approximate application, because the results of

---

[1] This subject of the approximate character of quantitative science is pursued, at some length, in my *Principles of Science*, chap. xxi., on " The Theory of Approximation," and elsewhere in the same work.

[2] Thomson and Tait's *Treatise on Natural Philosophy*, vol. i. p. 337.

the various and often unknown contours of the seas
do not admit of numerical verification. In this and
many other cases we have mathematical theory without the data requisite for precise calculation.

The greater or less accuracy attainable in a mathematical science is a matter of accident, and does not
affect the fundamental character of the science.
There can be but two classes of sciences—those
which are *simply logical*, and *those which, besides
being logical, are also mathematical.* If there be
any science which determines merely whether a thing
be or be not—whether an event will happen, or will
not happen—it must be a purely logical science; but
if the thing may be greater or less, or the event may
happen sooner or later, nearer or farther, then quantitative notions enter, and the science must be mathematical in nature, by whatever name we call it.

Capability of Exact Measurement

Many will object, no doubt, that the notions
which we treat in this science are incapable of any
measurement. We cannot weigh, nor gauge, nor
test the feelings of the mind; there is no unit of
labour, or suffering, or enjoyment. It might thus
seem as if a mathematical theory of Economics would
be necessarily deprived for ever of numerical data.

I answer, in the first place, that nothing is less
warranted in science than an uninquiring and un-
hoping spirit. In matters of this kind, those who

despair are almost invariably those who have never
tried to succeed. A man might be despondent had
he spent a lifetime on a difficult task without a
gleam of encouragement; but the popular opinions
on the extension of mathematical theory tend to
deter any man from attempting tasks which, however difficult, ought, some day, to be achieved.

If we trace the history of other sciences, we gather
no lessons of discouragement. In the case of almost
everything which is now exactly measured, we can go
back to the age when the vaguest notions prevailed.
Previous to the time of Pascal, who would have
thought of measuring *doubt* and *belief*? Who could
have conceived that the investigation of petty games
of chance would have led to the creation of perhaps
the most sublime branch of mathematical science—the
theory of probabilities? There are sciences which,
even within the memory of men now living, have
become exactly quantitative. While Quesnay and
Baudeau and Le Trosne and Condillac were founding
Political Economy in France, and Adam Smith in
England, electricity was a vague phenomenon, which
was known, indeed, to be capable of becoming greater
or less, but was not measured nor calculated: it is
within the last forty or fifty years that a mathematical
theory of electricity, founded on exact data, has been
established. We now enjoy precise quantitative
notions concerning heat, and can measure the
temperature of a body to less than $\frac{1}{5000}$ part of a
degree centigrade. Compare this precision with that

of the earliest makers of thermometers, the Academicians del Cimento, who used to graduate their instruments by placing them in the sun's rays to obtain a point of fixed temperature.[1]

De Morgan excellently said,[2] "As to some magnitudes, the clear idea of measurement comes soon : in the case of length, for example. But let us take a more difficult one, and trace the steps by which we acquire and fix the idea : say *weight.* What weight is, we need not know. . . . We know it as a magnitude before we give it a name : any child can discover the *more* that there is in a bullet, and the less that there is in a cork of twice its size. Had it not been for the simple contrivance of the balance, which we are well assured (how, it matters not here) enables us to poise equal weights against one another, that is, to detect equality and inequality, and thence to ascertain how many times the greater contains the less, we might not to this day have had much clearer ideas on the subject of weight, as a magnitude, than we have on those of talent, prudence, or self-denial, looked at in the same light. All who are ever so little of geometers will remember the time when their notions of an angle, as a magnitude, were as vague as, perhaps more so than, those of a moral quality ; and they will also remember the steps by which this vagueness became clearness and precision."

Now there can be no doubt that pleasure, pain,

---

[1] See *Principles of Science,* chap. xiii., on "The Exact Measurement of Phenomena," 3d ed. p. 270.   [2] *Formal Logic,* p. 175.

labour, utility, value, wealth, money, capital, etc., are
all notions admitting of quantity; nay, the whole of
our actions in industry and trade certainly depend
upon comparing quantities of advantage or disadvantage.   Even the theories of moralists have recognised the quantitative character of the subject.
Bentham's *Introduction to the Principles of Morals
and Legislation* is thoroughly mathematical in the
character of the method.   He tells us[1] to estimate
the tendency of an action thus : " Sum up all the
values of all the pleasures on the one side, and those
of all the pains on the other.   The balance, if it be
on the side of pleasure, will give the good tendency
of the act upon the whole, with respect to the
interests of that individual person ; if on the side of
pain, the bad tendency of it upon the whole."   The
mathematical character of Bentham's treatment of
moral science is also well exemplified in his remarkable tract entitled, "A Table of the Springs of Action,"
printed in 1817, as in p. 3, and elsewhere.

" But where," the reader will perhaps ask, " are
your numerical data for estimating pleasures and
pains in Political Economy ? "   I answer, that my
numerical data are more abundant and precise than
those possessed by any other science, but that we have
not yet known how to employ them.   The very
abundance of our data is perplexing.   There is not
a clerk nor book-keeper in the country who is not

[1] Chapter iv., on the " Value of a Lot of Pleasure or Pain, How
to be measured," sec. v. 5.

engaged in recording numerical facts for the economist. The private-account books, the great ledgers of merchants and bankers and public offices, the share lists, price lists, bank returns, monetary intelligence, Custom-house and other Government returns, are all full of the kind of numerical data required to render Economics an exact mathematical science. Thousands of folio volumes of statistical, parliamentary, or other publications await the labour of the investigator. It is partly the very extent and complexity of the information which deters us from its proper use. But it is chiefly a want of method and completeness in this vast mass of information which prevents our employing it in the scientific investigation of the natural laws of Economics.

I hesitate to say that men will ever have the means of measuring directly the feelings of the human heart. A unit of pleasure or of pain is difficult even to conceive; but it is the amount of these feelings which is continually prompting us to buying and selling, borrowing and lending, labouring and resting, producing and consuming; and *it is from the quantitative effects of the feelings that we must estimate their comparative amounts*. We can no more know nor measure gravity in its own nature than we can measure a feeling; but, just as we measure gravity by its effects in the motion of a pendulum, so we may estimate the equality or inequality of feelings by the decisions of the human mind. The will is our pendulum, and its oscillations are minutely registered in the price lists of the markets. I know not when we shall have a perfect system of statistics, but the want of it is the only insuperable obstacle in the way of making Economics an exact science. In the absence of complete statistics, the science will not be less mathematical, though it will be immensely less useful than if it were, comparatively speaking, exact. A correct theory is the first step towards improvement, by showing what we need and what we might accomplish.

Measurement of Feeling and Motives

Many readers may, even after reading the preceding remarks, consider it quite impossible to create such a calculus as is here contemplated, because we have no means of defining and measuring quantities of feeling, like we can measure a mile, or a right angle, or any other physical quantity. I have granted that we can hardly form the conception of a unit of pleasure or pain, so that the numerical expression of quantities of feeling seems to be out of the question. But we only employ units of measurement in other things to facilitate the comparison of quantities ; and if we can compare the quantities directly, we do not need the units. Now the mind of an individual is the balance which makes its own comparisons, and is the final judge of quantities of feeling. As Mr. Bain says,[1] " It is only an identical proposition to affirm

---

[1] *The Emotions and the Will*, 1st ed., p. 447.

that the greatest of two pleasures, or what appears such, sways the resulting action; for it is this resulting action that alone determines which is the greater."

Pleasures, in short, are, for the time being, as the mind estimates them; so that we cannot make a choice, or manifest the will in any way, without indicating thereby an excess of pleasure in some direction. It is true that the mind often hesitates and is perplexed in making a choice of great importance: this indicates either varying estimates of the motives, or a feeling of incapacity to grasp the quantities concerned. I should not think of claiming for the mind any accurate power of measuring and adding and subtracting feelings, so as to get an exact balance. We can seldom or never affirm that one pleasure is an exact multiple of another; but the reader who carefully criticises the following theory will find that it seldom involves the comparison of quantities of feeling differing much in amount. The theory turns upon those critical points where pleasures are nearly, if not quite, equal. I never attempt to estimate the whole pleasure gained by purchasing a commodity; the theory merely expresses that, when a man has purchased enough, he would derive equal pleasure from the possession of a small quantity more as he would from the money price of it. Similarly, the whole amount of pleasure that a man gains by a day's labour hardly enters into the question; it is when a man is doubtful whether to increase his hours of labour or not, that we discover an equality between the pain of that extension and the pleasure of the increase of possessions derived from it.

The reader will find, again, that there is never, in any single instance, an attempt made to compare the amount of feeling in one mind with that in another. I see no means by which such comparison can be accomplished. The susceptibility of one mind may, for what we know, be a thousand times greater than that of another. But, provided that the susceptibility was different in a like ratio in all directions, we should never be able to discover the difference. Every mind is thus inscrutable to every other mind, and no common denominator of feeling seems to be possible. But even if we could compare the feelings of different minds, we should not need to do so; for one mind only affects another indirectly. Every event in the outward world is represented in the mind by a corresponding motive, and it is by the balance of these that the will is swayed. But the motive in one mind is weighed only against other motives in the same mind, never against the motives in other minds. Each person is to other persons a portion of the outward world—the *non-ego* as the metaphysicians call it. Thus motives in the mind of A may give rise to phenomena which may be represented by motives in the mind of B; but between A and B there is a gulf. Hence the weighing of motives must always be confined to the bosom of the individual.

I must here point out that, though the theory

presumes to investigate the condition of a mind, and
bases upon this investigation the whole of Economics,
practically it is an aggregate of individuals which
will be treated.   The general forms of the laws of
Economics are the same in the case of individuals and
nations ; and, in reality, it is a law operating in the
case of multitudes of individuals which gives rise to
the aggregate represented in the transactions of a
nation.   Practically, however, it is quite impossible
to detect the operation of general laws of this kind in
the actions of one or a few individuals.   The motives
and conditions are so numerous and complicated, that
the resulting actions have the appearance of caprice,
and are beyond the analytic powers of science.   With
every increase in the price of such a commodity as
sugar, we ought, theoretically speaking, to find every
person reducing his consumption by a small amount,
and according to some regular law.   In reality, many
persons would make no change at all ; a few, probably,
would go to the extent of dispensing with the use of
sugar altogether so long as its cost continued to be
excessive.   It would be by examining the average
consumption of sugar in a large population that we
might detect a continuous variation, connected with
the variation of price by a constant law.   It would
not, of necessity, happen that the law would be
exactly the same in the case of aggregates and individuals, unless all those individuals were of the
same character and position as regards wealth and
habits ; but there would be a more or less regular

law to which the same kind of formulæ would apply. The use of an average, or, what is the same, an aggregate result, depends upon the high probability that accidental and disturbing causes will operate, in the long run, as often in one direction as the other, so as to neutralise each other. Provided that we have a sufficient number of independent cases, we may then detect the effect of any *tendency*, however slight. Accordingly, questions which appear, and perhaps are, quite indeterminate as regards individuals, may be capable of exact investigation and solution in regard to great masses and wide averages.[1]

Logical Method of Economics

The logical method of Economics as a branch of the social sciences is a subject on which much might be written, and on which very diverse opinions are held at the present day (1879). In this place I can only make a few brief remarks. I think that John Stuart Mill is substantially correct in considering our science to be a case of what he calls[2] the Physical or Concrete Deductive Method; he considers that we may start from some obvious psychological law, as for instance, that a greater gain is preferred to a smaller one, and we may then reason downwards, and predict the phenomena which will be produced in society by

---

[1] Concerning the meaning and employment of *Averages*, see *Principles of Science*, chap. xvi., on " The Method of Means."

[2] *System of Logic*, book vi., chap. ix. sec. 3.

such a law. The causes in action in any community
are, indeed, so complicated that we shall seldom be
able to discover the undisturbed effects of any one
law, but, so far as we can analyse the statistical
phenomena observed, we obtain a verification of our
reasoning. This view of the matter is almost identical
with that adopted by the late Professor Cairnes in
his lectures on " The Character and Logical Method
of Political Economy." [1]

The principal objection to be urged against this
treatment of the subject, is that Mill has described
the Concrete Deductive Method as if it were one of
many inductive methods. In my Elementary Lessons
in Logic (p. 258), I proposed to call the method the
Complete Method, as implying that it combines observation, deduction, and induction in the most complete and perfect way. But I subsequently arrived
at the conclusion that this so-called Deductive Method
is no special method at all, but simply induction
itself in its essential form. As I have fully explained,[2]
Induction is an *inverse operation*, the inverse of
Deduction, and can only be performed by the use of
deduction. Possessing certain facts of observation,
we frame an hypothesis as to the laws governing those
facts ; we reason from the hypothesis deductively to
the results to be expected ; and we then examine
these results in connection with the facts in question ;
coincidence confirms the whole reasoning ; conflict

[1] 2nd ed. (Macmillan), 1875.
[2] *Principles of Science*, chaps. vii., ix., xii., etc.

obliges us either to seek for disturbing causes, or else to abandon our hypothesis. In this procedure there is nothing peculiar; when properly understood it is found to be the method of all the inductive sciences.

The science of Economics, however, is in some degree peculiar, owing to the fact, pointed out by J. S. Mill and Cairnes, that its ultimate laws are known to us immediately by intuition, or, at any rate, they are furnished to us ready made by other mental or physical sciences. That every person will choose the greater apparent good; that human wants are more or less quickly satiated; that prolonged labour becomes more and more painful, are a few of the simple inductions on which we can proceed to reason deductively with great confidence. From these axioms we can deduce the laws of supply and demand, the laws of that difficult conception, value, and all the intricate results of commerce, so far as data are available. The final agreement of our inferences with *à posteriori* observations ratifies our method. But unfortunately this verification is often the least satisfactory part of the process, because, as J. S. Mill has fully explained, the circumstances of a nation are infinitely complicated, and we seldom get two or more instances which are comparable. To fulfil the conditions of inductive inquiry, we ought to be able to observe the effects of a cause coming singly into action, while all other causes remain unaltered. Entirely to prove the good effects of Free Trade in

England, for example, we ought to have the nation unaltered in every circumstance except the abolition of burdens and restrictions on trade.[1] But it is obvious that while Free Trade was being introduced into England, many other causes of prosperity were also coming into action——the progress of invention, the construction of railways, the profuse consumption of coal, the extension of the colonies, etc. etc. Although, then, the beneficent results of Free Trade are great and unquestionable, they could hardly be proved to exist *à posteriori*; they are to be believed because deductive reasoning from premises of almost certain truth leads us confidently to expect such results, and there is nothing in experience which in the least conflicts with our expectations. In spite of occasional revulsions, due to periodical fluctuations depending on physical causes, the immense prosperity of the country since the adoption of Free Trade confirms our anticipations as far as, under complex circumstances, facts are capable of doing so. It will thus be seen that Political Economy tends to be more deductive than many of the physical sciences, in which closely approximate verification is often possible; but, even so far as the science is inductive, it involves the use of deductive reasoning, as already explained.

Within the last year or two, much discussion has been raised concerning the Philosophical Method of Political Economy, by Mr. T. E. Cliffe Leslie's

---

[1] *Principles of Science*, chap. xix., on "Experiment."

interesting Essay on that subject,[1] as also by the recent
address of Dr. Ingram at the Dublin Meeting of the
British Association.[2] I quite concur with these able
and eminent economists so far as to allow that
historical investigation is of great importance in
Social Science. But, instead of converting our
present science of economics into an historical science,
utterly destroying it in the process, I would perfect
and develop what we already possess, and at the
same time erect a new branch of social science on an
historical foundation. This new branch of science, on
which many learned men, such as Richard Jones, De
Laveleye, Lavergne, Cliffe Leslie, Sir Henry Maine,
Thorold Rogers, have already laboured, is doubtless a
portion of what Herbert Spencer calls Sociology, the
Science of the Evolution of Social Relations. Political
Economy is in a chaotic state at present, because there
is need of subdividing a too extensive sphere of
knowledge. Quesnay, Sir James Steuart, Baudeau,
Le Trosne, and Condillac first differentiated Economics sufficiently to lead it to be regarded as a
distinct science ; it has since been loaded with great
accretions due to the progress of investigation. It is
only by subdivision, by recognising a branch of
Economic Sociology, together possibly with two or
three other branches of statistical, jural, or social
science, that we can rescue our science from its

---

[1] *Hermathena*, No. iv., Dublin, 1876, p. 1.
[2] *Statistical Journal*, January 1879, vol. xli. p. 602. Also reprint
by Longmans, 1878.

confused state. I have already endeavoured to show
the need of this step in a lecture delivered at the
University College, in October 1876,[1] and I shall
perhaps have a future opportunity of enlarging more
upon the subject.

To return, however, to the topic of the present
work, the theory here given may be described as *the
mechanics of utility and self-interest*. Oversights
may have been committed in tracing out its details,
but in its main features this theory must be the true
one. Its method is as sure and demonstrative as
that of kinematics or statics, nay, almost as self-
evident as are the elements of Euclid, when the real
meaning of the formulæ is fully seized.

I do not hesitate to say, too, that Economics
might be gradually erected into an exact science, if
only commercial statistics were far more complete
and accurate than they are at present, so that the
formulæ could be endowed with exact meaning by
the aid of numerical data. These data would consist
chiefly in accurate accounts of the quantities of
goods possessed and consumed by the community,
and the prices at which they are exchanged. There
is no reason whatever why we should not have those
statistics, except the cost and trouble of collecting
them, and the unwillingness of persons to afford
information. The quantities themselves to be measured
and registered are most concrete and precise. In a few

---

[1] *Fortnightly Review*, Dec. 1876 ; "The Future of Political Economy."
[Reprinted in the author's *Principles of Economics* (1905).]

cases we already have information approximating to completeness, as when a commodity like tea, sugar, coffee, or tobacco is wholly imported. But when articles are untaxed, and partly produced within the country, we have yet the vaguest notions of the quantities consumed. Some slight success is now, at last, attending the efforts to gather agricultural statistics ; and the great need felt by men engaged in the cotton and other trades to obtain accurate accounts of stocks, imports, and consumption, will probably lead to the publication of far more complete information than we have hitherto enjoyed.

The deductive science of Economics must be verified and rendered useful by the purely empirical science of Statistics. Theory must be invested with the reality and life of fact. But the difficulties of this union are immensely great, and I appreciate them quite as much as does Cairnes in his admirable lectures " On the Character and Logical Method of Political Economy." I make hardly any attempt to employ statistics in this work, and thus I do not pretend to any numerical precision. But, before we attempt any investigation of facts, we must have correct theoretical notions ; and of what are here presented, I would say, in the words of Hume, in his *Essay on Commerce*, " If false, let them be rejected : but no one has a right to entertain a prejudice against them merely because they are out of the common road."

Relation of Economics to Ethics

I wish to say a few words, in this place, upon the relation of Economics to Moral Science. The theory which follows is entirely based on a calculus of pleasure and pain ; and the object of Economics is to maximise happiness by purchasing pleasure, as it were, at the lowest cost of pain. The language employed may be open to misapprehension, and it may seem as if pleasures and pains of a gross kind were treated as the all-sufficient motives to guide the mind of man. I have no hesitation in accepting the Utilitarian theory of morals which does uphold the effect upon the happiness of mankind as the criterion of what is right and wrong. But I have never felt that there is anything in that theory to prevent our putting the widest and highest interpretation upon the terms used.

Jeremy Bentham put forward the Utilitarian theory in the most uncompromising manner. According to him, whatever is of interest or importance to us must be the cause of pleasure or of pain ; and when the terms are used with a sufficiently wide meaning, pleasure and pain include all the forces which drive us to action. They are explicitly or implicitly the matter of all our calculations, and form the ultimate quantities to be treated in all the moral sciences. The words of Bentham on this subject may require some explanation and qualification, but they are too grand and too full of truth to be omitted. "Nature," he says,[1] "has placed mankind under the governance of two sovereign masters — *pain* and *pleasure*. It is for them alone to point out what we ought to do, as well as to determine what we shall do. On the one hand the standard of right and wrong, on the other the chain of causes and effects, are fastened to their throne. They govern us in all we do, in all we say, in all we think : every effort we can make to throw off our subjection will serve but to demonstrate and confirm it. In words a man may pretend to abjure their empire ; but, in reality, he will remain subject to it all the while. The *principle of utility* recognises this subjection, and assumes it for the foundation of that system, the object of which is to rear the fabric of felicity by the hands of reason and of law. Systems which attempt to question it deal in sounds instead of sense, in caprice instead of reason, in darkness instead of light."

In connection with this passage we may take that of Paley, who says, with his usual clear brevity,[2] "I hold that pleasures differ in nothing but in continuance and intensity."

The acceptance or non-acceptance of the basis of the Utilitarian doctrine depends, in my mind, on the exact interpretation of the language used. As it seems to me, the feelings of which a man is capable

---

[1] *An Introduction to the Principles of Morals and Legislation*, by Jeremy Bentham.   Edition of 1823, vol. i. p. 1.

[2] *Principles of Moral and Political Philosophy*, book i., chap. vi.

are of various grades. He is always subject to mere physical pleasure or pain, necessarily arising from his bodily wants and susceptibilities. He is capable also of mental and moral feelings of several degrees of elevation. A higher motive may rightly overbalance all considerations belonging even to the next lower range of feelings; but so long as the higher motive does not intervene, it is surely both desirable and right that the lower motives should be balanced against each other. Starting with the lowest stage —it is a man's duty, as it is his natural inclination, to earn sufficient food and whatever else may best satisfy his proper and moderate desires. If the claims of a family or of friends fall upon him, it may become desirable that he should deny his own desires and even his physical needs their full customary gratification. But the claims of a family are only a step to a higher grade of duties.

The safety of a nation, the welfare of great populations, may happen to depend upon his exertions, if he be a soldier or a statesman: claims of a very strong kind may now be overbalanced by claims of a still stronger kind. Nor should I venture to say that, at any point, we have reached the highest rank —the supreme motives which should guide the mind. The statesman may discover a conflict between motives; a measure may promise, as it would seem, the greatest good to great numbers, and yet there may be motives of uprightness and honour that may hinder his promoting the measure. How such difficult questions may be rightly determined it is not my purpose to inquire here.

The utilitarian theory holds, that all forces influencing the mind of man are pleasures and pains; and Paley went so far as to say that all pleasures and pains are of one kind only. Mr. Bain has carried out this view to its complete extent, saying,[1] "No amount of complication is ever able to disguise the general fact, that our voluntary activity is moved by only two great classes of stimulants; either a pleasure or a pain, present or remote, must lurk in every situation that drives us into action." The question certainly appears to turn upon the language used. Call any motive which attracts us to a certain course of conduct, pleasure; and call any motive which deters us from that conduct, pain; and it becomes impossible to deny that all actions are governed by pleasure and pain. But it then becomes indispensable to admit that a single higher pleasure will sometimes neutralise a vast extent and continuance of lower pains. It seems hardly possible to admit Paley's statement, except with an interpretation that would probably reverse his intended meaning. Motives and feelings are certainly of the same kind to the extent that we are able to weigh them against each other; but they are, nevertheless, almost incomparable in power and authority.

My present purpose is accomplished in pointing out this hierarchy of feeling, and assigning a proper

[1] *The Emotions and the Will*, 1st ed., p. 460.

place to the pleasures and pains with which the Economist deals. It is the lowest rank of feelings which we here treat. The calculus of utility aims at supplying the ordinary wants of man at the least cost of labour. Each labourer, in the absence of other motives, is supposed to devote his energy to the accumulation of wealth. A higher calculus of moral right and wrong would be needed to show how he may best employ that wealth for the good of others as well as himself. But when that higher calculus gives no prohibition, we need the lower calculus to gain us the utmost good in matters of moral indifference. There is no rule of morals to forbid our making two blades of grass grow instead of one, if, by the wise expenditure of labour, we can do so. And we may certainly say, with Francis Bacon, "while philosophers are disputing whether virtue or pleasure be the proper aim of life, do you provide yourself with the instruments of either."

CHAPTER II

Pleasure and Pain as Quantities

PROCEEDING to consider how pleasure and pain can be estimated as magnitudes, we must undoubtedly accept what Bentham has laid down upon this subject. "To a person," he says,[1] "considered *by himself*, the value of a pleasure or pain, considered *by itself*, will be greater or less according to the four following circumstances :—

(1) Its *intensity*.

(2) Its *duration*.

(3) Its *certainty* or *uncertainty*.

(4) Its *propinquity* or *remoteness*.

These are the circumstances which are to be considered in estimating a pleasure or a pain considered each of them by itself."

[1] *An Introduction to the Principles of Morals and Legislation*, 2nd ed., 1823, vol. i. p. 49. The earliest writer who, so far as I know, has treated Pleasure and Pain in a definitely quantitative manner, is Francis Hutcheson, in his *Essay on the Nature and Conduct of the Passions and Affections*, 1728, pp. 34-43, 126, etc.

Bentham[1] goes on to consider three other circumstances which relate to the ultimate and complete
result of any act or feeling; these are—

(5) *Fecundity*, or the chance a feeling has of
     being followed by feelings of the same kind :
     that is, pleasures, if it be a pleasure ; pains,
     if it be a pain.

(6) *Purity*, or the chance it has of not being fol-
     lowed by feelings of an opposite kind.   And

(7) *Extent*, or the number of persons to whom it
     extends, and who are affected by it.

These three last circumstances are of high importance
as regards the theory of morals ; but they will not
enter into the more simple and restricted problem
which we attempt to solve in Economics.

A feeling, whether of pleasure or of pain, must
be regarded as having two dimensions, or modes of
varying in regard to quantity.   Every feeling must
last some time, and it may last a longer or shorter
time ; while it lasts, it may be more or less acute
and intense.   If in two cases the duration of feeling
is the same, that case will produce the greater
quantity which is the more intense ; or we may say
that, with the same duration, the quantity will be
proportional to the intensity.   On the other hand,
if the intensity of a feeling were to remain constant,
the quantity of feeling would increase with its
duration.   Two days of the same degree of happiness

[1] Introduction, p. 50.

are to be twice as much desired as one day; two
days of suffering are to be twice as much feared.   If
the intensity ever continued fixed, the whole quantity
would be found by multiplying the number of units
of intensity into the number of units of duration.
Pleasure and pain, then, are quantities possessing
two dimensions, just as superficies possesses the two
dimensions of length and breadth.

In almost every case, however, the intensity of
feeling will change from moment to moment.   In-

FIG. 1.

cessant variation characterises our states of mind, and
this is the source of the main difficulties of the
subject.   Nevertheless, if these variations can be
traced out at all, or any approach to method and law
can be detected, it will be possible to form a conception of the resulting quantity of feeling.   We may
imagine that the intensity changes at the end of
every minute, but remains constant in the intervals.
The quantity during each minute may be represented,
as in fig. 1, by a rectangle whose base is supposed
to correspond to the duration of a minute, and whose

height is proportional to the intensity of the feeling during the minute in question. Along the line *ox* we measure *time,* and along parallels to the perpendicular line *oy* we measure *intensity.* Each of the rectangles between *pm* and *qn* represents the feeling of one minute. The aggregate quantity of feeling generated during the time *mn* will then be represented by the aggregate area of the rectangles

Fig. 2.

between *pm* and *qn.* In this case the intensity of the feeling is supposed to be gradually declining.

But it is an artificial assumption that the intensity would vary by sudden steps and at regular intervals. The error thus introduced will not be great if the intervals of time are very short, and will be less the shorter the intervals are made. To avoid all error, we must imagine the intervals of time to be infinitely short; that is, we must treat the intensity as varying continuously. Thus the proper representation of the variation of feeling is found in a curve of more or less complex character.

In fig. 2 the height of each point of the curve pq, above the horizontal line ox, indicates the intensity of feeling in a moment of time; and the whole quantity of feeling generated in the time mn is measured by the area bounded by the lines pm, qn, mn, and pq. The feeling belonging to any other time, ma, will be measured by the space $mabp$ cut off by the perpendicular line ab.

Pain the Negative of Pleasure

It will be readily conceded that pain is the opposite of pleasure; so that to decrease pain is to increase pleasure; to add pain is to decrease pleasure. Thus we may treat pleasure and pain as positive and negative quantities are treated in algebra. The algebraic sum of a series of pleasures and pains will be obtained by adding the pleasures together and the pains together, and then striking the balance by subtracting the smaller amount from the greater. Our object will always be to maximise the resulting sum in the direction of pleasure, which we may fairly call the positive direction. This object we shall accomplish by accepting everything, and undertaking every action of which the resulting pleasure exceeds the pain which is undergone; we must avoid every object or action which leaves a balance in the other direction.

The most important parts of the theory will turn upon the exact equality, without regard to sign, of the pleasure derived from the possession of an object, and the pain encountered in its acquisition. I am glad, therefore, to quote the following passage from Mr. Bain's treatise on *The Emotions and the Will*,[1] in which he exactly expresses the opposition of pleasure and pain :—" When pain is followed by pleasure, there is a tendency in the one, more or less, to neutralise the other. When the pleasure exactly assuages the pain, we say that the two are equivalent, or equal in amount, although of opposite nature, like hot and cold, positive and negative ; and when two different kinds of pleasure have the power of satiating the same amount of pain, there is fair ground for pronouncing them of equal emotional power. Just as acids are pronounced equivalent when in amount sufficient to neutralise the same portion of alkali, and as heat is estimated by the quantity of snow melted by it, so pleasures are fairly compared as to their total efficacy on the mind, by the amount of pain that they are capable of submerging. In this sense there may be an effective estimate of degree."

Anticipated Feeling

Bentham has stated[2] that one of the main elements in estimating the force of a pleasure or pain is its *propinquity* or *remoteness*. It is certain that a very large part of what we experience in life depends not on the actual circumstances of the

---

[1] 1st ed., p. 30.   [2] See above, p. 28.

moment so much as on the anticipation of future events.   As Mr. Bain says,[1] " The foretaste of pleasure is pleasure begun : every actual delight casts before it a corresponding ideal."   Every one must have felt that the enjoyment actually experienced at any moment is but limited in amount, and usually fails to answer to the anticipations which have been formed.   " Man never is but always to be blest " is a correct description of our ordinary state of mind ; and there is little doubt that, in minds of much intelligence and foresight, the greatest force of feeling and motive arises from the anticipation of a long-continued future.

Now, between the actual amount of feeling anticipated and that which is felt there must be some natural relation, very variable no doubt according to circumstances, the intellectual standing of the race, or the character of the individual ; and yet subject to some general laws of variation.   The intensity of present anticipated feeling must, to use a mathematical expression, be *some function of the future actual feeling and of the intervening time,* and it must increase as we approach the moment of realisation.   The change, again, must be less rapid the farther we are from the moment, and more rapid as we come nearer to it.   An event which is to happen a year hence affects us on the average about as much one day as another ; but an event of importance, which is to take place three days hence, will probably

[1] *The Emotions and the Will,* 1st ed., p. 74.

affect us on each of the intervening days more acutely than the last.[1]

This power of anticipation must have a large influence in Economics; for upon it is based all accumulation of stocks of commodity to be consumed at a future time. That class or race of men who have the most foresight will work most for the future. The untutored savage, like the child, is wholly occupied with the pleasures and the troubles of the moment; the morrow is dimly felt; the limit of his horizon is but a few days off. The wants of a future year, or of a lifetime, are wholly unforeseen. But, in a state of civilisation, a vague though powerful feeling of the future is the main incentive to industry and saving. The cares of the moment are but ripples on the tide of achievement and hope. We may safely call that man happy who, however lowly his position and limited his possessions, can always hope for more than he has, and can feel that every moment of exertion tends to realise his aspirations. He, on the contrary, who seizes the enjoyment of the passing moment without regard to coming times, must discover sooner or later that his stock of pleasure is on the wane, and that even hope begins to fail.

Uncertainty of Future Events

In admitting the force of anticipated feeling, we are compelled to take account of the uncertainty of

---

[1] Meaning presumably: '. . . more acutely than on the previous day.'—[Ed.]

all future events. We ought never to estimate the value of that which may or may not happen as if it would certainly happen. When it is as likely as not that I shall receive £100, the chance is worth but £50, because if, for a great many times in succession, I purchase the chance at this rate, I shall almost certainly neither lose nor gain. The test of correct estimation of probabilities is that the calculations agree with fact on the average. If we apply this rule to all future interests, we must reduce our estimate of any feeling in the ratio of the numbers expressing the probability of its occurrence. If the probability is only one in ten that I shall have a certain day of pleasure, I ought to anticipate the pleasure with one-tenth of the force which would belong to it if certain. In selecting a course of action which depends on uncertain events, as, in fact, does everything in life, I should multiply the quantity of feeling attaching to every future event by the fraction denoting its probability. A great casualty, which is very unlikely to happen, may not be so important as a slight casualty which is nearly sure to happen. Almost unconsciously we make calculations of this kind more or less accurately in all the ordinary affairs of life ; and in systems of life, fire, marine, or other insurance, we carry out the calculations to great perfection. In all industry directed to future purposes, we must take similar account of our want of knowledge of what is to be.

CHAPTER III

Definition of Terms

PLEASURE and pain are undoubtedly the ultimate objects of the Calculus of Economics. To satisfy our wants to the utmost with the least effort—to procure the greatest amount of what is desirable at the expense of the least that is undesirable—in other words, *to maximise pleasure,* is the problem of Economics. But it is convenient to transfer our attention as soon as possible to the physical objects or actions which are the source to us of pleasures and pains. A very large part of the labour of any community is spent upon the production of the ordinary necessaries and conveniences of life, such as food, clothing, buildings, utensils, furniture, ornaments, etc.; and the aggregate of these things, therefore, is the immediate object of our attention.

It is desirable to introduce at once, and to define, some terms which facilitate the expression of the Principles of Economics. By a *commodity* we shall understand any object, substance, action, or service, which can‑afford pleasure or ward off pain. The name was originally abstract, and denoted the quality of anything by which it was capable of serving man. Having acquired, by a common process of confusion, a concrete signification, it will be well to retain the word entirely for that signification, and employ the term *utility* to denote the abstract quality whereby an object serves our purposes, and becomes entitled to rank as a commodity. Whatever can produce pleasure or prevent pain *may* possess utility. J.-B. Say has correctly and briefly defined utility as " la faculté qu'ont les choses de pouvoir servir à l'homme, de quelque manière que ce soit." The food which prevents the pangs of hunger, the clothes which fend off the cold of winter, possess incontestable utility ; but we must beware of restricting the meaning of the word by any moral considerations. Anything which an individual is found to desire and to labour for must be assumed to possess for him utility. In the science of Economics we treat men not as they ought to be, but as they are. Bentham, in establishing the foundations of Moral Science in his great *Introduction to the Principles of Morals and Legislation* (page 3), thus comprehensively defines the term in question : " By utility is meant that property in any object, whereby it tends to produce benefit, advantage, pleasure, good, or happiness (all this, in the present case, comes to the same thing), or (what comes again to the same thing) to prevent the happening of mis-

chief, pain, evil, or unhappiness to the party whose
interest is considered."

This perfectly expresses the meaning of the word
in Economics, provided that the will or inclination
of the person immediately concerned is taken as the
sole criterion, for the time, of what is or is not useful.

The Laws of Human Want

Economics must be founded upon a full and
accurate investigation of the conditions of utility;
and, to understand this element, we must necessarily
examine the wants and desires of man.   We, first of
all, need a theory of the consumption of wealth.
J. S. Mill, indeed, has given an opinion inconsistent
with this.   " Political economy," he says,[1] " has
nothing to do with the consumption of wealth, further
than as the consideration of it is inseparable from that
of production, or from that of distribution.   We know
not of any laws of the consumption of wealth, as the
subject of a distinct science; they can be no other
than the laws of human enjoyment."

But it is surely obvious that Economics does rest
upon the laws of human enjoyment; and that, if
those laws are developed by no other science, they
must be developed by economists.   We labour to
produce with the sole object of consuming, and the
kinds and amounts of goods produced must be determined with regard to what we want to consume.

[1] *Essays on some Unsettled Questions of Political Economy*, p. 132.

Every manufacturer knows and feels how closely he must anticipate the tastes and needs of his customers : his whole success depends upon it; and, in like manner, the theory of Economics must begin with a correct theory of consumption.   Many economists have had a clear perception of this truth.   Lord Lauderdale distinctly states,[1] that "the great and important step towards ascertaining the causes of the direction which industry takes in nations . . . seems to be the discovery of what dictates the proportion of demand for the various articles which are produced." Senior, in his admirable treatise, has also recognised this truth, and pointed out what he calls the *Law of Variety* in human requirements.   The necessaries of life are so few and simple, that a man is soon satisfied in regard to these, and desires to extend his range of enjoyment.   His first object is to vary his food ; but there soon arises the desire of variety and elegance in dress ; and to this succeeds the desire to build, to ornament, and to furnish—tastes which, where they exist, are absolutely insatiable, and seem to increase with every improvement in civilisation.[2]

Many French economists also have observed that human wants are the ultimate subject-matter of Economics ; Bastiat, for instance, in his *Harmonies*

---

[1] *Inquiry into the Nature and Origin of Public Wealth*, 2nd ed., 1819, p. 306 (1st ed. 1804).

[2] *Encyclopædia Metropolitana*, article "Political Economy," p. 133. 5th ed. of Reprint, p. 11.

of Political Economy, says,[1] " *Wants, Efforts, Satisfaction*—this is the circle of Political Economy."

In still later years, Courcelle-Seneuil actually commenced his treatise with a definition of *want*—" Le
besoin économique est un désir qui a pour but la
possession et la jouissance d'un objet matériel." [2]   And
I conceive that he has given the best possible statement of the problem of Economics when he expresses
its object as " à satisfaire nos besoins avec la moindre
somme de travail possible." [3]

Professor Hearn also begins his excellent treatise,
entitled *Plutology, or the Theory of Efforts to
supply Human Wants,* with a chapter in which he
considers the nature of the wants impelling man to
exertion.

The writer, however, who seems to me to have
reached the deepest comprehension of the foundations
of Economics is T. E. Banfield.   His course of lectures
delivered in the University of Cambridge in 1844, and
published under the title of *The Organisation of
Labour,* is highly interesting, though not always
correct.   In the following passage [4] he profoundly
points out that the scientific basis of Economics is in
a theory of consumption : I need make no excuse for
quoting this passage at full length.

" The lower wants man experiences in common

[1] *Harmonies of Political Economy,* translated by P. J. Stirling,
1860, p. 65.

[2] *Traité Théorique et Pratique d'Economie Politique,* par J. G.
Courcelle-Seneuil, 2me ed., Paris, 1867, tom. i. p. 25.

[3] *Ib.,* p. 33.   [4] 2nd ed., p. 11.

with brutes.   The cravings of hunger and thirst, the
effects of heat and cold, of drought and damp, he
feels with more acuteness than the rest of the animal
world.   His sufferings are doubtless sharpened by the
consciousness that he has no right to be subject to
such inflictions.   Experience, however, shows that
privations of various kinds affect men differently in
degree according to the circumstances in which they
are placed.   For some men the privation of certain
enjoyments is intolerable, whose loss is not even felt
by others.   Some, again, sacrifice all that others hold
dear for the gratification of longings and aspirations
that are incomprehensible to their neighbours.   Upon
this complex foundation of low wants and high
aspirations the Political Economist has to build the
theory of production and consumption.

"An examination of the nature and intensity of
man's wants shows that this connection between them
gives to Political Economy its scientific basis.   The
first proposition of the theory of consumption is, that
*the satisfaction of every lower want in the scale
creates a desire of a higher character.*   If the higher
desire existed previous to the satisfaction of the
primary want, it becomes more intense when the
latter is removed.   The removal of a primary want
commonly awakens the sense of more than one
secondary privation : thus a full supply of ordinary
food not only excites to delicacy in eating, but
awakens attention to clothing.   The highest grade in
the scale of wants, that of pleasure derived from the

beauties of nature and art, is usually confined to men
who are exempted from all the lower privations.　Thus
the demand for, and the consumption of, objects of
refined enjoyment has its lever in the facility with
which the primary wants are satisfied.　This, therefore,
is the key to the true theory of value.　Without
relative value in the objects to the acquirement
of which we direct our power, there would be no
foundation for Political Economy as a science."

Utility is not an Intrinsic Quality

My principal work now lies in tracing out the
exact nature and conditions of utility.　It seems
strange indeed that economists have not bestowed
more minute attention on a subject which doubtless
furnishes the true key to the problem of Economics.

In the first place, utility, though a quality of
things, is *no inherent quality*.　It is better described
as *a circumstance of things* arising out of their
relation to man's requirements.　As Senior most
accurately says, " Utility denotes no intrinsic quality
in the things which we call useful ; it merely expresses
their relations to the pains and pleasures of mankind."
We can never, therefore, say absolutely that some
objects have utility and others have not.　The ore
lying in the mine, the diamond escaping the eye of
the searcher, the wheat lying unreaped, the fruit
ungathered for want of consumers, have no utility at
all.　The most wholesome and necessary kinds of

food are useless unless there are hands to collect and mouths to eat them sooner or later. Nor, when we consider the matter closely, can we say that all portions of the same commodity possess equal utility. Water, for instance, may be roughly described as the most useful of all substances. A quart of water per day has the high utility of saving a person from dying in a most distressing manner. Several gallons a day may possess much utility for such purposes as cooking and washing ; but after an adequate supply is secured for these uses, any additional quantity is a matter of comparative indifference. All that we can say, then, is, that water, up to a certain quantity, is indispensable ; that further quantities will have various degrees of utility ; but that beyond a certain quantity the utility sinks gradually to zero ; it may even become negative, that is to say, further supplies of the same substance may become inconvenient and hurtful.

Exactly the same considerations apply more or less clearly to every other article. A pound of bread per day supplied to a person saves him from starvation, and has the highest conceivable utility. A second pound per day has also no slight utility : it keeps him in a state of comparative plenty, though it be not altogether indispensable. A third pound would begin to be superfluous. It is clear, then, that *utility is not proportional to commodity* : the very same articles vary in utility according as we already possess more or less of the same article. The like may be said of other things. One suit of clothes per annum is necessary, a second convenient, a third desirable, a fourth not unacceptable; but we, sooner or later, reach a point at which further supplies are not desired with any perceptible force, unless it be for subsequent use.

Law of the Variation of Utility

Let us now investigate this subject a little more closely. Utility must be considered as measured by, or even as actually identical with, the addition made to a person's happiness. It is a convenient name for the aggregate of the favourable balance of feeling produced—the sum of the pleasure created and the pain prevented. We must now carefully discriminate between the *total utility* arising from any commodity and the utility attaching to any particular portion of it. Thus the total utility of the food we eat consists in maintaining life, and may be considered as infinitely great; but if we were to subtract a tenth part from what we eat daily, our loss would be but slight. We should certainly not lose a tenth part of the whole utility of food to us. It might be doubtful whether we should suffer any harm at all.

Let us imagine the whole quantity of food which a person consumes on an average during twenty-four hours to be divided into ten equal parts. If his food be reduced by the last part, he will suffer but little; if a second tenth part be deficient, he will feel the want distinctly; the subtraction of the third tenth part will be decidedly injurious ; with every subsequent subtraction of a tenth part his sufferings will be more and more serious, until at length he will be upon the verge of starvation.   Now, if we call each of the tenth parts *an increment*, the meaning of these facts is, that each increment of food is less necessary, or possesses less utility, than the previous one.   To explain this variation of utility we may make use of space-representations, which I have found convenient

Fig. 3.

in illustrating the laws of Economics in my College lectures during fifteen years past.

Let the line *ox* be used as a measure of the quantity of food, and let it be divided into ten equal parts to correspond to the ten portions of food mentioned above.   Upon these equal lines are constructed rectangles, and the area of each rectangle may be assumed to represent the utility of the increment of food corresponding to its base.   Thus the utility of the last increment is small, being proportional to the small rectangle on x.   As we approach towards *o*, each increment bears a larger rectangle, that standing upon III being the largest complete rectangle. The utility of the next increment, II, is undefined, as also that of I, since these portions of food would be indispensable to life, and their utility, therefore, infinitely great.

We can now form a clear notion of the utility of the whole food, or of any part of it, for we have only to add together the proper rectangles. The utility of the first half of the food will be the sum of the rectangles standing on the line oa; that of the second half will be represented by the sum of the smaller rectangles between a and b. The total utility of the food will be the whole sum of the rectangles, and will be infinitely great.

The comparative utility of the several portions is, however, the most important point. Utility may be treated [1] as *a quantity of two dimensions*, one dimension consisting in the quantity of the commodity, and another in the intensity of the effect produced upon the consumer. Now, the quantity of the commodity is measured on the horizontal line ox, and the intensity of utility will be measured by the length of the upright lines, or *ordinates*. The intensity of utility of the third increment is measured either by pq, or $p'q'$, and its utility is the product of the units in pp' multiplied by those in pq.

But the division of the food into ten equal parts is an arbitrary supposition. If we had taken twenty

---

[1] The theory of dimensions of utility is fully stated in a subsequent section.

or a hundred or more equal parts, the same general
principle would hold true, namely, that each small
portion would be less useful and necessary than the
last.   The law may be considered to hold true theoretically, however small the increments are made ; and
in this way we shall at last reach a figure which is
undistinguishable from a continuous curve.   The
notion of infinitely small quantities of food may seem
absurd as regards the consumption of one individual ;
but, when we consider the consumption of a nation
as a whole, the consumption may well be conceived
to increase or diminish by quantities which are, practically speaking, infinitely small compared with the
whole consumption.   The laws which we are about to
trace out are to be conceived as theoretically true of
the individual ; they can only be practically verified
as regards the aggregate transactions, productions, and
consumptions of a large body of people.   But the
laws of the aggregate depend of course upon the laws
applying to individual cases.

The law of the variation of the degree of utility
of food may thus be represented by a continuous curve
pbq (fig. 4), and the perpendicular height of each
point of the curve above the line *ox*, represents the
degree of utility of the commodity when a certain
amount has been consumed.

Thus, when the quantity *oa* has been consumed,
the degree of utility corresponds to the length of the
line *ab* ; for if we take a very little more food, *aa′*,
its utility will be the product of *aa′* and *ab* very

nearly, and more nearly the less is the magnitude of
aa'. The degree of utility is thus properly measured

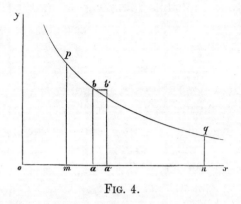

FIG. 4.

by the height of a very narrow rectangle corresponding to a very small quantity of food, which theoretically ought to be infinitely small.

Total Utility and Degree of Utility

We are now in a position to appreciate perfectly
the difference between the *total utility* of any commodity and *the degree of utility* of the commodity at
any point.   These are, in fact, quantities of altogether
different kinds, the first being represented by an area,
and the second by a line.   We must consider how
we may express these notions in appropriate mathematical language.

Let x signify, as is usual in mathematical books,
the quantity which varies independently — in this
case the quantity of commodity.   Let u denote the
whole utility proceeding from the consumption of x.

Then u will be, as mathematicians say, *a function of* x; that is, it will vary in some continuous and regular, but probably unknown, manner, when x is made to vary. Our great object at present, however, is to express the *degree of utility*.

Mathematicians employ the sign Δ prefixed to a sign of quantity, such as x, to signify that a quantity of the same nature as x, but small in proportion to x, is taken into consideration. Thus Δx means a small portion of x, and $x + \Delta x$ is therefore a quantity a little greater than x. Now, when x is a quantity of commodity, the utility of $x + \Delta x$ will be more than that of x as a general rule. Let the whole utility of $x + \Delta x$ be denoted by $u + \Delta u$; then it is obvious that the increment of utility Δu belongs to the increment of commodity Δx; and if, for the sake of argument, we suppose the degree of utility uniform over the whole of Δx, which is nearly true owing to its smallness, we shall find the corresponding degree of utility by dividing Δu by Δx.

We find these considerations fully illustrated by fig. 4, in which oa represents x, and ab is the degree of utility at the point a. Now, if we increase x by the small quantity aa', or Δx, the utility is increased by the small rectangle $abb'a'$, or Δu; and, since a rectangle is the product of its sides, we find that the length of the line ab, the degree of utility, is represented by the fraction $\dfrac{\Delta u}{\Delta x}$.

As already explained, however, the utility of a

commodity may be considered to vary with perfect
continuity, so that we commit a small error in assuming it to be uniform over the whole increment Δx.
To avoid this we must imagine Δx to be reduced to
an infinitely small size, Δu decreasing with it. The
smaller the quantities are the more nearly we shall
have a correct expression for ab, the degree of utility

at the point a. Thus the *limit* of this fraction $\dfrac{\Delta u}{\Delta x}$,

or, as it is commonly expressed, $\dfrac{du}{dx}$, is the degree of

utility corresponding to the quantity of commodity x.
The degree of utility is, in mathematical language,
*the differential coefficient of u considered as a func-
tion of x*, and will itself be another function of x.

We shall seldom need to consider the degree of
utility except as regards the last increment which has
been consumed, or, which comes to the same thing,
the next increment which is about to be consumed.
I shall therefore commonly use the expression *final
degree of utility*, as meaning the degree of utility of
the last addition, or the next possible addition of a
very small, or infinitely small, quantity to the existing stock. In ordinary circumstances, too, the final
degree of utility will not be great compared with
what it might be. Only in famine or other extreme
circumstances do we approach the higher degrees of
utility. Accordingly, we can often treat the lower
portions of the curves of variation (*pbq*, fig. 4) which
concern ordinary commercial transactions, while we

leave out of sight the portions beyond p or q. It is also evident that we may know the degree of utility at any point while ignorant of the total utility, that is, the area of the whole curve. To be able to estimate the total enjoyment of a person would be an interesting thing, but it would not be really so important as to be able to estimate the additions and subtractions to his enjoyment, which circumstances occasion. In the same way a very wealthy person may be quite unable to form any accurate statement of his aggregate wealth; but he may nevertheless have exact accounts of income and expenditure, that is, of additions and subtractions.

Variation of the Final Degree of Utility

The final degree of utility is that function upon which the Theory of Economics will be found to turn. Economists, generally speaking, have failed to discriminate between this function and the total utility, and from this confusion has arisen much perplexity. Many commodities which are most useful to us are esteemed and desired but little. We cannot live without water, and yet in ordinary circumstances we set no value on it. Why is this? Simply because we usually have so much of it that its final degree of utility is reduced nearly to zero. We enjoy, every day, the almost infinite utility of water, but then we do not need to consume more than we have. Let the supply run short by drought, and we begin

to feel the higher degrees of utility, of which we
think but little at other times.

The variation of the function expressing the final
degree of utility is the all-important point in economic
problems. We may state as a general law, that *the
degree of utility varies with the quantity of commodity, and ultimately decreases as that quantity
increases*. No commodity can be named which we
continue to desire with the same force, whatever be
the quantity already in use or possession. All our
appetites are capable of *satisfaction* or *satiety* sooner
or later, in fact, both these words mean, etymologically, that we have had *enough*, so that more is of no
use to us. It does not follow, indeed, that the degree
of utility will always sink to zero. This may be the
case with some things, especially the simple animal
requirements, such as food, water, air, etc. But the
more refined and intellectual our needs become, the
less are they capable of satiety. To the desire for
articles of taste, science, or curiosity, when once
excited, there is hardly a limit.

This great principle of the ultimate decrease of
the final degree of utility of any commodity is implied
in the writings of many economists, though seldom
distinctly stated. It is the real law which lies at the
basis of Senior's so-called " Law of Variety." Indeed,
Senior incidentally states the law itself. He says :
" It is obvious that our desires do not aim so much
at quantity as at diversity. Not only are there
limits to the pleasure which commodities of any given

class can afford, but the pleasure diminishes in a rapidly increasing ratio long before those limits are reached. Two articles of the same kind will seldom afford twice the pleasure of one, and still less will ten give five times the pleasure of two. In proportion, therefore, as any article is abundant, the number of those who are provided with it, and do not wish, or wish but little, to increase their provision, is likely to be great; and, so far as they are concerned, the additional supply loses all, or nearly all, its utility. And, in proportion to its scarcity, the number of those who are in want of it, and the degree in which they want it, are likely to be increased; and its utility, or, in other words, the pleasure which the possession of a given quantity of it will afford, increases proportionally." [1]

Banfield's "Law of the Subordination of Wants" also rests upon the same basis. It cannot be said, with accuracy, that the satisfaction of a lower want *creates* a higher want; it merely permits the higher want to manifest itself. We distribute our labour and possessions in such a way as to satisfy the more pressing wants first. If food runs short, the all-absorbing question is, how to obtain more, because, at the moment, more pleasure or pain depends upon food than upon any other commodity. But, when food is moderately abundant, its final degree of utility falls very low, and wants of a more complex and less satiable nature become comparatively prominent.

[1] *Encyclopædia Metropolitana*, p. 133. Reprint, p. 12.

The writer, however, who appears to me to have most clearly appreciated the nature and importance of the law of utility, is Richard Jennings, who, in 1855, published a small book called the *Natural Elements of Political Economy.*[1] This work treats of the physical groundwork of Economics, showing its dependence on physiological laws. It displays great insight into the real basis of Economics; yet I am not aware that economists have bestowed the slightest attention on Jennings's views.[2] I give, therefore, a full extract from his remarks on the nature of utility. It will be seen that the law, as I state it, is no novelty, and that careful deduction from principles in our possession is alone needed to give us a correct Theory of Economics.

" To turn from the relative effect of commodities, in producing sensations, to those which are absolute, or dependent only on the quantity of each commodity, it is but too well known to every condition of men, that the degree of each sensation which is produced, is by no means commensurate with the quantity of the commodity applied to the senses. . . . These effects require to be closely observed, because they are the foundation of the changes of money price, which valuable objects command in times of varied scarcity and abundance; we shall therefore

---

[1] London : Longmans.

[2] Cairnes is, however, an exception. See his work on *The Character and Logical Method of Political Economy.* London, 1857, p. 81. 2nd ed. (Macmillan), 1875, pp. 56, 110, 224 App. B.

here direct our attention to them for the purpose of ascertaining the nature of the law according to which the sensations that attend on consumption vary in degree with changes in the quantity of the commodity consumed.

" We may gaze upon an object until we can no longer discern it, listen until we can no longer hear, smell until the sense of odour is exhausted, taste until the object becomes nauseous, and touch until it becomes painful ; we may consume food until we are fully satisfied, and use stimulants until more would cause pain. On the other hand, the same object offered to the special senses for a moderate duration of time, and the same food or stimulants consumed when we are exhausted or weary, may convey much gratification. If the whole quantity of the commodity consumed during the interval of these two states of sensation, the state of satiety and the state of inanition, be conceived to be divided into a number of equal parts, each marked with its proper degrees of sensation, the question to be determined will be, what relation does the difference in the degrees of the sensation bear to the difference in the quantities of the commodity ?

" First, with respect to all commodities, our feelings show that the degrees of satisfaction do not proceed *pari passu* with the quantities consumed ; they do not advance equally with each instalment of the commodity offered to the senses, and then suddenly stop ; but diminish gradually, until they

ultimately disappear, and further instalments can
produce no further satisfaction. In this progressive
scale the increments of sensation resulting from
equal increments of the commodity are obviously
less and less at each step,—each degree of sensation
is less than the preceding degree. Placing ourselves
at that middle point of sensation, the *juste milieu*, the
aurea mediocritas, the ἄριστον μέτρον of sages, which
is the most usual status of the mass of mankind,
and which, therefore, is the best position that can
be chosen for measuring deviations from the usual
amount, we may say that the law which expresses
the relation of degrees of sensation to quantities of
commodities is of this character : if the average or
temperate quantity of commodities be increased, the
satisfaction derived is increased in a less degree, and
ultimately ceases to be increased at all; if the
average or temperate quantity be diminished, the
loss of more and more satisfaction will continually
ensue, and the detriment thence arising will ultimately become exceedingly great." [1]

Disutility and Discommodity

A few words will suffice to suggest that as utility
corresponds to the production of pleasure, or, at
least, a favourable alteration in the balance of pleasure and pain, so negative utility will consist in the
production of pain, or the unfavourable alteration of
the balance. In reality we must be almost as often

[1] Pp. 96-9.

concerned with the one as with the other; nevertheless, economists have not employed any distinct technical terms to express that production of pain, which accompanies so many actions of life. They have fixed their attention on the more agreeable aspect of the matter. It will be allowable, however, to appropriate the good English word *discommodity*, to signify any substance or action which is the opposite of *commodity*, that is to say, *anything which we desire to get rid of*, like ashes or sewage. Discommodity is, indeed, properly an abstract form signifying inconvenience, or disadvantage; but, as the noun *commodities* has been used in the English language for four hundred years at least as a concrete term,[1] so we may now convert discommodity into a concrete term, and speak of *discommodities* as substances or things which possess the quality of causing inconvenience or harm. For the abstract notion, the opposite or negative of utility, we may invent the term *disutility*, which will mean something different from inutility, or the absence of utility. It is obvious that utility passes through inutility before changing into disutility, these notions being related as +, 0 and —.

Distribution of Commodity in different Uses

The principles of utility may be illustrated by

---

[1] It is used precisely in its present economic sense in the remarkable "Processe of the Libelle of English Policie," probably written in the fifteenth century, and printed in Hakluyt's *Voyages*.

considering the mode in which we distribute a commodity when it is capable of several uses.   There
are articles which may be employed for many distinct purposes : thus, barley may be used either to
make beer, spirits, bread, or to feed cattle ; sugar
may be used to eat, or for producing alcohol; timber
may be used in construction, or as fuel ; iron and
other metals may be applied to many different purposes.   Imagine, then, a community in the possession
of a certain stock of barley ; what principles will
regulate their mode of consuming it ?   Or, as we have
not yet reached the subject of exchange, imagine an
isolated family, or even an individual, possessing an
adequate stock, and using some in one way and some
in another.   The theory of utility gives, theoretically
speaking, a complete solution of the question.

Let s be the whole stock of some commodity, and
let it be capable of two distinct uses.   Then we may
represent the two quantities appropriated to these
uses by x_1 and y_1, it being a condition that $x_1 + y_1 = s$.
The person may be conceived as successively expend-
ing small quantities of the commodity.   Now it is
the inevitable tendency of human nature to choose
that course which appears to offer the greatest
advantage at the moment.   Hence, when the person
remains satisfied with the distribution he has made,
it follows that no alteration would yield him more
pleasure ; which amounts to saying that an increment
of commodity would yield exactly as much utility in
one use as in another.   Let Δu_1, Δu_2, be the incre-

ments of utility, which might arise respectively from consuming an increment of commodity in the two different ways. When the distribution is completed, we ought to have $\Delta u_1 = \Delta u_2$; or at the limit we have the equation

$$\frac{du_1}{dx} = \frac{du_2}{dy},$$

which is true when x, y are respectively equal to x_1, y_1. We must, in other words, have the *final degrees of utility* in the two uses equal.

The same reasoning which applies to uses of the same commodity will evidently apply to any two uses, and hence to all uses simultaneously, so that we obtain a series of equations less numerous by a unit than the number of ways of using the commodity. The general result is that commodity, if consumed by a perfectly wise being, must be consumed with a maximum production of utility.

We should often find these equations to fail. Even when x is equal to $\frac{99}{100}$ of the stock, its degree of utility might still exceed the utility attaching to the remaining $\frac{1}{100}$ part in either of the other uses. This would mean that it was preferable to give the whole commodity to the first use. Such a case might perhaps be said to be not the exception but the rule; for, whenever a commodity is capable of only one use, the circumstance is theoretically represented by saying, that the final degree of utility in this employment always exceeds that in any other employment.

Under peculiar circumstances great changes may take place in the consumption of a commodity. In a time of scarcity the utility of barley as food might rise so high as to exceed altogether its utility, even as regards the smallest quantity, in producing alcoholic liquors ; its consumption in the latter way would then cease. In a besieged town the employment of articles becomes revolutionised. Things of great utility in other respects are ruthlessly applied to strange purposes. In Paris a vast stock of horses were eaten, not so much because they were useless in other ways, as because they were needed more strongly as food. A certain stock of horses had, indeed, to be retained as a necessary aid to locomotion, so that the equation of the degrees of utility never wholly failed.

Theory of Dimensions of Economic Quantities

In the recent progress of physical science, it has been found requisite to use notation for the purpose of displaying clearly the natures and relations of its various kinds of quantities concerned. Each different sort of quantity is, of course, expressed in terms of its own appropriate unit—length in terms of yards, or metres ; surface, or area, in terms of square yards or square metres ; time in terms of seconds, days, or years ; and so forth. But the more complicated quantities are evidently related to the simpler ones. Surface is measured by the *square yard*—that is to say, the unit of length is involved twice over, and if by L we denote one dimension of length, then the dimensions of surface are LL, or L^2. The dimensions of cubic capacity are in like manner LLL, or L^3.

In these cases the dimensions all enter *positively*, because the number of units in the cubical body, for instance, is found by *multiplying* the numbers of units in its length, breadth, and depth. In other cases a dimension enters *negatively*. Thus denoting time by T, it is easy to see that the dimensions of velocity will be L *divided by* T, or LT^{-1}, because the number of units in the velocity of a body is found by *dividing* the units of length passed over by the units of time occupied in passing. In expressing the dimensions of thermal and electric quantities, fractional exponents often become necessary, and the subject assumes the form of a theory of considerable complexity. The reader to whom this branch of science is new will find a section briefly describing it in my *Principles of Science*, 3rd ed., p. 325, or he may refer to the works there mentioned.[1]

Now, if such a theory of dimensions is requisite in dealing with the precise ideas of physical magnitudes, it seems to be still more desirable as regards the quantities with which we are concerned in Economics. One of the first and most difficult steps in a science is to conceive clearly the nature of the magnitudes

[1] J. D. Everett's *Illustrations of the Centimetre-gramme-second System of Units*, 1875 [5th ed., 1902]; Fleeming Jenkin's *Text-Book of Electricity and Magnetism*, 1873; Clerk-Maxwell's *Theory of Heat*, or the commencement of his great *Treatise on Electricity*, vol. i. p. 2.

about which we are arguing. Heat was long the
subject of discussion and experiment before physicists
formed any definite idea how its quantity could be
measured and connected with other physical quantities. Yet, until that was done, it could not be considered the subject of an exact science. For one or
two centuries economists have been wrangling about
wealth, demand and supply, value, production, capital,
interest, and the like ; but hardly any one could say
exactly what were the natures of the quantities in
question. Believing that it is in forming these
primary ideas that we require to exercise the greatest
care, I have thought it well worth the trouble and
space to enter fully into a discussion of the dimensions
of economic quantities.

Beginning with the easiest and simplest ideas, the
dimensions of commodity, regarded merely as a physical quantity, will be *the dimensions of mass*. It is
true that commodities are measured in various ways,—
thread by length, carpet by length, corn and liquids
by cubic measure, eggs by number, metals and most
other goods by weight. But it is obvious that,
though the carpet be sold by length, the breadth and
the weight of the cloth are equally taken into account
in fixing the terms of sale. There will generally be a
tacit reference to weight, and through weight to mass
of materials in all measurement of commodity. Even
if this be not always the case, we may, for the sake of
simplifying our symbols in the first treatment of the
subject, assume that it is so. We need hardly recede

to any ultimate analysis of the physical conditions of the commodity, but may take it to be measured by *mass*, symbolised by M, the sign usually employed in physical science to denote this dimension.

A little consideration will show, however, that we have really little to do with absolute quantities of commodity. One hundred sacks of corn regarded merely by themselves can have no important meaning for the economist. Whether the quantity is large or small, enough or too much, depends in the first place upon the number of consumers for whom it is intended, and, in the second place, upon the time for which it is to last them. We may perhaps throw out of view the number of consumers in this theory, by supposing that we are always dealing with the single average individual, the unit of which population is made up. Still, we cannot similarly get rid of the element of time. Quantity of supply must necessarily be estimated by the number of units of commodity divided by the number of units in the time over which it is to be expended. Thus it will involve M positively and T negatively, and its dimensions will be presented by MT^{-1}. Thus in reality *supply should be taken to mean not supply absolutely, but rate of supply.*

Consumption of commodity must have the same dimensions. For goods must be consumed in time; any action or effect endures a greater or less time, and commodity which will be abundant for a less time may be scanty for a greater time. To say that a town consumes fifty million gallons of water is unmeaning *per se*.   Before we can form any judgment about the statement, we must know whether it is consumed in a day, or a week, or a month.

Following out this course of thought we shall arrive at the conclusion that time enters into all economic questions.   We live in time, and think and act in time; we are in fact altogether the creatures of time.   Accordingly it is rate of supply, rate of production, rate of consumption, per unit of time that we shall be really treating; but it does not follow that T^{-1} enters into all the dimensions with which we deal.

As was fully explained in Chapter II., the ultimate quantities which we treat in Economics are Pleasures and Pains, and our most difficult task will be to express their dimensions correctly.   In the first place, pleasure and pain must be regarded as measured upon the same scale, and as having, therefore, the same dimensions, being quantities of the same kind, which can be added and subtracted; they differ only in sign or direction.   Now, the only dimension belonging properly to feeling seems to be *intensity*, and this intensity must be independent both of time and of the quantity of commodity enjoyed.   *The intensity of feeling must mean, then, the instantaneous state produced by an elementary or infinitesimal quantity of commodity consumed.*

Intensity of feeling, however, is only another name for degree of utility, which represents the favourable effect produced upon the human frame by the consumption of commodity, that is by an elementary or infinitesimal quantity of commodity. Putting U to indicate this dimension, we must remember that U will not represent even the full dimensions of the instantaneous state of pleasure or pain, much less the continued state which extends over a certain duration of time. The instantaneous state depends upon the sufficiency or insufficiency of supply of commodity. To enjoy a highly pleasurable condition, a person must want a good deal of commodity, and must be well supplied with it. Now, this supply is, as already explained, rate of supply, so that we must multiply U by MT^{-1} in order to arrive at the real instantaneous state of feeling. The kind of quantity thus symbolised by MUT^{-1} must be interpreted as meaning *so much commodity producing a certain amount of pleasurable effect per unit of time.* But this quantity will not be *quantity of utility* itself. It will only be that quantity which, when multiplied by time, will produce quantity of utility. Pleasure, as was stated at the outset, has the dimensions of intensity and duration. It is then this *intensity* which is symbolised by MUT^{-1}, and we must multiply this last symbol by T in order to obtain the dimensions of utility or quantity of pleasure produced. But in making this multiplication, $MUT^{-1}T$ reduces to MU, which must therefore be taken to denote the dimensions of *quantity of utility.*

We here meet with an explanation of the fact, so

long perplexing to me, that the element of time does not appear throughout the diagrams and problems of this theory relating to utility and exchange. All goes on in time, and time is a necessary element of the question; yet it does not explicitly appear. Recurring to our diagrams, that for instance on p. 46, it is obvious that the dimension U, or degree of utility, is measured upon the perpendicular axis oy. The horizontal axis must, therefore, be that upon which rate of supply of commodity or MT^{-1} is measured, strictly speaking. If now we introduce the duration of the utility, we should apparently need a third axis, perpendicular to the plane of the page, upon which to denote it. But were we to introduce this third dimension, we should obtain a solid figure, representing a quantity truly of three dimensions. This would be erroneous, because the third dimension T enters negatively into the quantity represented by the horizontal axis. Thus time eliminates itself, and we arrive at a quantity of two dimensions correctly represented by a curvilinear area, one dimension of which corresponds to each of the factors in MU.

This result is at first sight paradoxical; but the difficulty is exactly analogous to that which occurs in the question of interest, and which led so profound a mathematician as Dean Peacock into a blunder, as will be shown in the Chapter upon Capital. Interest of money is proportional to the length of time for which the principal is lent, and also to the amount of money lent and the rate of interest. But this rate of interest involves time negatively, so that time is ultimately eliminated, and interest emerges with the same dimensions as the principal sum. In the case of utility we begin with a certain absolute stock of commodity, M. In expending it we must spread it over more or less time, so that it is really rate of supply which is to be considered; but it is this rate MT^{-1}, not simply M, which influences the final degree of utility, U, at which it is consumed. If the same commodity be made to last a longer time, the degree of utility will be higher, because the necessity of the consumer will be less satisfied. Thus the absolute amount of utility produced will, as a general rule, be greater as the time of expenditure is greater; but this will also be the case with the quantity symbolised by MU, because the quantity U will under those circumstances be greater, while M remains constant.

To clear up the matter still further if possible, I will recapitulate the results we have arrived at.

M means absolute amount of commodity.

MT^{-1} means amount of commodity applied, so much per unit of time.

U means the resulting pleasurable effect of any increment of that supply, an infinitesimal quantity supplied per unit of time.

MUT^{-1} means therefore so much pleasurable effect produced per unit of commodity per unit of time.[1]

---

[1] Reference to the lines in italics on p. 66 shows that this should read : " MUT^{-1} means therefore so much pleasurable effect produced by *so much* commodity per unit of time."—[Ed.]

$MUT^{-1}T$, or MU, means therefore so much absolute pleasurable effect produced by commodity in an unspecified duration of time.

Actual, Prospective, and Potential Utility

The difficulties of Economics are mainly the difficulties of conceiving clearly and fully the conditions of utility. Even at the risk of being tiresome, I will therefore point out more minutely how various are the senses in which a thing may be said to have utility.

It is quite usual, and perhaps correct, to call iron or water or timber a useful substance ; but we may mean by these words at least three distinct facts. We may mean that a particular piece of iron is at the present moment actually useful to some person ; or that, although not actually useful, it is expected to be useful at a future time ; or we may only mean that it would be useful if it were in the possession of some person needing it. The iron rails of a railway, the iron which composes the Britannia Bridge,[1] or an ocean steamer, is actually useful ; the iron lying in a merchant's store is not useful at present, though it is expected soon to be so ; but there is a vast quantity of iron existing in the bowels of the earth, which has all the physical properties of iron, and might be useful

---

[1] Over the Menai Straits, North Wales. This tubular bridge was considered a feat of engineering at the time of its completion in 1850, and for many years after.—[Ed.]

if extracted, though it never will be. These are instances of *actual, prospective, and potential utility.*

It will be apparent that *potential utility* does not really enter into the science of Economics, and when I speak of *utility* simply, I do not mean to include potential utility. It is a question of physical science whether a substance possesses qualities which might make it suitable to our needs if it were within our reach. Only when there arises some degree of probability, however slight, that a particular object will be needed, does it acquire *prospective utility*, capable of rendering it a desirable possession. As Condillac correctly remarks : [1] " On diroit que les choses ne commencent à exister pour eux, qu'au moment où ils ont un intérêt à savoir qu'elles existent." But a very large part in industry, and the science of industry, belongs to *prospective utility.* We can at any one moment use only a very small fraction of what we possess. By far the greater part of what we hold might be allowed to perish at any moment, without harm, if we could have it re-created with equal ease at a future moment, when need of it arises.

We might also distinguish, as is customary with French economists, between *direct* and *indirect utility.* Direct utility attaches to a thing like food, which we can actually supply to satisfy our wants. But things which have no direct utility may be the means of pro-

---

[1] Condillac, *Le Commerce et le Gouvernement*, Seconde Partie, Introduction. *Œuvres Complètes.* Paris, 1803. Tom. vii. p. 2.

curing us such by exchange, and they may therefore
be said to have indirect utility.[1] To the latter form
of utility I have elsewhere applied the name *acquired
utility*.[2] This distinction is not the same as that
which is made in the Theory of Capital between
mediate and *immediate utility*, the former being that
of any implement, machine, or other means of pro-
curing commodities possessing *immediate* and *direct
utility*—that is, the power of satisfying want.[3]

Distribution of a Commodity in Time

We have seen that, when a commodity is capable
of being used for different purposes, definite principles
regulate its application to those purposes. A similar
question arises when a stock of commodity is in hand,
and must be expended over a certain interval of time
more or less definite. The science of Economics must
point out the mode of consuming it to the greatest
advantage—that is, with a maximum result of utility.
If we reckon all future pleasures and pains as if they
were present, the solution will be the same as in the
case of different uses. If a commodity has to be distributed over n days' use, and v_1, v_2, etc., be the final
degrees of utility on each day's consumption, then we
ought clearly to have

$$v_1 = v_2 = v_3 = \ldots = v_n.$$

---

[1] Garnier, *Traité d'Economie Politique*, 5me ed., p. 11.

[2] See chap. iv., p. 137.

[3] See chap. vii. [These terms are not used in chap. vii., or elsewhere in this book.—Ed.]

It may, however, be uncertain during how many days we may require the stock to last. The commodity might be of a perishable nature, so that if we were to keep some of it for ten days, it might become unserviceable, and its utility be sacrificed. Assuming that we can estimate more or less exactly the probability of its remaining good, let $p_1, p_2, p_3 \ldots p_{10}$, be these probabilities. Then, on the principle (p. 36) that a future pleasure or pain must be reduced in proportion to its want of certainty, we have the equations

$$v_1 p_1 = v_2 p_2 = \ldots = v_{10} p_{10}.$$

The general result is, that as the probability is less, the commodity assigned to each day is less, so that v, its final degree of utility, will be greater.

So far we have taken no account of the varying influence of an event according to its propinquity or remoteness. The distribution of commodity described is that which should be made, and would be made by a being of perfect good sense and foresight. To secure a maximum of benefit in life, all future events, all future pleasures or pains, should act upon us with the same force as if they were present, allowance being made for their uncertainty. The factor expressing the effect of remoteness should, in short, always be unity, so that time should have no influence. But no human mind is constituted in this perfect way : a future feeling is always less influential than a present one. To take this fact into account, let q_1, q_2, q_3, etc., be the undetermined fractions which express the

ratios of the present pleasures or pains to those future
ones from whose anticipation they arise. Having a
stock of commodity in hand, our tendency will be to
distribute it so that the following equations will hold
true—

$$v_1 p_1 q_1 = v_2 p_2 q_2 = v_3 p_3 q_3 = \ldots = v_n p_n q_n.$$

It will be an obvious consequence of these
equations that less commodity will be assigned to
future days in some proportion to the intervening
time.

An illustrative problem, involving questions of
prospective utility and probability, is found in the
case of a vessel at sea, which is insufficiently victualled
for the probable length of the voyage to the nearest
port. The actual length of the voyage depends on
the winds, and must be uncertain ; but we may
suppose that it will almost certainly last ten days or
more, but not more than thirty days. It is apparent
that if the food were divided into thirty equal parts,
partial famine and suffering would be certainly endured for the first ten days, to ward off later evils
which may not be encountered. To consume one-tenth
part of the food on each of the first ten days would
be still worse, as almost certainly entailing starvation
on the following days. To determine the most
beneficial distribution of the food, we should require
to know the probability of each day between the tenth
and thirtieth days forming part of the voyage, and
also the law of variation of the degree of utility of
food. The whole stock ought then to be divided into

thirty portions, allotted to each of the thirty days, and of such magnitudes that the final degrees of utility multiplied by the probabilities may be equal. Thus, let v_1, v_2, v_3, etc., be the final degrees of utility of the first, second, third, and other days supplied, and p_1, p_2, p_3, etc., the probabilities that the days in question will form part of the voyage; then we ought to have

$$p_1\, v_1 = p_2\, v_2 = p_3\, v_3 = \ldots = p_{29}\, v_{29} = p_{30}\, v_{30}.$$

If these equations did not hold true, it would be beneficial to transfer a small portion from one lot to some other lot. As the voyage is supposed certainly to last the first ten days, we have

$$p_1 = p_2 = \ldots = p_{10} = 1 ;$$

hence we must have

$$v_1 = v_2 = \ldots = v_{10} ;$$

that is to say, the allotments to the first ten days should be equal. They should afterwards decrease according to some regular law; for, as the probability decreases, the final degree of utility should increase in inverse proportion.

CHAPTER IV

THEORY OF EXCHANGE

Importance of Exchange in Economics

EXCHANGE is so important a process in the maximising of utility and the saving of labour, that some economists have regarded their science as treating of this operation alone. Utility arises from commodities being brought in suitable quantities and at the proper times into the possession of persons needing them; and it is by exchange, more than any other means, that this is effected. Trade is not indeed the only method of economising : a single individual may gain in utility by a proper consumption of the stock in his possession. The best employment of labour and capital by a single person is also a question disconnected from that of exchange, and which must yet be treated in the science. But, with these exceptions, I am perfectly willing to agree with the high importance attributed to exchange.

It is impossible to have a correct idea of the science of Economics without a perfect comprehension of the Theory of Exchange ; and I find it both possible and desirable to consider this subject before introducing any notions concerning labour or the production of commodities. In these words of J. S. Mill I thoroughly concur : " Almost every speculation respecting the economical interests of a society thus constituted, implies some theory of Value : the smallest error on that subject infects with corresponding error all our other conclusions ; and anything vague or misty in our conception of it creates confusion and uncertainty in everything else." But when he proceeds to say, " Happily, there is nothing in the laws of Value which remains for the present or any future writer to clear up ; the theory of the subject is complete " [1]—he utters that which it would be rash to say of any of the sciences.

Ambiguity of the term Value

I must, in the first place, point out the thoroughly ambiguous and unscientific character of the term *value.* Adam Smith noticed the extreme difference of meaning between *value in use* and *value in exchange* ; and it is usual for writers on Economics to caution their readers against the confusion of thought to which they are liable. But I do not believe that either writers or readers can avoid the confusion so long as they use the word. In spite of the most acute feeling of the danger, I often detect myself

---

[1] *Principles of Political Economy,* book iii., chap. i. sec. 1.

using the word improperly; nor do I think that the best authors escape the danger.

Let us turn to Mill's definition of Exchange Value,[1] and we see at once the misleading power of the term. He tells us—"Value is a relative term. The value of a thing means the quantity of some other thing, or of things in general, which it exchanges for." Now, if there is any fact certain about exchange value, it is, that it means not an object at all, but a circumstance of an object. Value implies, in fact, a relation; but if so, it cannot possibly be *some other thing*. A student of Economics has no hope of ever being clear and correct in his ideas of the science if he thinks of value as at all a *thing* or an *object*, or even as anything which lies in a thing or object. Persons are thus led to speak of such a nonentity as *intrinsic value*. There are, doubtless, qualities inherent in such a substance as gold or iron which influence its value; but the word Value, so far as it can be correctly used, merely expresses *the circumstance of its exchanging in a certain ratio for some other substance*.

Value expresses Ratio of Exchange

If a ton of pig-iron exchanges in a market for an ounce of standard gold, neither the iron is value nor the gold; nor is there value in the iron nor in the gold. The notion of value is concerned only in the

---

[1] *Principles of Political Economy*, book iii., chap. vi.

fact or circumstance of one exchanging for the other.
Thus it is scientifically incorrect to say that the value
of the ton of iron *is* the ounce of gold : we thus convert value into a concrete thing ; and it is, of course,
equally incorrect to say that the value of the ounce
of gold is the ton of iron.   The more correct and safe
expression is, that *the value of the ton of iron is equal
to the value of the ounce of gold,* or that their values
are as one to one.

Value in exchange expresses nothing but a ratio,
and the term should not be used in any other sense.
To speak simply of the value of an ounce of gold is as
absurd as to speak of the *ratio of the number seventeen.*
What is the ratio of the number seventeen ?   The
question admits no answer, for there must be another
number named in order to make a ratio ; and the
ratio will differ according to the number suggested.
What is the value of iron compared with that of gold ?
—is an intelligible question.   The answer consists in
stating the ratio of the quantities exchanged.

Popular use of the term Value

In the popular use of the word value no less than
three distinct though connected meanings seem to be
confused together.   These may be described as
   (1) Value in use ;
   (2) Esteem, or urgency of desire ;
   (3) Ratio of exchange.
Adam Smith, in the familiar passage already referred

to, distinguished between the first and the third meanings. He said,[1] "The word value, it is to be observed, has two different meanings, and sometimes expresses the power of purchasing other goods which the possession of that object conveys. The one may be called 'value in use'; the other 'value in exchange.' The things which have the greatest value in use have frequently little or no value in exchange; and, on the contrary, those which have the greatest value in exchange have frequently little or no value in use. Nothing is more useful than water: but it will purchase scarce anything; scarce anything can be had in exchange for it. A diamond, on the contrary, has scarce any value in use; but a very great quantity of other goods may frequently be had in exchange for it."

It is sufficiently plain that, when Smith speaks of water as being highly useful and yet devoid of purchasing power, he means *water in abundance*, that is to say, water so abundantly supplied that it has exerted its full useful effect, or its *total utility*. Water, when it becomes very scarce, as in a dry desert, acquires exceedingly great purchasing power. Thus Smith evidently means by value in use, *the total utility of a substance of which the degree of utility has sunk very low, because the want of such substance has been well nigh satisfied.* By purchasing power he clearly means the ratio of exchange for other commodities. But here he fails to point out that the

[1] *Wealth of Nations*, book i., chap. iv., near the end.

quantity of goods received in exchange depends just as much upon the nature of the goods received, as on the nature of those given for them. In exchange for a diamond we can get a great quantity of iron, or corn, or paving-stones, or other commodity of which there is abundance ; but we can get very few rubies, sapphires, or other precious stones. Silver is of high purchasing power compared with zinc, or lead, or iron, but of small purchasing power compared with gold, platinum, or iridium. Yet we might well say in any case that diamond and silver are things of high value. Thus I am led to think that the word value is often used in reality to mean *intensity of desire or esteem for a thing.* A silver ornament is a beautiful object apart from all ideas of traffic ; it may thus be valued or esteemed simply because it suits the taste and fancy of its owner, and is the only one possessed. Even Robinson Crusoe must have looked upon each of his possessions with varying esteem and desire for more, although he was incapable of exchanging with any other person. Now, in this sense value seems to be identical with the final degree of utility of a commodity, as defined in a previous page (p. 51) ; it is measured by the intensity of the pleasure or benefit which would be obtained from a new increment of the same commodity. No doubt there is a close connection between value in this meaning, and value as ratio of exchange. Nothing can have a high purchasing power unless it be highly esteemed in itself ; but it may be highly esteemed apart from all com-

parison with other things; and, though highly
esteemed, it may have a low purchasing power,
because those things against which it is measured
are still more esteemed.

Thus I come to the conclusion that, in the use of
the word value, three distinct meanings are habitu-
ally confused together, and require to be thus distinguished—

(1) Value in use = total utility ;
(2) Esteem = final degree of utility ;
(3) Purchasing power = ratio of exchange.

It is not to be expected that we could profitably
discuss such matters as economic doctrines, while the
fundamental ideas of the subject are thus jumbled
up together in one ambiguous word. The only
thorough remedy consists in substituting for the
dangerous name *value* that one of the three stated
meanings which is intended in each case. In this
work, therefore, I shall discontinue the use of the
word value altogether, and when, as will be most
often the case in the remainder of the book, I need
to refer to the third meaning, often called by economists *exchange or exchangeable value*, I shall substitute the wholly unequivocal expression *Ratio of
Exchange*, specifying at the same time what are the
two articles exchanged. When we speak of the ratio
of exchange of pig-iron and gold, there can be no
possible doubt that we intend to refer to the ratio of
the number of units of the one commodity to the

number of units of the other commodity for which
it exchanges, the units being arbitrary concrete
magnitudes, but the ratio an abstract number.

When I proposed, in the first edition of this book,
to use Ratio of Exchange instead of the word value,
the expression had been so little, if at all, employed
by English economists, that it amounted to an in-
novation. J. S. Mill, indeed, in his chapters on
Value, speaks once and again of things exchanging
for each other "in the ratio of their cost of production"; but he always omits to say distinctly that
exchange value is itself a matter of ratio. As to
Ricardo, Malthus, Adam Smith, and other great
English economists, although they usually discourse
at some length upon the meanings of the word value,
I am not aware that they ever explicitly apply the
name *ratio* to exchange or exchangeable value. Yet
ratio is unquestionably the correct scientific term,
and the only term which is strictly and entirely
correct.

It is interesting, therefore, to find that, although
overlooked by English economists, the expression had
been used by two or more of the truly scientific
French economists, namely, Le Trosne and Condillac.
Le Trosne carefully defines value in the following
terms : [1] " La valeur consiste dans le rapport d'échange
qui se trouve entre telle chose et telle autre, entre
telle mesure d'une production et telle mesure des
autres." Condillac apparently adopts the words of

[1] *De l'Intérêt Social*, 1777, chap. i. sec. 4.

Le Trosne, saying[1] of value : " Qu'elle consiste dans le rapport d'échange entre telle chose et telle autre." Such economical works as those of Baudeau, Le Trosne, and Condillac were almost wholly unknown to English readers until attention was drawn to them by Mr. H. D. Macleod and Professor Adamson ; but I shall endeavour for the future to make proper use of them.

Dimension of Value

There is no difficulty in seeing that, when we use the word Value in the sense of ratio of exchange, its dimension will be simply zero.   Value will be expressed, like angular magnitude and other ratios in general, by abstract number.   Angular magnitude is measured by the ratio of a line to a line, the ratio of the arc subtended by the angle to the radius of the circle.   So value in this sense is a ratio of the quantity of one commodity to the quantity of some other commodity exchanged for it.   If we compare the commodities simply as physical quantities, we have the dimensions M divided by M, or MM^{-1}, or M^0.   Exactly the same result would be obtained if, instead of taking the mere physical quantities, we were to compare their utilities, for we should then have MU divided by MU or M^0U^0, which, as it really means *unity*,[2] is identical in meaning with M^0.

---

[1] *Le Commerce et le Gouvernement*, 1776 ; *Œuvres Complètes de Condillac*, 1803, tom. 6me, p. 20.

[2] Correctly *no dimensions* ; that is, mere number.—[Ed.]

When we use the word value in the sense of esteem, or urgency of desire, the feeling with which Oliver Twist must have regarded a few more mouthfuls when he "asked for more," the meaning of the word, as already explained, is identical with *degree of utility*, of which the dimension is U. Lastly, the *value in use* of Adam Smith, or the *total utility*, is the integral of U.dM, and has the dimensions MU. We may thus tabulate our results concerning the ambiguous uses of the word *value*—

Popular Expression of Meaning	Scientific Expression	Dimensions
(1) Value in use	Total Utility	MU
(2) Esteem, or Urgency of Desire for more	Final Degree of Utility .	U
(3) Purchasing Power	Ratio of Exchange . .	M^0

Definition of Market

Before proceeding to the Theory of Exchange, it will be desirable to place beyond doubt the meanings of two other terms which I shall frequently employ.

By a *Market* I shall mean much what commercial men use it to express. Originally a market was a public place in a town where provisions and other objects were exposed for sale; but the word has been generalised, so as to mean any body of persons who are in intimate business relations and carry on extensive transactions in any commodity. A great city may contain as many markets as there are important branches of trade, and these markets may or may not be localised. The central point of a market is the public exchange,—mart or auction rooms, where the traders agree to meet and transact business. In London, the Stock Market, the Corn Market, the Coal Market, the Sugar Market, and many others, are distinctly localised; in Manchester, the Cotton Market, the Cotton Waste Market, and others. But this distinction of locality is not necessary. The traders may be spread over a whole town, or region of country, and yet make a market, if they are, by means of fairs, meetings, published price lists, the post office, or otherwise, in close communication with each other. Thus, the common expression *Money Market* denotes no locality: it is applied to the aggregate of those bankers, capitalists, and other traders who lend or borrow money, and who constantly exchange information concerning the course of business.[1]

In Economics we may usefully adopt this term with a clear and well-defined meaning. By a market I shall mean two or more persons dealing in two or more commodities, whose stocks of those commodities and intentions of exchanging are known to all. It is also essential that the ratio of exchange between any

---

[1] I find that Cournot has long since defined the economic use of the word *market*, with admirable brevity and precision, but exactly to the same effect as the text above. He incidentally says in a footnote (*Récherches sur les Principes Mathématiques de la Théorie des Richesses*, Paris, 1838, p. 55), " On sait que les économistes entendent par *marché*, non pas un lieu déterminé ou se consomment les achats et les ventes, mais tout un territoire dont les parties sont unies par des rapports de libre commerce, en sorte que les prix s'y nivellent avec facilité et promptitude." [Translation by Bacon (Macmillan, 1897), p. 51 n.]

two persons should be known to all the others.   It is only so far as this community of knowledge extends that the market extends.   Any persons who are not acquainted at the moment with the prevailing ratio of exchange, or whose stocks are not available for want of communication, must not be considered part of the market.   Secret or unknown stocks of a commodity must also be considered beyond reach of a market so long as they remain secret and unknown. Every individual must be considered as exchanging from a pure regard to his own requirements or private interests, and there must be perfectly free competition, so that any one will exchange with any one else for the slightest apparent advantage.   There must be no conspiracies for absorbing and holding supplies to produce unnatural ratios of exchange. Were a conspiracy of farmers to withhold all corn from market, the consumers might be driven, by starvation, to pay prices bearing no proper relation to the existing supplies, and the ordinary conditions of the market would be thus overthrown.

The theoretical conception of a perfect market is more or less completely carried out in practice.   It is the work of brokers in any extensive market to organise exchange, so that every purchase shall be made with the most thorough acquaintance with the conditions of the trade.   Each broker strives to gain the best knowledge of the conditions of supply and demand, and the earliest intimation of any change. He is in communication with as many other traders as possible, in order to have the widest range of information, and the greatest chance of making suitable exchanges. It is only thus that a definite market price can be ascertained at every moment, and varied according to the frequent news capable of affecting buyers and sellers. By the mediation of a body of brokers a complete *consensus* is established, and the stock of every seller or the demand of every buyer brought into the market. It is of the very essence of trade to have wide and constant information. A market, then, is theoretically perfect only when all traders have perfect knowledge of the conditions of supply and demand, and the consequent ratio of exchange; and in such a market, as we shall now see, there can only be one ratio of exchange of one uniform commodity at any moment.

So essential is a knowledge of the real state of supply and demand to the smooth procedure of trade and the real good of the community, that I conceive it would be quite legitimate to compel the publication of any requisite statistics. Secrecy can only conduce to the profit of speculators who gain from great fluctuations of prices. Speculation is advantageous to the public only so far as it tends to equalise prices; and it is, therefore, against the public good to allow speculators to foster artificially the inequalities of prices by which they profit. The welfare of millions, both of consumers and producers, depends upon an accurate knowledge of the stocks of cotton and corn; and it would, therefore, be no unwarrantable interference with the liberty of the subject to require any information as to the stocks in hand. In Billingsgate fish market there was long ago a regulation to the effect that salesmen shall fix up in a conspicuous place every morning a statement of the kind and amount of their stock.[1] The same principle has long been recognised in the Acts of Parliament concerning the collection of statistics of the quantities and prices of corn sold in English market towns. More recently similar legislation has taken place as regards the cotton trade, in the Cotton Statistics Act of 1868. Publicity, whenever it can thus be enforced on markets by public authority, tends almost always to the advantage of everybody except perhaps a few speculators and financiers.

Definition of Trading Body

I find it necessary to adopt some expression for any number of people whose aggregate influence in a market, either in the way of supply or demand, we have to consider. By a *trading body* I mean, in the most general manner, any body either of buyers or sellers. The trading body may be a single individual in one case; it may be the whole inhabitants of a continent in another; it may be the individuals of a trade diffused through a country in a third. England and North America will be trading bodies if we are considering the corn we receive from

[1] Waterston's *Cyclopædia of Commerce*, ed. 1846, p. 466.

America in exchange for iron and other goods. The continent of Europe is a trading body as purchasing coal from England. The farmers of England are a trading body when they sell corn to the millers, and the millers both when they buy corn from the farmers and sell flour to the bakers.

We must use the expression with this wide meaning, because the principles of exchange are the same in nature, however wide or narrow may be the market considered. Every trading body is either an individual or an aggregate of individuals, and the law, in the case of the aggregate, must depend upon the fulfilment of law in the individuals. We cannot usually observe any precise and continuous variation in the wants and deeds of an individual, because the action of extraneous motives, or what would seem to be caprice, overwhelms minute tendencies. As I have already remarked (p. 15), a single individual does not vary his consumption of sugar, butter, or eggs from week to week by infinitesimal amounts, according to each small change in the price. He probably continues his ordinary consumption until accident directs his attention to a rise in price, and he then, perhaps, discontinues the use of the articles altogether for a time. But the aggregate, or what is the same, the average consumption, of a large community will be found to vary continuously or nearly so. The most minute tendencies make themselves apparent in a wide average. Thus, our laws of Economics will be theoretically true in the case of individuals, and practically true in the case of large aggregates ; but the general principles will be the same, whatever the extent of the trading body considered. We shall be justified, then, in using the expression with the utmost generality.

It should be remarked, however, that the economic laws representing the conduct of large aggregates of individuals will never represent exactly the conduct of any one individual. If we could imagine that there were a thousand individuals all exactly alike in regard to their demand for commodities, and their capabilities of supplying them, then the average laws of supply and demand deduced from the conduct of such individuals would agree with the conduct of any one individual. But a community is composed of persons differing widely in their powers, wants, habits, and possessions. In such circumstances the average laws applying to them will come under what I have elsewhere[1] called the " Fictitious Mean," that is to say, they are numerical results which do not pretend to represent the character of any existing thing. But average laws would not on this account be less useful, if we could obtain them ; for the movements of trade and industry depend upon averages and aggregates, not upon the whims of individuals.

The Law of Indifference

When a commodity is perfectly uniform or homogeneous in quality, any portion may be indifferently

---

[1] *Principles of Science*, 1st ed., vol. i. p. 422 ; 3d ed., p. 363.

used in place of an equal portion : hence, in the same market, and at the same moment, all portions must be exchanged at the same ratio. There can be no reason why a person should treat exactly similar things differently, and the slightest excess in what is demanded for one over the other will cause him to take the latter instead of the former. In nicely balanced exchanges it is a very minute scruple which turns the scale and governs the choice. A minute difference of quality in a commodity may thus give rise to preference, and cause the ratio of exchange to differ. But where no difference exists at all, or where no difference is known to exist, there can be no ground for preference whatever. If, in selling a quantity of perfectly equal and uniform barrels of flour, a merchant arbitrarily fixed different prices on them, a purchaser would of course select the cheaper ones ; and where there was absolutely no difference in the thing purchased, even an excess of a penny in the price of a thing worth a thousand pounds would be a valid ground of choice. Hence follows what is undoubtedly true, with proper explanations, that *in the same open market, at any one moment, there cannot be two prices for the same kind of article.* Such differences as may practically occur arise from extraneous circumstances, such as the defective credit of the purchasers, their imperfect knowledge of the market, and so on.

The principle above expressed is a general law of the utmost importance in Economics, and I propose to call it *The Law of Indifference*, meaning that, when two objects or commodities are subject to no important difference as regards the purpose in view, they will either of them be taken instead of the other with perfect indifference by a purchaser. Every such act of indifferent choice gives rise to an equation of degrees of utility, so that in this principle of indifference we have one of the central pivots of the theory.

Though the price of the same commodity must be uniform at any one moment, it may vary from moment to moment, and must be conceived as in a state of continual change. Theoretically speaking, it would not usually be possible to buy two portions of the same commodity *successively* at the same ratio of exchange, because, no sooner would the first portion have been bought than the conditions of utility would be altered. When exchanges are made on a large scale, this result will be verified in practice.[1] If a wealthy person invested £100,000 in the funds in the morning, it is hardly likely that the operation could be repeated in the afternoon at the same price. In any market, if a person goes on buying largely, he will ultimately

---

[1] It is, I believe, verified in the New York Stock Markets, where it is the practice to sell Stocks by auction in successive lots, without disclosing the total amount to be put up. When the amount offered begins to exceed what was expected, then each successive lot brings a less price, and those who bought the earlier lots suffer. But if the amount offered is small, the early buyers have the advantage. Such an auction sale only exhibits in miniature what is constantly going on in the markets generally on a large scale.

raise the price against himself. Thus it is apparent that extensive purchases would best be made gradually, so as to secure the advantage of a lower price upon the earlier portions. In theory this effect of exchange upon the ratio of exchange must be conceived to exist in some degree, however small may be the purchases made. Strictly speaking, the ratio of exchange at any moment is that of dy to dx, of an infinitely small quantity of one commodity to the infinitely small quantity of another which is given for it. The ratio of exchange is really a differential coefficient. The quantity of any article purchased is a function of the price at which it is purchased, and the ratio of exchange expresses the rate at which the quantity of the article increases compared with what is given for it.

We must carefully distinguish, at the same time, between the Statics and Dynamics of this subject. The real condition of industry is one of perpetual motion and change. Commodities are being continually manufactured and exchanged and consumed. If we wished to have a complete solution of the problem in all its natural complexity, we should have to treat it as a problem of motion—a problem of dynamics. But it would surely be absurd to attempt the more difficult question when the more easy one is yet so imperfectly within our power. It is only as a purely statical problem that I can venture to treat the action of exchange. Holders of commodities will be regarded not as continuously passing on these commodities in streams of trade, but as possessing certain fixed amounts which they exchange until they come to equilibrium.

It is much more easy to determine the point at which a pendulum will come to rest than to calculate the velocity at which it will move when displaced from that point of rest.   Just so, it is a far more easy task to lay down the conditions under which trade is completed and interchange ceases, than to attempt to ascertain at what rate trade will go on when equilibrium is not attained.

The difference will present itself in this form : dynamically we could not treat the ratio of exchange otherwise than as the ratio of dy and dx, infinitesimal quantities of commodity.   Our equations would then be regarded as differential equations, which would have to be integrated.   But in the statical view of the question we can substitute the ratio of the finite quantities y and x.   Thus, from the self-evident principle, stated on pp. 91-2, that there cannot, in the same market, at the same moment, be two different prices for the same uniform commodity, it follows that *the last increments in an act of exchange must be exchanged in the same ratio as the whole quantities exchanged.*   Suppose that two commodities are bartered in the ratio of x for y ; then every m^{th} part of x is given for the mth part of y, and it does not matter for which of the mth parts.   No part of the commodity can be treated differently from any other part.   We may carry this division to an indefinite

extent by imagining *m* to be constantly increased, so
that, at the limit, even an infinitely small part of *x*
must be exchanged for an infinitely small part of *y*, in
the same ratio as the whole quantities.   This result we
may express by stating that the increments concerned
in the process of exchange must obey the equation

$$\frac{dy}{dx} = \frac{y}{x}.$$

The use which we shall make of this equation will
be seen in the next section.

The Theory of Exchange

The keystone of the whole Theory of Exchange,
and of the principal problems of Economics, lies in
this proposition—*The ratio of exchange of any two
commodities will be the reciprocal of the ratio of the
final degrees of utility of the quantities of commodity
available for consumption after the exchange is completed.*   When the reader has reflected a little upon
the meaning of this proposition, he will see, I think,
that it is necessarily true, if the principles of human
nature have been correctly represented in previous
pages.

Imagine that there is one trading body possessing
only corn, and another possessing only beef.   It is
certain that, under these circumstances, a portion of
the corn may be given in exchange for a portion of
the beef with a considerable increase of utility.   How
are we to determine at what point the exchange will

cease to be beneficial? This question must involve both the ratio of exchange and the degrees of utility. Suppose, for a moment, that the ratio of exchange is approximately that of ten pounds of corn for one pound of beef: then if, to the trading body which possesses corn, ten pounds of corn are less useful than one of beef, that body will desire to carry the exchange further. Should the other body possessing beef find one pound less useful than ten pounds of corn, this body will also be desirous to continue the exchange. Exchange will thus go on until each party has obtained all the benefit that is possible, and loss of utility would result if more were exchanged. Both parties, then, rest in satisfaction and equilibrium, and the degrees of utility have come to their level, as it were.

This point of equilibrium will be known by the criterion, that an infinitely small amount of commodity exchanged in addition, at the same rate, will bring neither gain nor loss of utility. In other words, if increments of commodities be exchanged at the established ratio, their utilities will be equal for both parties. Thus, if ten pounds of corn were of exactly the same utility as one pound of beef, there would be neither harm nor good in further exchange at this ratio.

It is hardly possible to represent this theory completely by means of a diagram, but the accompanying figure may, perhaps, render it clearer. Suppose the line pqr to be a small portion of the curve of utility of one commodity, while the broken line $p'qr'$ is the like curve of another commodity which has been reversed and superposed on the other. Owing to this reversal, the quantities of the first commodity are measured along the base line from a towards b, whereas those of the second must be measured in the opposite direction. Let units of both commodities be represented by equal lengths : then the little line $a'a$ indicates an increase of the first commodity, and a decrease of the second. Assume the ratio of exchange to be that of unit for unit, or

FIG. 5.

1 to 1 : then, by receiving the commodity $a'a$ the person will gain the utility ad, and lose the utility $a'c$; or he will make a net gain of the utility corresponding to the mixtilinear figure cd. He will, therefore, wish to extend the exchange. If he were to go up to the point b', and were still proceeding, he would, by the next small exchange, receive the utility be, and part with $b'f$; or he would have a net loss of ef. He would, therefore, have gone too far ; and it is pretty obvious that the point of intersection, q, defines the place where he would stop with the greatest

advantage.   It is there that a net gain is converted into a net loss, or rather where, for an infinitely small quantity, there is neither gain nor loss.   To represent an infinitely small quantity, or even an exceedingly small quantity, on a diagram is, of course, impossible ; but on either side of the line mq I have represented the utilities of a small quantity of commodity more or less, and it is apparent that the net gain or loss upon the exchange of these quantities would be trifling.

Symbolic Statement of the Theory

To represent this process of reasoning in symbols, let Δx denote a small increment of corn, and Δy a small increment of beef exchanged for it.   Now our Law of Indifference comes into play.   As both the corn and the beef are homogeneous commodities, no parts can be exchanged at a different ratio from other parts in the same market : hence, if x be the whole quantity of corn given for y the whole quantity of beef received, Δy must have the same ratio to Δx as y to x ; we have then,

$$\frac{\Delta y}{\Delta x} = \frac{y}{x}, \quad \text{or} \quad \Delta y = \frac{y}{x}\Delta x.$$

In a state of equilibrium, the utilities of these increments must be equal in the case of each party, in order that neither more nor less exchange would be desirable.   Now the increment of beef, Δy, is $\frac{y}{x}$ times as great as the increment of corn, Δx, so that,

in order that their utilities shall be equal, the degree
of utility of beef must be $\dfrac{x}{y}$ times as great as the
degree of utility of corn. Thus we arrive at the
principle that *the degrees of utility of commodities
exchanged will be in the inverse proportion of the
magnitudes of the increments exchanged.*

Let us now suppose that the first body, A, originally possessed the quantity a of corn, and that the
second body, B, possessed the quantity b of beef.
As the exchange consists in giving x of corn for y of
beef, the state of things after exchange will be as
follows :—

> A holds $a - x$ of corn, and y of beef,
> B holds x of corn, and $b - y$ of beef.

Let $\phi_1(a - x)$ denote the final degree of utility of corn
to A, and $\phi_2 x$ the corresponding function for B.
Also let $\psi_1 y$ denote A's final degree of utility for
beef, and $\psi_2(b - y)$ B's similar function. Then, as
explained on p. 96, A will not be satisfied unless the
following equation holds true :—

$$\phi_1(a - x) \,.\, dx = \psi_1 y \,.\, dy \;;$$
$$\text{or} \quad \frac{\phi_1(a - x)}{\psi_1 y} = \frac{dy}{dx}.$$

Hence, substituting for the second member by the
equation given on p. 95, we have

$$\frac{\phi_1(a - x)}{\psi_1 y} = \frac{y}{x}.$$

What holds true of A will also hold true of B,

mutatis mutandis. He must also derive exactly
equal utility from the final increments, otherwise it
will be for his interest to exchange either more or
less, and he will disturb the conditions of exchange.
Accordingly the following equation must hold true :—

$$\psi_2(b-y) \cdot dy = \phi_2 x \cdot dx \; ;$$

or, substituting as before,

$$\frac{\phi_2 x}{\psi_2(b-y)} = \frac{y}{x}.$$

We arrive, then, at the conclusion, that whenever
two commodities are exchanged for each other, and
*more or less can be given or received in infinitely
small quantities*, the quantities exchanged satisfy two
equations, which may be thus stated in a concise form—

$$\frac{\phi_1(a-x)}{\psi_1 y} = \frac{y}{x} = \frac{\phi_2 x}{\psi_2(b-y)}.$$

The two equations are sufficient to determine the
results of exchange ; for there are only two unknown
quantities concerned, namely, x and y, the quantities
given and received.

A vague notion has existed in the minds of
economical writers, that the conditions of exchange
may be expressed in the form of an equation. Thus,
J. S. Mill has said :[1] "The idea of a *ratio*, as between
demand and supply, is out of place, and has no concern in the matter : the proper mathematical analogy
is that of an *equation*. Demand and supply, the
quantity demanded and the quantity supplied, will be

[1] *Principles of Political Economy*, book iii., chap. ii., sec. 4.

made equal." Mill here speaks of an equation as only a proper mathematical *analogy*. But if Economics is to be a real science at all, it must not deal merely with analogies ; it must reason by real equations, like all the other sciences which have reached at all a systematic character. Mill's equation, indeed, is not explicitly the same as any at which we have arrived above. His equation states that the quantity of a commodity given by A is equal to the quantity received by B. This seems at first sight to be a mere truism, for this equality must necessarily exist if any exchange takes place at all. The theory of value, as expounded by Mill, fails to reach the root of the matter, and show how the amount of demand or supply is caused to vary. And Mill does not perceive that, as there must be two parties and two quantities to every exchange, there must be two equations.

Nevertheless, our theory is perfectly consistent with the laws of supply and demand ; and if we had the functions of utility determined, it would be possible to throw them into a form clearly expressing the equivalence of supply and demand. We may regard x as the quantity demanded on one side and supplied on the other; similarly, y is the quantity supplied on the one side and demanded on the other. Now, when we hold the two equations to be simultaneously true, we assume that the x and y of one equation equal those of the other. The laws of supply and demand are thus a result of what seems to me the true theory of value or exchange.

Analogy to the Theory of the Lever

I have heard objections made to the general character of the equations employed in this book. It is remarked that the equations in question continually involve infinitesimal quantities, and yet they are not treated as differential equations usually are, that is integrated. There is, indeed, no reason why the process of integration should not be applied when it is required, and I will here show that the equations employed do not differ in general character from those which are really treated in many branches of physical science. Whenever, in fact, we deal with continuously varying quantities, the ultimate equations must lie between infinitesimals. The process of integration, if I understand the matter aright, only ascertains other equations, the truth of which follows from the fundamental differential equation.

The mode in which mechanics is usually treated in elementary work tends to disguise the real foundation of the science which is to be found in the so-called *theory of virtual velocities*. Let us take the description of the lever of the first order as it is given in some of the best modern elementary works, as, for instance, in Mr. Magnus's *Lessons in Elementary Mechanics*, p. 128. We here read as follows :—

" Let AB be a lever turning freely about C, the fulcrum, and let P be the force applied at A, and W the force exerted, or resistance overcome, or weight raised at B. Suppose the lever turned through the angle ACA', then the work done by P equals $P \times$ arc AA', and work done by W equals $W \times$ arc BB', if P and W act perpendicularly to the arm. Therefore, by the law of energy,

$$P \times AA' = W \times BB', \text{ and since } \frac{AA'}{BB'} = \frac{AC}{BC} \text{ we have}$$

$$P \times AC = W \times BC,$$

or, $P \times$ its arm $= W \times$ its arm."

Now, in such a statement as this, we seem to be dealing with plain finite quantities, and there is no apparent difficulty in the matter. In reality the difficulty is only disguised by assuming that P and W act perpendicularly to the arm through finite arcs. This condition is, indeed, carried out with approximate exactness in the problem of the wheel and axle,[1] which may be regarded as combining together an infinite series of straight levers, coming successively into operation. In this machine, therefore, the weights, roughly speaking, always act perpendicularly to arms of invariable length. But, in the generality of cases of the lever, the theory is only true for infinitely small displacements, and no sooner has the lever begun to move through any finite arc AA', than it ceases to be exactly true that the work done by P equals $P \times$ arc AA'. Nevertheless, the theory is quite correct as applied to the lever considered statically, that is, as in a state of

[1] See Magnus's *Lessons*, sec. 91.

rest and equilibrium, because the finite arcs of displacement, when it really is displaced, are exactly proportional to the infinitely small arcs, known as virtual velocities, through which it would be displaced, if instead of being at rest, it suffered an infinitely small displacement.

It is curious, moreover, that, when we take the theory of the lever treated according to the principle of virtual velocities, we get equations exactly similar in form to those of the theory of value as established above. The general principle of virtual velocities is to the effect that, if any number of forces be in equilibrium at one or more points of a rigid body, and if this body receive an infinitely small displacement, the algebraic sum of the products of each force into its displacement is equal to zero. In the case of a lever of the first order, this amounts to saying that one force multiplied into its displacement will be neutralised by the other force multiplied into its *negative* displacement. But inasmuch as the displacements are exactly proportional to the lengths of the arms of the lever, we obtain as a derivative equation, that the forces multiplied each by its own arm are equal to each other. No doubt in the quotation given above, $P \times AC = W \times BC$ is an equation between finite quantities; but the real equation derived immediately from the principle of virtual velocities, is $P \times AA' = W \times BB'$, in which P and W are finite, but AA' and BB' are in strictness infinitely small displacements. Let us write this equation in the form $\dfrac{W}{P} = \dfrac{AA'}{BB'}$; then as we also

have $\dfrac{AA'}{BB'} = \dfrac{AC}{BC}$ we can substitute; hence $\dfrac{W}{P} = \dfrac{AC}{BC}$.

I dwell upon this matter at some length because we here have exactly the forms of the equations of exchange. As we have seen, the original equation is of the general form $\dfrac{\phi x}{\psi y} = \dfrac{dy}{dx}$, where ψy and ϕx represent finite expressions for the degrees of utility of the commodities Y and X, as regards some individual, and dy and dx are infinitesimal quantities of those commodities exchanged. But these infinitesimals may in this case at least be eliminated, because, in virtue of the Law of Indifference, they are exactly proportional to the whole finite quantities exchanged. Hence for $\dfrac{dy}{dx}$ we substitute $\dfrac{y}{x}$. We may write the equations one below the other, so as to make the analogy visible—thus

$$\frac{W}{P} = \frac{AA'}{BB'} = \frac{AC}{BC}$$

$$\frac{\phi x}{\psi y} = \frac{dy}{dx} = \frac{y}{x}.$$

To put this analogy of the theories of exchange and of the lever in the clearest possible light, I give below a diagram, in which the several economic qualities are represented by the parts of the diagram to which they correspond or are proportional.

Now in statical problems no such process as

integration is applicable. The equation lies actually between imaginary infinitesimal quantities, and there is no effect to be summed up. Yet there is no statical problem which is not subject to the principle of virtual velocities, and Poisson, in his *Traité de*

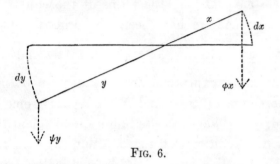

FIG. 6.

Mécanique, which commences with statical theorems, asserts explicitly,[1] "Dans cet ouvrage, j'emploierai exclusivement la méthode *des infiniment petits*."

Impediments to Exchange

We have hitherto treated the theory of exchange as if the action of exchange could be carried on without trouble or cost. In reality, the cost of conveyance is almost always of importance, and it is sometimes the principal element in the question. To the cost of mere transport must be added a variety of charges of brokers, agents, packers, dock, harbour, light dues, etc., together with any customs duties imposed either on the importation or exportation of commodities. All these charges, whether necessary

[1] Seconde Édition, Paris, 1833, sec. 12, vol. i. p. 14.

or arbitrary, are so many impediments to commerce, and tend to reduce its advantages. The effect of any one such charge, or of the aggregate of the costs of exchange, can be represented in our formulæ in a very simple manner.

In whatever modes the charges are payable, they may be conceived as paid by the surrender on importation of a certain fraction of the commodity received; for the amount of the charges will usually be proportional to the quantity of goods, and, if expressed in money, can be considered as turned into commodity.

Thus, if **A** gives x in exchange, this is not the quantity received by **B**; a part of x is previously subtracted, so that B receives say mx, which is less than x, and the terms of exchange must be adjusted on his part so as to agree with this condition. Hence the second equation will be

$$\frac{y}{mx} = \frac{\phi_2(mx)}{\psi_2(b-y)}.$$

Again, A, though giving x, will not receive the whole of y; but say ny, so that his equation similarly will be

$$\frac{\phi_1(a-x)}{\psi_1(ny)} = \frac{ny}{x}.$$

The result is, that there is not one ratio of exchange, but two ratios; and the more these differ, the less advantage will there be in exchange. It is obvious that A has either to remain satisfied with less of the second commodity than before, or has to give more

of his own in purchasing it. By an obvious transfer
of the factors m and n we may state the equations of
impeded exchange in the concise form—

$$\frac{\phi_1(a-x)}{n.\psi_1(ny)} = \frac{y}{x} = \frac{m.\phi_2(mx)}{\psi_2(b-y)}.$$

Illustrations of the Theory of Exchange

As stated above, the Theory of Exchange may
seem to be of a somewhat abstract and perplexing
character ; but it is not difficult to find practical
illustrations which will show how it is verified in the
actual working of a great market. The ordinary laws
of supply and demand, when properly stated, are the
practical manifestation of the theory. Considerable
discussion has taken place concerning these laws, in
consequence of Mr. W. T. Thornton's writings upon
the subject in the *Fortnightly Review*, and in his
work on the *Claims of Labour*. Mill, although he
had previously declared the Theory of Value to be
complete and perfect (see p. 76), was led by Mr.
Thornton's arguments to allow that modification was
required.

For my own part, I think that most of Mr.
Thornton's arguments are beside the question. He
suggests that there are no regular laws of supply and
demand, because he adduces certain cases in which no
regular variation can take place. Those cases might
be indefinitely multiplied, and yet the laws in question
would not be touched. Of course, laws which assume

a continuity of variation are inapplicable where continuous variation is impossible. Economists can never be free from difficulties unless they will distinguish between a theory and the *application of a theory*. Because, in retail trade, in English or Dutch auction, or other particular modes of traffic, we cannot at once observe the operation of the laws of supply and demand, it is not in the least to be supposed that those laws are false. In fact, Mr. Thornton seems to allow that, if prospective demand and supply are taken into account, they become substantially true. But, in the actual working of any market, the influence of future events should never be neglected, neither by a merchant nor an economist.

Though Mr. Thornton's objections are mostly beside the question, his remarks have served to show that the action of the laws of supply and demand was inadequately explained by previous economists. What constitutes the demand and the supply was not carefully enough investigated. As Mr. Thornton points out, there may be a number of persons willing to buy; but if their highest offer is ever so little short of the lowest price which the seller is willing to take, their influence is *nil*. If in an auction there are ten people willing to buy a horse at £20, but not higher, their demand instantly ceases when any one person offers £21. I am inclined not only to accept such a view, but to carry it further. Any change in the price of an article will be determined not with regard to the large numbers who might or might not buy it at other prices, but by the few who will or will not buy it according as a change is made close to the existing price.

The theory consists in carrying out this view to the point of asserting that it is only comparatively insignificant quantities of supply and demand which are at any moment operative on the ratio of exchange. This is practically verified by what takes place in any very large market—say that of the Consolidated Three Per Cent Annuities. As the whole amount of the English funds is nearly eight hundred millions sterling, the quantity bought or sold by any ordinary purchaser is inconsiderably small in comparison. Even £1000 worth of stock may be taken as an infinitesimally small increment, because it does not appreciably affect the total existing supply. Now the theory consists in asserting that the market price of the funds is affected from hour to hour not by the enormous amounts which *might* be bought or sold at extreme prices, but by the comparatively insignificant amounts which *are* being sold or bought at the existing prices. A change of price is always occasioned by the overbalancing of the inclinations of those who will or will not sell just about the point at which prices stand. When Consols are at $93\frac{1}{2}$, and business is in a tranquil state, it matters not how many buyers there are at 93, or sellers at 94. They are really off the market. Those only are operative who may be made to buy or sell by a rise or fall of an eighth. The question is, whether the price shall remain at $93\frac{1}{2}$,

or rise to 93⅝, or fall to 93⅜.   This is determined by
the sale or purchase of comparatively very small
amounts.   It is the purchasers who find a little stock
more profitable to them than the corresponding sum
of money who make the price rise by ⅛.   When the
price of the funds is very steady and the market
quiescent, it means that the stocks are distributed
among holders in such a way that the exchange of
more or less at the prevailing price is a matter of
indifference.

In practice, no market ever long fulfils the theoretical conditions of equilibrium, because, from the
various accidents of life and business, there are sure
to be people every day compelled to sell, or having
sudden inducements to buy.   There is nearly always,
again, the influence of prospective supply or demand,
depending upon the political intelligence of the
moment.   Speculation complicates the action of the
laws of supply and demand in a high degree, but does
not in the least degree arrest their action or alter
their nature.   We shall never have a Science of
Economics unless we learn to discern the operation of
law even among the most perplexing complications
and apparent interruptions.

Problems in the Theory of Exchange

We have hitherto considered only one simple case
of the Theory of Exchange.   In all other cases where
the commodities are capable of indefinite subdivision,

the principles will be exactly the same, but the particular conditions may be subject to variation.

We may, firstly, express the conditions of a great market where vast quantities of some stock are available, so that any one small trader will not appreciably affect the ratio of exchange. This ratio is, then, approximately a fixed number, and each trader exchanges at that ratio just so much as suits him. These circumstances may be represented by supposing A to be a trading body possessing two very large stocks of commodities, a and b. Let C be a person who possesses a comparatively small quantity c of the second commodity, and gives a portion of it, y, which is very small compared with b, in exchange for a portion x of a, which is very small compared with a. Then, after exchange, we shall find A in possession of the quantities $a - x$ and $b + y$, and C in possession of x and $c - y$. The equations will become

$$\frac{\phi_1(a - x)}{\psi_1(b + y)} = \frac{y}{x} = \frac{\phi_2 x}{\psi_2(c - y)}.$$

Since $a - x$ and $b + y$, by supposition, do not appreciably differ from a and b, we may substitute the latter quantities, and we have, for the first equation, approximately,

$$\frac{\phi_1 a}{\psi_1 b} = \frac{y}{x} = m.$$

The ratio of exchange being an approximately fixed ratio determined by the conditions of the trading body A, there is, in reality, only one undetermined quantity, x, the quantity of commodity which C finds it advantageous to purchase by expending part of c. This will now be determined by the equation

$$\frac{\phi_1 a}{\psi_1 b} = \frac{\phi_2 x}{\psi_2 (c - mx)}.$$

This equation will represent the condition in regard to any one distinct commodity of a very small country trading with a much larger one. It might represent, to some extent, the circumstances of trade between the Channel Islands and the great markets of England, though, of course, it is never absolutely verified, because the smallest purchasers do affect the market in some degree. The equation still more accurately represents the position of an individual consumer with regard to the aggregate trade of a large community, since he must buy at the current prices, which he cannot in an appreciable degree affect.

A still simpler formula, however, is needed to represent the conditions of a large part of our purchases. In many cases we want so little of a commodity, that an individual need not give more than a very small fraction of his possessions to obtain it. We may suppose, then, that y in the last problem is a very small part of c, so that $\psi_2(c - y)$ does not differ appreciably from $\psi_2 c$. Taking m as before to be the existing ratio of exchange, we have only one equation—

$$\frac{\phi_2 x}{\psi_2 c} = m,$$

or $\phi_2 x = m \cdot \psi_2 c.$

This means that C will buy of the commodity until its degree of utility falls below that of the commodity he gives. A person's expenditure on salt is in this country an inconsiderable item of expense; what he thus spends does not make him appreciably poorer; yet, if the established price or ratio is one penny for each pound of salt, he buys in any time, say one year, so many pounds of salt that an additional pound would not have so much utility to him as a penny. In the above equation $m \cdot \psi_2 c$ represents the utility to him of a penny, which being an inconsiderable fraction of his possessions, is approximately invariable in utility, and he buys salt until $\phi_2 x$, which is approximately the utility of the next pound, is equal to, or it may be somewhat less than that of the penny. But this case must not be confused with that of purchases which appreciably affect the possessions of the purchaser. Thus, if a poor family purchase much butchers'-meat, they will probably have to go without something else. The more they buy, the lower the final degree of utility of the meat, and *the higher the final degree of utility of something else*; and thus these purchases will be the more narrowly limited.

Complex Cases of the Theory

We have hitherto considered the Theory of Exchange as applying only to two trading bodies possessing and dealing in two commodities. Exactly the same principles hold true, however numerous and complicated may be the conditions. The main point to be remembered in tracing out the results of the theory is, that the same pair of commodities in the same market can have only one ratio of exchange, which must therefore prevail between each body and each other, the costs of conveyance being considered as *nil*. The equations become rapidly more numerous as additional bodies or commodities are considered; but we may exhibit them as they apply to the case of three trading bodies and three commodities.

Thus, suppose that

A possesses the stock a of cotton, and gives x_1 of it to B, x_2 to C.

B possesses the stock b of silk, and gives y_1 to A, y_2 to C.

C possesses the stock c of wool, and gives z_1 to A, z_2 to B.

We have here altogether six unknown quantities— x_1, x_2, y_1, y_2, z_1, z_2; but we have also sufficient means of determining them. They are exchanged as follows—

A gives x_1 for y_1, and x_2 for z_1.

B ,, y_1 for x_1, and y_2 for z_2.

C ,, z_1 for x_2, and z_2 for y_2.

These may be treated as independent exchanges; each body must be satisfied in regard to each of its exchanges, and we must therefore take into account the functions of utility or the final degrees of utility of each commodity in respect of each body. Let us express these functions as follows—

ϕ_1, ψ_1, χ_1 are the respective functions of utility for A.

ϕ_2, ψ_2, χ_2 .   .   .   . B.

ϕ_3, ψ_3, χ_3 .   .   .   . C.

Now A, after the exchange, will hold $a - x_1 - x_2$ of cotton and y_1 of silk; and B will hold x_1 of cotton and $b - y_1 - y_2$ of silk : their ratio of exchange, y_1 for x_1, will therefore be governed by the following pair of equations :—

$$\frac{\phi_1(a - x_1 - x_2)}{\psi_1 y_1} = \frac{y_1}{x_1} = \frac{\phi_2 x_1}{\psi_2(b - y_1 - y_2)}.$$

The exchange of A with C will be similarly determined by the ratio of the degrees of utility of wool and cotton on each side subsequent to the exchange; hence we have

$$\frac{\phi_1(a - x_1 - x_2)}{\chi_1 z_1} = \frac{z_1}{x_2} = \frac{\phi_3 x_2}{\chi_3(c - z_1 - z_2)}.$$

There will also be interchange between B and C which will be independently regulated on similar principles, so that we have another pair of equations to complete the conditions, namely—

$$\frac{\psi_2(b - y_1 - y_2)}{\chi_2 z_2} = \frac{z_2}{y_2} = \frac{\psi_3 y_2}{\chi_3(c - z_1 - z_2)}.$$

We might proceed in the same way to lay down the conditions of exchange between more numerous bodies, but the principles would be exactly the same. For every quantity of commodity which is given in exchange something must be received; and if portions of the same kind of commodity be received from several distinct parties, then we may conceive the quantity which is given for that commodity to be broken up into as many distinct portions. The exchanges in the most complicated case may thus always be decomposed into simple exchanges, and every exchange will give rise to two equations sufficient to determine the quantities involved. The same can also be done when there are two or more commodities in the possession of each trading body.

Competition in Exchange

One case of the Theory of Exchange is of considerable importance, and arises when two parties compete together in supplying a third party with a certain commodity. Thus, suppose that A, with the quantity of one commodity denoted by a, purchases another kind of commodity both from B and from C, who respectively possess b and c of it. All the quantities concerned are as follows—

A gives x_1 of a to B and x_2 to C,
B   „ y_1 of b to A,
C   „ y_2 of c to A.

As each commodity may be supposed to be perfectly homogeneous, the ratio of exchange must be the same in one case as in the other, so that we have one equation thus furnished—

$$\frac{y_1}{x_1} = \frac{y_2}{x_2}. \tag{1}$$

Now, provided that A gets the right commodity in the proper quantity, he does not care whence it comes, so that we need not, in his equation, distinguish the source or destination of the quantities; he simply gives $x_1 + x_2$, and receives in exchange $y_1 + y_2$. Observing, then, that by (1)

$$\frac{y_1 + y_2}{x_1 + x_2} = \frac{y_1}{x_1}$$

we have the usual equation of exchange—

$$\frac{\phi_1(a - x_1 - x_2)}{\psi_1(y_1 + y_2)} = \frac{y_1}{x_1}. \tag{2}$$

But B and C must both be separately satisfied with their shares in the transaction. Thus

$$\frac{\phi_2 x_1}{\psi_2(b - y_1)} = \frac{y_1}{x_1}; \tag{3}$$

$$\frac{\phi_3 x_2}{\psi_3(c - y_2)} = \frac{y_2}{x_2}. \tag{4}$$

There are altogether four unknown quantities— x_1, x_2, y_1, y_2; and we have four equations by which to determine them. Various suppositions might be made as to the comparative magnitudes of the quantities b and c, or the character of the functions concerned; and conclusions could then be drawn as to the effect upon the trade. The general result would be, that the smaller holder must more or less conform to the prices of the larger holder.

Failure of the Equations of Exchange

Cases constantly occur in which equations of the kind set forth in the preceding pages fail to hold true, or lead to impossible results. Such failure may indicate that no exchange at all takes place, but it may also have a different meaning.

In the first case, it may happen that the commodity possessed by A has a high degree of utility to A, and a low degree to B, and that *vice versâ* B's commodity has a high degree of utility to B and less to A. This difference of utility might exist to such an extent, that though B were to receive very little of A's commodity, yet the final degree of utility to him would be less than that of his own commodity, of which he enjoys much more. In such a case no benefit can arise from exchange, and no exchange will consequently take place. This failure of exchange will be indicated by a failure of the equations.

It may also happen that the whole quantities of commodity possessed are exchanged, and yet the equations fail. A may have so low a desire for consuming his own commodity, that the very last increment of it has less degree of utility to him than a small addition to the commodity received in exchange. The same state of things might happen to exist with B as regards his commodity : under these circumstances the whole possessions of one might be exchanged for the whole of the other, and the ratio of exchange would of course be defined by the ratio of these quantities. Yet each party might desire the last increment of the commodity received more than he desires the last increment of that given, so that the equations would fail to be true. This case will hardly occur practically in international trade, since two nations usually trade in many commodities, a fact which would alter the conditions.

Again, the equations of exchange will fail to be possible when the commodity or useful article possessed on one or both sides is indivisible. We have always assumed hitherto that more or less of a commodity may be had, down to infinitely small quantities. This is approximately true of all ordinary trade, especially international trade between great industrial nations. Any one sack of corn or any one bar of iron is practically infinitesimal compared with the quantities exchanged by America and England; and even one cargo or parcel of corn or iron is a small fraction of the whole. But, in exceptional cases, even international trade might involve indivisible articles. We might conceive the British Government giving the Koh-i-noor diamond to the Khedive of Egypt in exchange for Pompey's Pillar, in which case it would certainly not answer the purpose to break up one article or the other.[1] When an island or portion of

---

[1] Since the above was written the value of Cleopatra's Needle has actually formed the subject of decision in the Admiralty Court, in connection with the award of salvage. The fact, however, is that in the absence of any act of exchange concerning such an object, the notion of value is not applicable at all. At the best the value assigned, namely £25,000, is a mere fiction arbitrarily invented to represent what might conceivably be given for such an object if there were a purchaser. It is, moreover, curious that since the first edition was printed Russia has actually made an exchange of islands with Japan. [In 1875 Japan ceded the southern portion of Saghalien to Russia in exchange for the northern half of the Kurile islands.—Ed.]

territory is transferred from one possessor to another, it is often necessary to take the whole, or none. America, in purchasing Alaska from Russia, would hardly have consented to purchase less than the whole. In every sale of a house, factory, or other building, it is usually impracticable to make any division without greatly lessening the utility of the whole. In all such cases our equations must fail to exist, because we cannot contemplate the existence of an increment or a decrement to an indivisible article.

Suppose, for example, that A and B each possess a book: they cannot break up the books, and must therefore exchange them entire, if at all. Under what conditions will they do so? Plainly on the condition that each makes a gain of utility by so doing. Here we deal not with the final degree of utility depending on an infinitesimal quantity, but on the *whole utility of the complete article*. Now let us assign the symbols as follows :—

$$u_1 = \text{the utility of A's book to A,}$$
$$u_2 \quad ,, \quad\quad ,, \quad \text{A's} \quad ,, \quad \text{to B,}$$
$$v_1 \quad ,, \quad\quad ,, \quad \text{B's} \quad ,, \quad \text{to A,}$$
$$v_2 \quad ,, \quad\quad ,, \quad \text{B's} \quad ,, \quad \text{to B.}$$

Then the conditions of exchange are simply

$$v_1 > u_1,$$
$$u_2 > v_2.$$

We might indeed theoretically contemplate the case where the utilities were exactly equal on one side; thus

$$v_1 > u_1,$$
$$u_2 = v_2 ;$$

B would then be wholly indifferent to the exchange, and I do not see any means of deciding whether he would or would not consent to it. But we need hardly consider the case, as it could seldom practically occur. Were the utilities exactly equal on both sides in respect to both objects, there would obviously be no motive to exchange. Again, the slightest loss of utility on either side would be a complete bar to the transaction, because we are not supposing, at present, that any other commodities are in possession so as to allow of separate inducements, or that any other motives than such as arise out of simple desire of one's own convenience enter into the question.

A much more difficult problem arises when we suppose an indivisible article exchanged for a divisible commodity. When Russia sold Alaska this was a practically indivisible thing; but it was bought with money of which more or less might be given to indefinitely small quantities. A bargain of this kind is exceedingly common; indeed it occurs in the case of every house, mansion, estate, factory, ship, or other complete whole, which is sold for money. Our former equations of exchange certainly fail, for they involve increments of commodity on both sides. The theory seems to give a very unsatisfactory answer, for the problem proves to be, within certain limits, indeterminate.

Let X be the indivisible article ; u_1 its utility to

its possessor A, and u_2 its utility to B.   Let y be the
quantity of commodity given for it, a commodity
which is supposed to be divisible *ad infinitum* ; let v_1
be the total utility of y to A, and v_2 its total utility
to B.   Then it is quite evident that, in order to give
rise to exchange, v_1 must be greater than u_1, and u_2
must be greater than v_2 ; that is, there must, as before,
be a gain of utility on each side.   The quantity y
must not be so great then as to deprive B of gain,
nor so small as to deprive A of gain.   The following
is an extract from Mr. Thornton's work which exactly
expresses the problem :—

"There are two opposite extremes—one above
which the price of a commodity cannot rise, the other
below which it cannot fall.   The upper of these limits
is marked by the utility, real or supposed, of the
commodity to the customer ; the lower, of its utility
to the dealer.   No one will give for a commodity a
quantity of money or money's worth, which, in his
opinion, would be of more use to him than the commodity itself.   No one will take for a commodity a
quantity of money or of anything else which he thinks
would be of less use to himself than the commodity.
The price eventually given and taken may be either
at one of the opposite extremes, or may be anywhere
intermediate between them." [1]

Three distinct cases might occur, which can best
be illustrated by a concrete example.   Suppose we can

[1] Thornton, *On Labour; its Wrongful Claims and Rightful Dues*
(1869), p. 58.

read the thoughts of the parties in the sale of a house. If A says £1200 is the least price which will satisfy him, and B holds that £800 is the highest price which it will be profitable for him to give, no exchange can possibly take place.   If A should find £1000 to be his lowest limit, while B happens to name the same sum for his highest limit, the transaction can be closed, and the price will be exactly defined.   But supposing, finally, that A is really willing to sell at £900, and B is prepared to buy at £1100, in what manner can we theoretically determine the price ?   I see no mode of solving the question.   Any price between £900 and £1100 will leave a profit on each side, and both parties will lose if they do not come to terms.   I conceive that such a transaction must be settled upon other than strictly economic grounds.   The result of the bargain will greatly depend upon the comparative amount of knowledge of each other's position and needs which either bargainer may possess or manage to obtain in the course of the transaction. Thus the power of reading another man's thoughts is of high importance in business, and the art of bargaining mainly consists in the buyer ascertaining the lowest price at which the seller is willing to part with his object, without disclosing if possible the highest price which he, the buyer, is willing to give.   The disposition and force of character of the parties, their comparative persistency, their adroitness and experience in business, or it may be feelings of justice or of kindliness, will also influence the decision.   These

are motives more or less extraneous to a theory of
Economics, and yet they appear necessary considerations in this problem. It may be that indeterminate
bargains of this kind are best arranged by an arbi-
trator or third party.

The equations of exchange may fail again when
commodities are divisible, but not to infinitely small
quantities. There is always, in retail trade, a convenient unit ʹbelow which we do not descend in
purchases. Paper may be bought in quires, or even
in packets, which it may not be desirable to break up.
Wine cannot be bought from the wine merchant
in less than a bottle at a time. In all such cases
exchange cannot, theoretically speaking, be perfectly
adjusted, because it will be infinitely improbable that
an integral number of units will precisely verify the
equations of exchange. In a large proportion of
cases, indeed, the unit may be so small compared
with the whole quantities exchanged as practically to
be infinitely small. But suppose that a person be
buying ink which is only to be had, under the circumstances, in one-shilling bottles. If one bottle be
not quite enough, how will he decide whether to take
a second or not ? Clearly by estimating the aggregate
utility of the bottle of ink compared with the shilling.
If there be an excess, he will certainly purchase it,
and proceed to consider whether a third be desirable
or not.

This case might be illustrated by fig. 7, in
which the spaces $o\,q_1$, $p_1\,q_2$, $p_2\,q_3$, etc., represent the

total utilities of successive bottles of ink ; while the
equal spaces $o\,r_1$, $p_1\,r_2$, etc., represent the total utilities
of successive shillings, which we may assume to be
practically invariable.   There is no doubt that three
bottles will be purchased, but the fourth will not

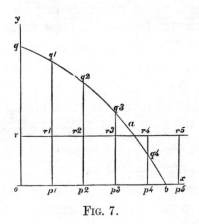

FIG. 7.

be purchased unless the mixtilinear figure $p_3\,q_3\,q_4\,p_4$
exceed in area the rectangle $p_3\,r_3\,r_4\,p_4$.

Cases of this kind are similar to those treated in
pp. 120-4, where the things exchanged are indivisible,
except that the question of exchange or no exchange
occurs over and over again with respect to each
successive unit, and is decided in respect to each by
the excess of the total utility of the unit to be
received over the total utility of that to be given.
There is indeed perfect harmony between the cases
where equations can and where they cannot be
established ; for we have only to imagine the indivisible units of commodity to be indefinitely lessened in

size to enable us to pass gradually down to the case
where equality of the increments of utility is ultimately established.

Negative and Zero Value

Only a few economists, notably Mr. H. D. Macleod
in several of his publications, have noticed the fact
that there may be such a thing as negative value.
Yet there cannot be the least doubt that people often
labour, or pay money to other labourers, in order to
get rid of things, and they would not do this unless
such things were hurtful, that is, had the opposite
quality to utility—disutility. Water, when it gets
into a mine, is a costly thing to get out again, and
many people have been ruined by wet mines. Quarries
and mines usually produce great quantities of valueless rock or earth, variously called duff, spoil, waste,
rubbish, and no inconsiderable part of the cost of
working arises from the need of raising and carrying
this profitless mass of matter and then finding land
on which to deposit it. Every furnace yields cinders,
dross, or slag, which can seldom be sold for any
money, and every household is at the expense of
getting rid, in one way or another, of sewage, ashes,
swill, and other *rejectanea*. Reflection soon shows,
in short, that no inconsiderable part of the values
with which we deal in practical economics must be
negative values.

It will hardly be needful to show at full length

that this negative value may be regarded as varying continuously in the same way as positive value. If after a long drought rain begins to fall heavily, it is at first hailed as a great benefit; the rain-water may be so valuable as to produce a crop, when otherwise successful agriculture would have been impossible. Rain may thus avert famine; but after the rain has fallen for a certain length of time, the farmer begins to think he has had enough of it; more rain will retard his operations, or injure the growing plants. As the rain continues to fall he fears further injury; water begins to flood his land, and there is even danger of the soil and crops being all washed away together. But the rain unfortunately pours down more and more heavily, until at length perhaps the crops, soil, house, stock,—nay, the farmer himself, are all swept bodily away. That same water, then, which in moderate quantity would have been of the greatest possible benefit, has only to be supplied in greater and greater quantities to become injurious, until it ends with occasioning the ruin, and even the death, of the individual. Those acquainted with the floods and droughts of Australia know that this is no fancy sketch.[1]

In many other cases it might be shown similarly that matter, we can hardly call it commodity, acquires a higher and higher degree of *disutility* the greater

---

[1] See the author's "History of the Floods and Droughts of New South Wales," in the *Australian Almanack*, Sydney, 1859, p. 61. Also Mr. H. C. Russell's *Climate of New South Wales.*

the quantity which has to be disposed of. Such is
the case with the sewage of great towns, the foul or
poisoned water from mines, dye-works, etc. Any
obstacle, however, may be regarded as so much discommodity, whether it be a mountain which has to
be bored through to make a railway, or a hollow
which has to be filled up with an expensive embankment. If a building site requires a certain expenditure in levelling and draining before it can be made
use of, the cost of this work is, of course, subtracted
from the value which the land would otherwise
possess. As every advantage in property gives rise
to value, so every disadvantage must be set against
that value.

We now come to the question how negative value
is to be represented in our equations. Let us suppose
a person possessing a of some commodity to find it
insufficient : then it has positive degree of utility for
him, that is to say $\phi(a)$ is positive. Suppose x to
be added to a and gradually increased : $\phi(a + x)$ will
gradually decrease. Let us assume that for a certain
value of x it becomes zero; then, if the further increase of x turns utility into disutility, $\phi(a + x)$ will
become a negative quantity. How will this negative
sign affect the validity of the equations which we
have been employing in preceding pages, and in which
each member has appeared to be both formally and
intrinsically positive ? It is plain that we cannot
equate a positive to a negative quantity; but it will
be found that if, at the same time that we introduce

negative utility, we also assign to each increment of commodity the positive or negative sign, according as it is added to or subtracted from the exchanger's possessions, that is to say, received or given in exchange, no such difficulty arises.

Suppose A and B respectively to hold a and b, and to exchange dx and dy of the commodities X and Y. Then it will be apparent from the general character of the argument on pp. 98-100, that the fundamental equation there adopted will be included in the more general form—

$$\phi(a \pm x) . dx + \psi(b \pm y) . dy = 0.$$

In this equation either factor of either term may be intrinsically negative, while the alternative signs before x and y allow for every possible case of giving and receiving in exchange.

Four possible cases will arise. In the first case, both commodities have utility for each person, that is to say, ϕ and ψ are both positive functions; but A gives some of X in return for some of Y. This means that dx is negative, and dy positive, while the quantities in possession after exchange are $a - x$, and $b + y$. Thus the equation becomes

$$-\phi(a - x) . dx + \psi(b + y) . dy = 0.$$

We should have merely to transpose the negative term to the other side of the equation, and to assume $b = 0$, to obtain the equation on p. 99.

As the second case, suppose that Y possesses disutility for A, so that the function ψ becomes for him negative; in order to get rid of y, he must also pay x with it, and both these quantities as well as dy and dx receive the negative sign. Then the equation takes the shape

$$\phi(a - x) \times (- dx) - \psi(b - y) \times (- dy) = 0,$$

or

$$- \phi(a - x) . dx + \psi(b - y) . dy = 0.$$

The third case is the counterpart of the last, and represents B's position, who receives both x and y, on the ground that one of these quantities is *discommodity* to him. But putting the matter as the case of A, we may assume ϕ to be positive, ψ negative, and giving the positive sign to all of x, y, dx, and dy, we obtain the equation—

$$\phi(a + x) . dx - \psi(b + y) . dy = 0.$$

It is possible to conceive yet a fourth case in which people should be exchanging two discommodities; that is to say, getting rid of one hurtful substance by accepting in place of it what is felt to be less hurtful, though still possessing disutility. In this case we have both ϕ and ψ negative, as well as one of the quantities exchanged; taking x and dx as positive, and y and dy as negative, the equation assumes the form

$$- \phi(a + x) . dx - \psi(b - y) . (- dy) = 0,$$

or

$$- \phi(a + x) . dx + \psi(b - y) . dy = 0.$$

It might be difficult to discover any distinct cases of this last kind of exchange. Generally speaking,

when a person receives assistance in getting rid of
some inconvenient possession, he pays in money or
other commodity for the service of him who helps
to remove the burden. It must naturally be a very
rare case that the remover has some burden which it
would suit the other party to receive in exchange.
Yet the contingency may, and no doubt does, sometimes occur. Two adjacent landowners, for instance,
might reasonably agree that, if A allows B to throw
the spoil of his mine on A's land, then A shall be
allowed to drain his mine into B's mine. It might
happen that B was comparatively more embarrassed
by the great quantity of his spoil than by water, and
that A had room for the spoil, but could not get rid
of the water in other ways without great difficulty.
An exchange of inconveniences would then be plainly
beneficial.

Looking at the equations obtained in the four
cases as stated above, it is apparent that the general
equation of exchange consists in equating to zero the
sum of one positive and one negative term, so that
the signs, both of the utility functions and of the
increments, may be disregarded. Thus the fundamental equation may be written in the general form

$$\frac{\phi(a \pm x)}{\psi(b \pm y)} = \frac{dy}{dx}.$$

We may express the result of this theory in general
terms by saying that the algebraic sum of the utility
or disutility received or parted with, as regards the
last increments concerned in an act of traffic, will

always be zero. It also follows that, without
regard to sign, the increments are in magnitude inversely as their degrees of utility or disutility. The
reader will not fail to notice the remarkable analogy
between this theory and that of the equilibrium of two
forces regarded according to the principle of virtual
velocities. A rigid lever will remain in equilibrium
under the action of two forces, provided that the algebraic sum of the forces, each multiplied by its infinitely
small displacement, be zero. Substitute for force degree of utility, positive or negative, and for infinitely
small displacements infinitely small quantities of commodity exchanged, and the principles are identical.

It still remains to consider the imaginary case in
which substances possess or are supposed to possess
neither utility nor disutility, and are yet exchanged
in finite quantities. Substituting the ratio of y and
x for that of dy and dx, the general equation

$$\frac{\phi(a \pm x)}{\psi(b \pm y)} = \frac{y}{x}$$

will give the value $\frac{y}{x} = \frac{0}{0}$, both the functions of utility

being zero. This means that the quantities exchanged
will be indeterminate so far as the theory of utility
goes. If one substance possesses utility, and the
other does not, the ratio of exchange becomes either

$\frac{y}{0}$ or $\frac{0}{y}$, infinity or zero, indicating that there can be

no comparison in our theory between things which do
and those which do not possess utility. Practically

speaking, such cases do not occur except in an approximate manner. Such things as cinders, shavings, night-soil, etc., have either low degrees of utility or disutility. If the dustman takes them away for nothing, they must have utility for him sufficient to pay the cost of removal. When the dust is riddled, one part is usually found to have utility just sufficient to balance the disutility of the remainder, giving us an instance of the second or third form of the equation of exchange according as we regard the matter from the householder's or the dustman's point of view.

Equivalence of Commodities

Much confusion is thrown into the statistical investigation of questions of supply and demand by the circumstance that one commodity can often replace another, and serve the same purposes more or less perfectly. The same, or nearly the same, substance is often obtained from two or three sources. The constituents of wheat, barley, oats, and rye are closely similar, if not identical. Vegetable structures are composed mainly of the same chemical compound in nearly all cases. Animal meat, again, is of nearly the same composition from whatever animal derived. There are endless differences of flavour and quality, but these are often insufficient to prevent one kind from serving in place of another.

Whenever different commodities are thus applicable to the same purposes, their conditions of demand and exchange are not independent. Their mutual

ratio of exchange cannot vary much, for it will be
closely defined by the ratio of their utilities. Beef
and mutton, for instance, differ so slightly, that
people eat them almost indifferently. But the whole-
sale price of mutton, on an average, exceeds that of
beef in the ratio of 9 to 8, and we must therefore
conclude that people generally esteem mutton more
than beef in this proportion, otherwise they would
not buy the dearer meat. It follows that the final
degrees of utility of these meats are in this ratio, or
that if ϕx be the degree of utility of mutton, and
ψy that of beef, we have

$$8 \cdot \phi x = 9 \cdot \psi y.$$

This equation would doubtless not hold true in
extreme circumstances ; if mutton became comparatively scarce, there would probably be some persons
willing to pay a higher price, merely because it would
then be considered a delicacy. But this is certain,
that, so long as the equation of utilities holds true,
the ratio of exchange between mutton and beef will
not diverge from that of 8 to 9. If the supply of
beef falls off to a small extent, people will not pay a
higher price for it, but will eat more mutton ; and if
the supply of mutton falls off, they will eat more beef
The conditions of supply will have no effect upon the
ratio of exchange ; we must, in fact, treat beef and
mutton as one commodity of two different strengths,
just as gold at eighteen and gold at twenty carats are
hardly considered as two but rather as one commodity,

of which twenty parts of one are equivalent to eighteen of the other.

It is upon this principle that we must explain, in harmony with Cairnes' views, the extraordinary permanence of the ratio of exchange of gold and silver, which from the commencement of the eighteenth century up to recent years never diverged much from 15 to 1. That this fixedness of ratio did not depend entirely upon the amount or cost of production is proved by the very slight effect of the Australian and Californian gold discoveries, which never raised the gold price of silver more than about $4\frac{2}{3}$ per cent, and failed to have a permanent effect of more than $1\frac{1}{2}$ per cent. This permanence of relative values may have been partially due to the fact, that gold and silver can be employed for exactly the same purposes, but that the superior brilliancy of gold occasions it to be preferred, unless it be about 15 or $15\frac{1}{2}$ times as costly as silver. Much more probably, however, the explanation of the fact is to be found in the fixed ratio of $15\frac{1}{2}$ to 1, according to which these metals are exchanged in the currency of France and some other continental countries. The French Currency Law of the Year XI established an artificial equation—

$$\text{Utility of gold} = 15\tfrac{1}{2} \times \text{Utility of silver} ;$$

and it is probably not without some reason that Wolowski and other recent French economists attributed to this law of replacement an important effect in preventing disturbance in the relations of gold and silver.

Since the first edition of this work was published, the views of Wolowski have received striking verification in the unprecedented fall in the value of silver which has occurred in the last three or four years. The ratio of equivalent weights of silver and gold, which had never before risen much above 16 to 1, commenced to rise in 1874, and was at one time (July 1876) as high as 22·5 to 1 in the London market. Though it has since fallen, the ratio continues to be subject to frequent considerable oscillations. The great production of silver in Nevada may contribute somewhat to this extraordinary result, but the principal cause must be the suspension of the French Law of the Double Standard, and the demonetisation of silver in Germany, Scandinavia, and elsewhere. As I have treated the subject of the value of silver and the Double Standard elsewhere,[1] I need not pursue it here.

Acquired Utility of Commodities

The Theory of Exchange, as explained above, rests entirely on the consideration of quantities of utility, and no reference to labour or cost of produc-

---

[1] *Serious Fall in the Value of Gold*, 1863, p. 33 (reprinted in *Investigations in Currency and Finance*, 1884). *Money and the Mechanism of Exchange* (International Scientific Series ; also translated into French, German, and Italian, see Appendix IV.), chap. xii. This chapter has been translated by M. H. Gravez, and reprinted in the *Bibliothèque Utile*, vol. xliv. (Germer Baillière), Paris, 1878. See also Papers on the Silver Question read before the American Social Science Association at Saratoga, Sept. 5, 1877, Boston, 1877, and *Bankers' Magazine*, Dec. 1877 (reprinted in *Investigations in Currency and Finance*, 1884 and 1908).

tion has been made.   The *value* of a divisible commodity, if I may for a moment use the dangerous
term, is measured, not, indeed, by its total utility,
but by its final degree of utility, that is by the
intensity of the need we have for *more* of it.   But
the power of exchanging one commodity for another
greatly extends the range of utility.   We are no
longer limited to considering the degree of utility
of a commodity as regards the wants of its immediate
possessor; for it may have a higher usefulness to
some other person, and can be transferred to that
person in exchange for some commodity of a higher
degree of utility to the purchaser.   The general result
of exchange is, that all commodities sink, as it were,
to the same level of utility in respect of the last
portions consumed.

In the Theory of Exchange we find that the
possessor of any divisible commodity will exchange
such a portion of it, that the next increment would
have exactly equal utility with the increment of other
produce which he would receive for it.   This will
hold good however various may be the kinds of commodity he requires.   Suppose that a person possesses
one single kind of commodity, which we may consider to be money, or income, and that p, q, r, s, t,
etc., are quantities of other commodities which he
purchases with portions of his income.   Let x be the
uncertain quantity of money which he will desire not
to exchange; what relation will exist between these
quantities x, p, q, r, etc. ?   This relation will partly

depend upon the ratio of exchange, partly on the final degree of utility [1] of these commodities. Let us assume, for a moment, that all the ratios of exchange are equalities, or that a unit of one is always to be purchased with a unit of another. Then, plainly, we must have the degrees of utility equal, otherwise there would be advantage in acquiring more of that possessing the higher degree of utility. Let the sign ϕ denote the function of utility, which will be different in each case ; then we have simply the equations—

$$\phi_1 x = \phi_2 p = \phi_3 q = \phi_4 r = \phi_5 s = \text{etc.}$$

But, as a matter of fact, the ratio of exchange is seldom or never that of unit for unit ; and when the quantities exchanged are unequal, the degrees of utility will not be equal. If for one pound of silk I can have three of cotton, then the degree of utility of cotton must be a third that of silk, otherwise I should gain by exchange. Thus the general result of the facility of exchange prevailing in a civilised country is, that *a person procures such quantities of commodities that the final degrees of utility of any pair of commodities are inversely as the ratios of exchange of the commodities.*

Let x_1, x_2, x_3, x_4, etc., be the portions of his income given for p, q, r, s, etc., respectively, then we must have

$$\frac{\phi_2 p}{\phi_1 x} = \frac{x_1}{p}, \qquad \frac{\phi_3 q}{\phi_1 x} = \frac{x_2}{q}, \qquad \frac{\phi_4 r}{\phi_1 x} = \frac{x_3}{r},$$

---

[1] Strictly : "on the functions of final degree of utility," *i.e.* the shapes of the curves.—[Ed.]

and so on.   The theory thus represents the fact, that
a person distributes his income in such a way as to
equalise the utility of the final increments of all commodities consumed.   As water runs into hollows until
it fills them up to the same level, so wealth runs into
all the branches of expenditure.   This distribution
will vary greatly with different individuals, but it is
self-evident that the want which an individual feels
most acutely at the moment will be that upon which
he will expend the next increment of his income.
It obviously follows that *in expending a person's
income to the greatest advantage, the algebraic sum
of the quantities of commodity received or parted
with, each multiplied by its final degree of utility
[after the exchange], will be zero.*

We can now conceive, in an accurate manner, the
utility of money, or of that supply of commodity
which forms a person's income.   Its final degree of
utility is measured by that of any of the other commodities which he consumes.   What, for instance, is
the utility of one penny to a poor family earning fifty
pounds a year?   As a penny is an inconsiderable
portion of their income, it may represent one of the
infinitely small increments, and its utility is equal to
the utility of the quantity of bread, tea, sugar, or
other articles which they could purchase with it, this
utility depending upon the extent to which they were
already provided with those articles.   To a family
possessing one thousand pounds a year, the utility of
a penny may be measured in an exactly similar

manner ; but it will be much less, because their want
of any given commodity will be satiated or satisfied
to a much greater extent, so that the urgency of need
for a pennyworth more of any article is much reduced.

The general result of exchange is thus to produce
a certain equality of utility between different commodities, as regards the same individual ; but between
different individuals no such equality will tend to be
produced.[1]   In Economics we regard only commercial
transactions, and no equalisation of wealth from
charitable motives is considered.   The degree of
utility of wealth to a very rich man will be governed
by its degree of utility in that branch of expenditure
in which he continues to feel the most need of further
possessions.   His primary wants will long since have
been fully satisfied ; he could find food, if requisite,
for a thousand persons, and so, of course, he will have
supplied himself with as much as he in the least
desires.   But so far as is consistent with the inequality
of wealth in every community, all commodities are
distributed by exchange so as to produce the maximum of benefit.   Every person whose wish for a certain thing exceeds his wish for other things, acquires
what he wants provided he can make a sufficient
sacrifice in other respects.   No one is ever required

---

[1] Since, in equilibrium, final degrees of utility are proportional to
market prices, the "certain" equality of utility here said to exist between
different commodities is that between marginal portions of such
relative size that they are purchasable with the same small sum of
money ; *e.g.* between a "shilling's worth" of one and of other commodities.—[Ed.]

to give what he more desires for what he less desires, so that perfect freedom of exchange must be to the advantage of all.

The Gain by Exchange

It is a most important result of this theory that the ratio of exchange gives no indication of the real benefit derived from the action of exchange. So many trades are occupied in buying and selling, and make their profits by buying low and selling high, that there arises a fallacious tendency to believe that the whole benefit of trade depends upon the differences of prices. It is implied that to pay a high price is worse than doing without the article, and the whole financial system of a great nation may be distorted in the effort to carry out a false theory.

This is the result to which some of J. S. Mill's remarks, in his *Theory of International Trade*, would lead. That theory is always ingenious, and as it seems to me, nearly always true; but he draws from it the following conclusion :[1]—" The countries which carry on their foreign trade on the most advantageous terms are those whose commodities are most in demand by foreign countries, and which have themselves the least demand for foreign commodities. From which, among other consequences, it follows that the richest countries, *cæteris paribus*, gain the

[1] *Principles of Political Economy*, book iii., chap. xviii., end of the 8th section.

least by a given amount of foreign commerce : since, having a greater demand for commodities generally, they are likely to have a greater demand for foreign commodities, and thus modify the terms of interchange to their own disadvantage. Their aggregate gains by foreign trade, doubtless, are generally greater than those of poorer countries, since they carry on a greater amount of such trade, and gain the benefit of cheapness on a larger consumption : but their gain is less on each individual article consumed."

In the absence of any explanation to the contrary, this passage must be taken to mean that the advantage of foreign trade depends upon the terms of exchange, and that international trade is less advantageous to a rich than to a poor country. But such a conclusion involves confusion between two distinct things—the price of a commodity and its total utility. A country is not merely like a great mercantile firm buying and selling goods, and making a profit out of the difference of price ; it buys goods in order to consume them. But, in estimating the benefit which a consumer derives from a commodity, it is the total utility which must be taken as the measure, not the final degree of utility on which the terms of exchange depend.

To illustrate this truth we may employ the curves in fig. 8 to represent the functions of utility of two commodities. Let the wool of Australia be represented by the line *ob*, and its total utility to

Australia by the area of the curvilinear figure *obrp*. Let the utility of a second commodity, say cotton goods, to Australia be similarly represented in the lower curve, so that the quantity of commodity measured by $o'b'$ gives a total utility represented by

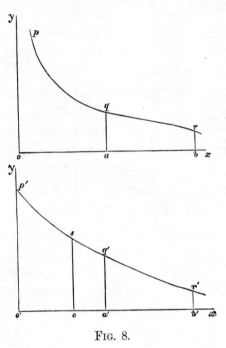

FIG. 8.

the figure $o'p'r'b'$. Then, if Australia gives half its wool, ab, for the quantity of cotton goods represented by $o'a'$, it loses the utility $aqrb$, but gains that represented by the larger area $o'p'q'a'$. There is accordingly a considerable net gain of utility, which is the real object of exchange. Even had Australia sold its wool at a lower price, obtaining cotton goods only to the amount of $o'c$, the utility of this amount, $o'p'sc$, would have exceeded that of the wool given for it.

So far is Mill's statement from being fundamentally correct, that I believe the truth lies in the opposite direction.   As a general rule, the greatness of the price which a country is willing and able to pay for the productions of other countries, measures, or at least manifests, the greatness of the benefit which it derives from such imports.   He who pays a high price must either have a very great need of that which he buys, or very little need of that which he pays for it; on either supposition there is gain by exchange.   In questions of this sort there is but one rule which can be safely laid down, namely, that no one will buy a thing unless he expects advantage from the purchase; and perfect freedom of exchange, therefore, tends to the maximising of utility.

One advantage of the Theory of Economics, carefully studied, will be to make us very careful in our conclusions when the matter is not of the simplest possible nature.   The fact that we can most imperfectly estimate the total utility of any one commodity should prevent us, for instance, from attempting to measure the benefit of any trade.   Accordingly, when Mill proceeds from his theory of international trade to that of taxation, and arrives at the conclusion that one nation may, by means of taxes on commodities imported, " appropriate to itself, at the expense of foreigners, a larger share than would otherwise belong

to it of the increase in the general productiveness of
the labour and capital of the world,"[1] I venture to
question the truth of his results.   I conceive that his
arguments involve a confusion between the ratio of
exchange and the total utility of a commodity, and a
far more accurate knowledge of economic laws than
any one yet possesses would be required to estimate
the true effect of a tax.   Customs duties may be
requisite as a means of raising revenue, but the time
is past when any economist should give the slightest
countenance to their employment for manipulating
trade, or for interfering with the natural tendency of
exchange to increase utility.

Numerical Determination of the Laws of Utility

The future progress of Economics as a strict
science must greatly depend upon our acquiring more
accurate notions of the variable quantities concerned
in the theory.   We cannot really tell the effect of
any change in trade or manufacture until we can with
some approach to truth express the laws of the variation of utility numerically.   To do this we need
accurate statistics of the quantities of commodities
purchased by the whole population at various prices.
The price of a commodity is the only test we have of
the utility of the commodity to the purchaser ; and
if we could tell exactly how much people reduce their
consumption of each important article when the price

---

[1] *Principles of Political Economy*, book v., chap. iv. sec. 6.

rises, we could determine, at least approximately, the variation of the final degree of utility—the all-important element in Economics.

In such calculations we may at first make use of the simpler equation given on p. 113. For the first approximation we may assume that the general utility of a person's income is not affected by the changes of price of the commodity ; so that, if in the equation

$$\phi x = m \cdot \psi c$$

we may have many different corresponding values for x and m, we may treat ψc, the utility of money, as a constant, and determine the general character of the function ϕx, the final degree of utility. This function would doubtless be a purely empirical one—a mere aggregate of terms devised so that their sum shall vary in accordance with statistical facts. The subject is too complex to allow of our expecting any simple precise law like that of gravity. Nor, when we have got the laws, shall we be able to give any exact explanation of them. They will be of the same character as the empirical formulæ used in many of the physical sciences—mere aggregates of mathematical symbols intended to replace a tabular statement.[1] Nevertheless, their determination will render Economics a science as exact as many of the physical sciences ; as exact, for instance, as Meteorology is likely to be for a very long time to come.

[1] See Jevons' *Principles of Science*, chap. xxii., new ed., pp. 487-489, and the references there given.

The method of determining the function of utility explained above will hardly apply, however, to the main elements of expenditure. The price of bread, for instance, cannot be properly brought under the equation in question, because, when the price of bread rises much, the resources of poor persons are strained, money becomes scarcer with them, and ψc, the utility of money, rises. The natural result is, the lessening of expenditure in other directions ; that is to say, all the wants of a poor person are supplied to a less degree of satisfaction when food is dear than when it is cheap. When in the long course of scientific progress a sufficient supply of suitable statistics has been at length obtained, it will become a mathematical problem of no great difficulty how to disentangle the functions expressing the degrees of utility of various commodities. One of the first steps, no doubt, will be to ascertain what proportion of the expenditure of poor people goes to provide food, at various prices of that food. But great difficulty is thrown in the way of all such inquiries by the vast differences in the condition of persons ; and still greater difficulties are created by the complicated ways in which one commodity replaces or serves instead of another.

Opinions as to the Variation of Price

There is no difficulty in finding in works of Economists remarks upon the relation between a change in the supply of a commodity and the consequent rise of price.   The general principles of the variation of utility have been familiar to many writers.

As a general rule the variation of price is much more marked in the case of necessaries of life than in the case of luxuries.   This result would follow from the fact observed by Adam Smith, that "The desire for food is limited in every man by the narrow capacity of the human stomach; but the desire of the conveniences and ornaments of building, dress, equipage, and household furniture, seems to have no limit or certain boundary."   As I assert that value depends upon desire for more, it follows that any excessive supply of food will lower its price very much more than in the case of articles of luxury.   Reciprocally, a deficiency of food will raise its price much more than would happen in the case of less necessary articles.   This conclusion is in harmony with facts; for Chalmers says:[1] "The necessaries of life are far more powerfully affected in the price of them by a variation in their quantity than are the luxuries of life.   Let the crop of grain be deficient by one-third in its usual amount, or rather, let the supply of grain in the market, whether from the home produce or by importation, be curtailed to the same extent, and this will create a much greater addition than of one-third to the price of it.   It is not an unlikely prediction that its cost would be more than doubled by the short-coming of one-third or one-fourth in the supply."

[1] Chalmers' *Christian and Economic Polity of a Nation*, vol. ii. p. 240.

He goes on to explain, at considerable length, that the same would not happen with such an article as rum. A deficiency in the supply of rum from the West Indies would occasion a rise of price, but not to any great extent, because there would be a substitution of other kinds of spirits, or else a reduction in the amount consumed. Men can live without luxuries, but not without necessaries. "A failure in the general supply of esculents to the extent of one-half would more than quadruple the price of the first necessaries of life, and would fall with very aggravated pressure on the lower orders. A failure to the same extent in all the vineyards of the world would most assuredly not raise the price of wine to anything near this proportion. Rather than pay four times the wonted price for Burgundy, there would be a general descent to claret, or from that to port, or from that to the home-made wines of our own country, or from that to its spirituous, or from that to its fermented liquors."[1] He points to sugar especially as an article which would be extensively thrown out of consumption by any great rise in price,[2] because it is a luxury, and at the same time forms a considerable element in expenditure. But he thinks that, if an article occasions a total expenditure of very small amount, variations of price will not much affect its consumption.

Speaking of nutmeg, he says: "There is not sixpence a year consumed of it for each family in Great

---

[1] Chalmers' *Christian and Economic Polity of a Nation*, vol. ii. p. 242.   [2] *Ibid.*, p. 251.

Britain; and perhaps not one family that spends more than a guinea on this article alone. Let the price then be doubled or trebled; this will have no perceptible effect on the demand; and the price will far rather be paid than that the wonted indulgence should in any degree be foregone. .... The same holds true of cloves, and cinnamon, and Cayenne pepper, and all the precious spiceries of the East; and it is thus that while, in the general, the price of necessaries differs so widely from that of luxuries, in regard to the extent of oscillation, there is a remarkable approximation in this matter between the very commonest of these necessaries and the very rarest of these luxuries." [1]

In these interesting observations Chalmers correctly distinguishes between the effect of desire for the commodity in question and that for other commodities. The cost of nutmeg does not appreciably affect the general expenditure on other things, and the equation on p. 113 therefore applies. But if sugar becomes scarce, to consume as before would necessitate a reduction of consumption in other directions; and as the degree of utility of more necessary articles rises much more rapidly than that of sugar, it is the latter article which is thrown out of use by preference. This is a far more complex case, which includes also the case of corn and all large articles of consumption.

Chalmers' remarks on the price of sugar are strongly supported by facts concerning the course of

[1] Chalmers' *Christian and Economic Polity of a Nation*, vol. ii. p. 252.

the sugar markets in 1855-6.   In the year 1855, as
is stated in Tooke's *History of Prices*,[1] attention was
suddenly drawn to a considerable reduction which
had taken place in the stocks of sugar.   The price
rapidly advanced, but before it had reached the
highest point the demand became almost wholly
suspended.   Not only did retail dealers avoid re-
plenishing their stocks, but there was an immediate
and sometimes entire cessation of consumption among
extensive classes.   There were instances among the
retail grocers of their not selling a single pound of
sugar until prices receded to what the public was
satisfied was a reasonable rate.

Variation of the Price of Corn

As to Chalmers' ingenious remarks upon the consumption of nutmeg, he seems to be at least partially
correct.   To a certain extent he brings into view the
principle explained above, that when only a small
quantity of income is required to purchase a certain
kind of commodity in sufficient abundance, the degree
of utility of income will not be appreciably affected
by the price paid, that is to say (p. 113) ψc remains
approximately constant.   It follows that $\dfrac{\phi x}{m}$ is constant, or in other words the final degree of utility of
the small commodity purchased must be directly proportional to the price.   If then the price rise much,

---

[1] Vol. v., p. 324, etc.

either the consumer must relinquish the use of that commodity almost entirely, or else he must feel such need of it, that a small decrease of consumption is irksome to him ; that is to say, looking to our curves of utility, either we must recede to a part of the curve very close to the axis of y, or else the curve must be one which rises rapidly as we move towards the origin. Now Chalmers assumes that with nutmeg the latter is the case. People accustomed to use it in his time were so fond of it that they would pay a much higher price rather than decrease their consumption considerably. This means that it possessed a high degree of utility to them, which could only be overbalanced by some serious increase in the value of ψc, which would ultimately mean the need of the necessaries of life.

It is very curious that in this subject, which reaches to the very foundations of Political Economy, we owe more to early than later writers. Before our science could be said to exist at all, writers on Political Arithmetic had got about as far as we have got at present. In a pamphlet of 1737,[1] it is remarked that " People who understand trade will readily agree with me, that the tenth part of a commodity in a market, more than there is a brisk demand for, is apt to lower the market, perhaps, twenty or thirty per cent, and that a deficiency of a tenth part will cause as exorbitant an advance." Sir J. Dalrymple,[2] again,

---

[1] Quoted in Lauderdale's *Inquiry into the Nature and Origin of Public Wealth*, 2nd ed., 1819, pp. 51, 52.   [2] *Ibid.*

says : "Merchants observe, that if the commodity in market is diminished one-third beneath its mean quantity, it will be nearly doubled in value; and that if it is augmented one-third above its mean quantity, it will sink near one-half in its value; or that, by further diminishing or augmenting the quantity, these disproportions between the quantity and prices vastly increase." These remarks bear little signs of accuracy, indeed, for the writers have spoken of commodities in general as if they all varied in price in a similar degree. It is probable that they were thinking of corn or other kinds of the more necessary food. In the *Spectator* we find a conjecture,[1] that the production of one-tenth part more of grain than is usually consumed would diminish the value of the grain one-half. I know nothing more strange and discreditable to statists and economists than that in so important a point as the relations of price and supply of the main article of food, we owe our most accurate estimates to writers who lived from one to two centuries ago.

There is a celebrated estimate of the variation of the price of corn which I have found quoted in innumerable works on Economics. It is commonly attributed to Gregory King, whose name should be held in honour as one of the fathers of statistical science in England. Born at Lichfield in 1648, King devoted himself much to mathematical studies, and was often occupied in surveying. His principal public appointments were those of Lancaster Herald and

[1] No. 200, quoted by Lauderdale, p. 50.

Secretary to the Commissioners of Public Accounts; but he is known to fame by the remarkable statistical tables concerning the population and trade of England, which he completed in the year 1696. His treatise was entitled *Natural and Political Observations and Conclusions upon the State and Condition of England*, 1696. It was never printed in the author's lifetime, but the contents were communicated in a most liberal manner to Dr. Davenant, who, making suitable acknowledgments as to the source of his information, founded thereupon his *Essay upon the Probable Methods of making a People gainers in the Balance of Trade.*[1] Our knowledge of Gregory King's conclusions was derived from this and other essays of Davenant, until George Chalmers printed the whole treatise at the end of the third edition of his well-known *Estimate of the Comparative Strength of Great Britain.*

The estimate of which I am about to speak is given by Davenant in the following words:[2] "We take it, that a defect in the harvest may raise the price of corn in the following proportions :—

Defect		Above the Common Rate
1 Tenth		3 Tenths
2 Tenths	raises	8 Tenths
3 Tenths	the	1·6 Tenths
4 Tenths	price	2·8 Tenths
5 Tenths		4·5 Tenths

So that when corn rises to treble the common rate,

---

[1] *The Political and Commercial Works of Charles Davenant*, vol. ii. p. 163.   [2] *Ibid.*, p. 224.

it may be presumed that we want above $\frac{1}{3}$ of the common produce; and if we should want $\frac{5}{10}$, or half the common produce, the price would rise to near five times the common rate."

Though this estimate has always been attributed to Gregory King, I cannot find it in his published treatise; nor does Davenant, who elsewhere makes full acknowledgments of what he owes to King, here attribute it to his friend. It is therefore, perhaps, due to Davenant.

We may re-state this estimate in the following manner, taking the average harvest and the average price of corn as unity :—

Quantity of Corn	1·0	·9	·8	·7	·6	·5
Price	1·0	1·3	1·8	2·6	3·8	5·5

Many writers have commented on this estimate. Thornton [1] observes that it is probably exceedingly inaccurate, and that it is not clear whether the total stock, or only the harvest of a single year, is to be taken as deficient. Tooke,[2] however, than whom on such a point there is no higher authority, believes that King's estimate " is not very wide of the truth, judging from the repeated occurrence of the fact that the price of corn in this country has risen from one hundred to two hundred per cent and upwards when the utmost computed deficiency of the crops has not been more than between one-sixth and one-third of an average."

[1] *An Inquiry into the Nature and Effects of the Paper Credit of Great Britain*, pp. 270, 271.   [2] *History of Prices*, vol. i. pp. 13-15.

I have endeavoured to ascertain the law to which Davenant's figures conform, and the mathematical function obtained does not greatly differ from what we might have expected. It is probable that the price of corn should never sink to zero, as, if abundant, it could be used for feeding horses, poultry, and cattle, or for other purposes for which it is too costly at present. It is said that in America corn, no doubt Indian corn, has been occasionally used as fuel. On the other hand, when the quantity is much diminished, the price should rise rapidly, and should become infinite before the quantity is zero, because famine would then be impending. The substitution of potatoes and other kinds of food renders the famine point very uncertain; but I think that a total deficiency of corn could not be made up by other food. Now a function of the form $\dfrac{a}{(x-b)^n}$ fulfils these conditions; for it becomes infinite when x is reduced to b, but for greater values of x always decreases as x increases. An inspection of the numerical data shows that n is about equal to 2, and, assuming it to be exactly 2, I find that the most probable values of a and b are $a = \cdot824$ and $b = \cdot12$. The formula thus becomes

$$\text{price of corn} = \frac{\cdot824}{(x - \cdot12)^2},$$

or approximately, $= \dfrac{5}{6\left(x - \frac{1}{8}\right)^2}.$

The following numbers show the degree of

approximation between the first of these formulæ and the data of Davenant :—

Harvest . . .	1·0	·9	·8	·7	·6	·5
Price (Davenant)	1·0	1·3	1·8	2·6	3·8	5·5
Price calculated	1·06	1·36	1·78	2·45	3·58	5·71

I cannot undertake to say how nearly Davenant's estimate agrees with experience ; but, considering the close approximation in the above numbers, we may safely substitute the empirical formula for his numbers ; and there are other reasons already stated for supposing that this formula is not far from the truth.[1] Roughly speaking, the price of corn may be said to vary inversely as the square of the supply, provided that this supply be not unusually small. I find that this is nearly the same conclusion as Whewell drew from the same numbers. He says :[2] "If the above numbers were to be made the basis of a mathematical rule, it would be found that the price varies inversely as the square of the supply, or rather in a higher ratio."

There is further reason for believing that the price of corn varies more rapidly than in the inverse ratio of the quantity. Tooke estimates[3] that in 1795 and 1796 the farmers of England gained seven millions sterling in each year by a deficiency of one-eighth part in the wheat crop, not including the considerable profit on the rise of price of other agricultural pro-

---

[1] See Preface to Fourth Edition.

[2] Six Lectures on Political Economy.   Cambridge, 1862.

[3] *History of Prices.*

duce. In each of the years 1799 and 1800, again, farmers probably gained eleven millions sterling by deficiency. If the price of wheat varied in the simple inverse proportion of the quantity, they would neither gain nor lose, and the fact that they gained considerably agrees with our formula as given above.

The variation of utility has not been overlooked by mathematicians, who had observed, as long ago as the early part of last century—before, in fact, there was any science of Political Economy at all— that the theory of probabilities could not be applied to commerce or gaming without taking notice of the very different utility of the same sum of money to different persons. Suppose that an even and fair bet is made between two persons, one of whom has £10,000 a year, the other £100 a year; let it be an equal chance whether they gain or lose £50. The rich person will, in neither case, feel much difference; but the poor person will receive far more harm by losing £50 than he can be benefited by gaining it. The utility of money to a poor person varies rapidly with the amount; to a rich person less so. Daniel Bernoulli, accordingly, distinguished in any question of probabilities between the *moral expectation* and the *mathematical expectation*, the latter being the simple chance of obtaining some possession, the former the chance as measured by its utility to the person. Having no means of ascertaining numerically the variation of utility, Bernoulli had to make assumptions of an arbitrary kind, and was then able to obtain reasonable answers to many important questions.   It is almost self-evident that the utility of money decreases as a person's total wealth increases ; if this be granted, it follows at once that gaming is, in the long run, a sure way to lose utility ; that every person should, when possible, divide risks, that is, prefer two equal chances of £50 to one similar chance of £100 ; and the advantage of insurance of all kinds is proved from the same theory. Laplace drew a similar distinction between the *fortune physique*, or the actual amount of a person's income, and the *fortune morale*, or its benefit to him.[1]

In answer to the objections of an ingenious correspondent, it may be remarked that when we say gaming is a sure way to lose utility, we take no account of the utility—that is, the pleasure—attaching to the pursuit of gaming itself ; we regard only the commercial loss or gain.   If a person with a certain income prefers to run the risk of losing a portion of it at play, rather than spending it in any other way, it must no doubt be conceded that the political economist, as such, can make no conclusive objection.   If the gamester is so devoid of other tastes that to spend money over the gaming-table is the best use he can discover for it, economically speaking, there is nothing further to be said.   The question then becomes a moral, legislative, or political one.   A source of amusement which, like gaming, betting, dram-

[1] Todhunter's *History of the Theory of Probability*, chap. xi., etc.

drinking, or opium-eating, is not in itself always pernicious, may come to be regarded as immoral, if in a considerable proportion of cases it leads to excessive and disastrous results. But this question evidently leads us into a class of subjects which could not be appropriately discussed in this work treating of pure economic theory.

The Origin of Value

The preceding pages contain, if I am not mistaken, an explanation of the nature of value which will, for the most part, harmonise with previous views upon the subject. Ricardo has stated, like most other economists, that utility is absolutely essential to value; but that "possessing utility, commodities derive their exchangeable value from two sources: from their scarcity, and from the quantity of labour required to obtain them."[1] Senior, again, has admirably defined wealth, or objects possessing value, as "those things, and those things only, which are transferable, are limited in supply, and are directly or indirectly productive of pleasure or preventive of pain." Speaking only of things which are transferable, or capable of being passed from hand to hand, we find that two of the clearest definitions of value recognise *utility* and *scarcity* as the essential qualities. But the moment that we distinguish between the total utility of a mass of commodity and the degree of

[1] *Principles of Political Economy and Taxation*, 3rd ed, p. 2.

utility of different portions, we may say that it is scarcity which prevents the fall in the final degree of utility. Bread has the almost infinite utility of maintaining life, and when it becomes a question of life or death, a small quantity of food exceeds in value all other things. But when we enjoy our ordinary supplies of food, a loaf of bread has little value, because the utility of an additional loaf is small, our appetites being satiated by our customary meals.

I have pointed out the excessive ambiguity of the word Value, and the apparent impossibility of using it safely. When intended to express the mere fact of certain articles exchanging in a particular ratio, I have proposed to substitute the unequivocal expression—*ratio of exchange*. But I am inclined to believe that a ratio is not the meaning which most persons attach to the word Value. There is a certain sense of esteem or desirableness, which we may have with regard to a thing apart from any distinct consciousness of the ratio in which it would exchange for other things. I may suggest that this distinct feeling of value is probably identical with the final degree of utility. While Adam Smith's often-quoted *value in use* is the total utility of a commodity to us, the *value in exchange* is defined by the *terminal utility*, the remaining desire which we or others have for possessing more.

There remains the question of labour as an element of value. Economists have not been wanting who put forward labour as the *cause of value*, asserting that all objects derive their value from the fact that labour has been expended on them; and it is thus implied, if not stated, that value will be proportional to labour. This is a doctrine which cannot stand for a moment, being directly opposed to facts. Ricardo disposes of such an opinion when he says : [1] " There are some commodities, the value of which is determined by their scarcity alone. No labour can increase the quantity of such goods, and therefore their value cannot be lowered by an increased supply. Some rare statues and pictures, scarce books and coins, wines of a peculiar quality, which can be made only from grapes grown on a particular soil, of which there is a very limited quantity, are all of this description. Their value is wholly independent of the quantity of labour originally necessary to produce them, and varies with the varying wealth and inclinations of those who are desirous to possess them."

The mere fact that there are many things, such as rare ancient books, coins, antiquities, etc., which have high values, and which are absolutely incapable of production now, disperses the notion that value depends on labour. Even those things which are producible in any quantity by labour seldom exchange exactly at the corresponding values. [2] The market

[1] *On the Principles of Political Economy and Taxation*, 3rd ed., 1821, p. 2.

[2] Mr. W. L. Sargant, in his *Recent Political Economy*, 8vo, London, 1867, p. 99, states that contracts have been made to manufacture the Enfield Rifle, of identically the same pattern, at prices ranging from 70s. each down to 20s., or even lower. The wages of the workmen

price of corn, cotton, iron, and most other things is, in the prevalent theories of value, allowed to fluctuate above or below its natural or cost value. There may, again, be any discrepancy between the quantity of labour spent upon an object and the value ultimately attaching to it. A great undertaking like the Great Western Railway, or the Thames Tunnel, may embody a vast amount of labour, but its value depends entirely upon the number of persons who find it useful. If no use could be found for the *Great Eastern* steamship, its value would be *nil*, except for the utility of some of its materials.[1] On the other hand, a successful undertaking, which happens to possess great utility, may have a value, for a time at least, far exceeding what has been spent upon it, as in the case of the [first] Atlantic Cable. The fact is, that *labour once spent has no influence on the future value of any article:* it is gone and lost for ever. In commerce bygones are for ever bygones; and we are always starting clear at each moment, judging the values of things with a view to future utility. Industry is essentially prospective, not retrospective; and seldom

varied from 40s. or 50s. down to 15s. a week. Such an instance renders it obvious that it is scarcity which governs value, and that it is the value of the produce which determines the wages of the producers.

[1] This statement has been justified by the fact. The *Great Eastern* steamship, built to the design of Brunel and Russell in 1858, with six masts and a displacement of 32,160 tons, proved a white elephant, being irremediably slow for passenger traffic, and too great in draft and general unwieldiness for cargo. She was sold two or three years ago for her value as old iron, and broken up at Glasgow.—[Ed.]

does the result of any undertaking exactly coincide with the first intentions of its promoters.

But though labour is never the cause of value, it is in a large proportion of cases the determining circumstance, and in the following way :— *Value depends solely on the final degree of utility. How can we vary this degree of utility ?—By having more or less of the commodity to consume. And how shall we get more or less of it ?—By spending more or less labour in obtaining a supply.* According to this view, then, there are two steps between labour and value. Labour affects supply, and supply affects the degree of utility, which governs value, or the ratio of exchange. In order that there may be no possible mistake about this all-important series of relations, I will re-state it in a tabular form, as follows :—

> *Cost of production determines supply ;*
> *Supply determines final degree of utility ;*
> *Final degree of utility determines value.*

But it is easy to go too far in considering labour as the regulator of value ; it is equally to be remembered that labour is itself of unequal value. Ricardo, by a violent assumption, founded his theory of value on quantities of labour considered as one uniform thing. He was aware that labour differs infinitely in quality and efficiency, so that each kind is more or less scarce, and is consequently paid at a higher or lower rate of wages. He regarded these differences as disturbing circumstances which would have to be allowed for; but his theory rests on the assumed equality of labour. This theory rests on a wholly different ground. I hold labour to be *essentially variable,* so that *its value must be determined by the value of the produce, not the value of the produce by that of the labour.* I hold it to be impossible to compare *à priori* the productive powers of a navvy, a carpenter, an iron-puddler, a schoolmaster, and a barrister. Accordingly, it will be found that not one of my equations represents a comparison between one man's labour and another's. The equation, if there is one at all, is between the same person in two or more different occupations. The subject is one in which complicated action and reaction takes place, and which we must defer until after we have described, in the next chapter, the Theory of Labour.

CHAPTER V

THEORY OF LABOUR

Definition of Labour

ADAM SMITH said, "The real price of everything, what everything really costs to the man who wants to acquire it, is the toil and trouble of acquiring it. . . . Labour was the first price, the original purchase-money, that was paid for all things."[1] If subjected to a very searching analysis, this celebrated passage might not prove to be so entirely true as it would at first sight seem to most readers to be. Yet it is substantially true, and luminously expresses the fact that labour is the beginning of the processes treated by economists, as consumption is the end and purpose. Labour is the painful exertion which we undergo to ward off pains of greater amount, or to procure pleasures which leave a balance in our favour. Courcelle-Seneuil[2] and Hearn have stated the problem of Economics with the utmost

[1] *Wealth of Nations*, book i., chap. v.
[2] *Traité Théorique et Pratique d'Economie Politique*, 2nd ed., vol. i. p. 33.

truth and brevity in saying, that it is *to satisfy our wants with the least possible sum of labour.*

In defining *labour* for the purposes of the economist we have a choice between two courses. In the first place, we may, if we like, include in it *all exertion of body or mind.* A game of cricket would, in this case, be labour; but if it be undertaken solely for the sake of the enjoyment attaching to it, the question arises whether we need take it under our notice. All exertion not directed to a distant and distinct end must be repaid simultaneously. There is no account of good or evil to be balanced at a future time. We are not prevented in any way from including such cases in our Theory of Economics; in fact, our Theory of Labour will, of necessity, apply to them. But we need not occupy our attention by cases which demand no calculus. When we exert ourselves for the sole amusement of the moment, there is but one rule needed, namely, to stop when we feel inclined—when the pleasure no longer equals the pain.

It will probably be better, therefore, to take the second course and concentrate our attention on such exertion as is not completely repaid by the immediate result. This would give us a definition nearly the same as that of Say, who defined labour as "*Action suivée, dirigée vers un but.*" Labour, I should say, is *any painful exertion of mind or body undergone partly or wholly with a view to future good.*[1] It is

---

[1] I have altered this definition as it stood in the first edition by inserting the words *partly or wholly*, and I only give it now as pro-

true that labour may be both agreeable at the time
and conducive to future good; but it is only agreeable in a limited amount, and most men are compelled
by their wants to exert themselves longer and more
severely than they would otherwise do. When a
labourer is inclined to stop, he clearly feels something
that is irksome, and our theory will only involve the
point where the exertion has become so painful as to
nearly balance all other considerations. Whatever
there is that is wholesome or agreeable about labour
before it reaches this point may be taken as a net
profit of good to the labourer; but it does not enter
into the problem. It is only when labour becomes
effort that we take account of it, and, as Hearn truly
says,[1] "such effort, as the very term seems to imply,
is more or less troublesome." In fact, we must, as
will shortly appear, measure labour by the amount of
pain which attaches to it.

visionally the best I can suggest. The subject presents itself to me
as one of great difficulty, and it is possible that the true solution
will consist in treating labour as a case of negative utility, or
negative mingled with positive utility. We should thus arrive at a
higher generalisation .which appears to be foreshadowed in the
remarkable work of Hermann Heinrich Gossen described in the
preface to this edition. Every act, whether of production or of
consumption, may be regarded as producing what Bentham calls a
lot both of pleasures and pains, and the distinction between the two
processes will consist in the fact that the algebraic value of the lot in
the case of consumption yields a balance of positive utility, while that
of production yields a negative or painful balance, at least in that part of
the labour involving most effort. In a happy life the negative balance
involved in production is more than cleared off by the positive balance
of pleasure arising from consumption.   [1] *Plutology*, p. 24.

Quantitative Notions of Labour

Let us endeavour to form a clear notion of what we mean by amount of labour. It is plain that duration will be one element of it; for a person labouring *uniformly* during two months must be allowed to labour twice as much as during one month. But labour may vary also in intensity. In the same time a man may walk a greater or less distance; may saw a greater or less amount of timber; may pump a greater or less quantity of water; in short, may exert more or less muscular and nervous force. Hence amount of labour will be a quantity of two dimensions, the product of intensity and time when the intensity is uniform, or the sum represented by the area of a curve when the intensity is variable.

But intensity of labour may have more than one meaning; it may mean the quantity of work done, or the painfulness of the effort of doing it. These two things must be carefully distinguished, and both are of great importance for the theory. The one is the reward, the other the penalty, of labour. Or rather, as the produce is only of interest to us so far as it possesses utility, we may say that there are three quantities involved in the theory of labour—the amount of painful exertion, the amount of produce, and the amount of utility gained. The variation of utility, as depending on the quantity of commodity possessed, has already been considered; the variation of the

amount of produce will be treated in the next chapter ;
we will here give attention to the variation of the
painfulness of labour.

Experience shows that as labour is prolonged the
effort becomes as a general rule more and more painful.
A few hours' work per day may be considered agreeable
rather than otherwise ; but so soon as the overflowing
energy of the body is drained off, it becomes irksome to
remain at work.   As exhaustion approaches, continued
effort becomes more and more intolerable.   Jennings
has so clearly stated this law of the variation of
labour, that I must quote his words.[1]   " Between these
two points, the point of incipient effort and the point
of painful suffering, it is quite evident that the degree
of toilsome sensations endured does not vary directly
as the quantity of work performed, but increases
much more rapidly, like the resistance offered by
an opposing medium to the· velocity of a moving
body.

" When this observation comes to be applied to
the toilsome sensations endured by the working
classes, it will be found convenient to fix on a middle
point, the average amount of toilsome sensation
attending the average amount of labour, and to
measure from this point the degrees of variation.   If,
for the sake of illustration, this average amount be
assumed to be of ten hours' duration, it would follow
that, if at any period the amount were to be supposed
to be reduced to five hours, the sensations of labour

[1] *Natural Elements of Political Economy*, p. 119.

would be found, at least by the majority of mankind, to be almost merged in the pleasures of occupation and exercise, whilst the amount of work performed would only be diminished by one-half; if, on the contrary, the amount were to be supposed to be increased to twenty hours, the quantity of work produced would only be doubled, whilst the amount of toilsome suffering would become insupportable. Thus, if the quantity produced, greater or less than the average quantity, were to be divided into any number of parts of equal magnitude, the amount of toilsome sensation attending each succeeding increment would be found greater than that which would attend the increment preceding; and the amount of toilsome sensation attending each succeeding decrement would be found less than that which would attend the decrement preceding."

There can be no question of the general truth of the above statement, although we may not have the data for assigning the exact law of the variation. We may imagine the painfulness of labour in proportion to produce to be represented by some such curve as *abcd* in fig. 9. In this diagram the height of points above the line *ox* denotes pleasure, and depths below it pain. At the moment of commencing labour it is usually more irksome than when the mind and body are well bent to the work. Thus, at first, the pain is measured by *oa*. At *b* there is neither pain nor pleasure. Between *b* and *c* an excess of pleasure is represented as due to the exertion itself.

But after *c* the energy begins to be rapidly exhausted, and the resulting pain is shown by the downward tendency of the line *cd*.

We may at the same time represent the degree of utility of the produce by some such curve as *pq*, the amount of produce being measured along the line *ox*. Agreeably to the theory of utility, already given, the curve shows that, the larger the wages earned, the

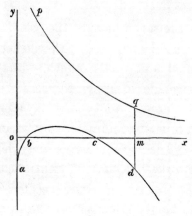

Fig. 9.

less is the pleasure derived from a further increment. There will, of necessity, be some point *m* such that $qm = dm$, that is to say, such that the pleasure gained is exactly equal to the labour endured. Now, if we pass the least beyond this point, a balance of pain will result : there will be an ever-decreasing motive in favour of labour, and an ever-increasing motive against it. The labourer will evidently cease, then, at the point *m*. It would be inconsistent with human nature for a man to work when the pain of work exceeds the desire of possession, including all the motives for exertion.

We must consider the duration of labour as measured by the number of hours' work per day. The alternation of day and night on the earth has rendered man essentially periodic in his habits and actions. In a natural and wholesome condition a man should return each twenty-four hours to exactly the same state; at any rate, the cycle should be closed within the seven days of the week. Thus the labourer must not be supposed to be either increasing or diminishing his normal strength. But the theory might also be made to apply to cases where special exertion is undergone for many days or weeks in succession, in order to complete work, as in collecting the harvest. Adequate motives may lead to and warrant overwork, but, if long continued, excessive labour reduces the strength and becomes insupportable; and the longer it continues the worse it is, the law being somewhat similar to that of periodic labour.

Symbolic Statement of the Theory

In attempting to represent these conditions of labour with accuracy, we shall find that there are no less than four quantities concerned; let us denote them as follows :—

$t =$ time, or duration of labour;

$l =$ amount of labour, as meaning the aggregate balance of pain accompanying it, irrespective of the produce;

$x =$ amount of commodity produced ;
$u =$ total utility of that commodity.

The amount of commodity produced will be very
different in different cases.   In any one case the rate
of production will be determined by dividing the
whole quantity produced by the time of production,
provided that the rate of production has been
uniform; it will then be $\frac{x}{t}$.   But if the rate of production be variable, it can only be determined at any
moment by comparing a small quantity of produce
with the small portion of time occupied in its production.   More strictly speaking, we must ascertain
the ratio of an infinitely small quantity of produce to
the corresponding infinitely small portion of time.
Thus *the rate of production* is properly denoted by
$\frac{\Delta x}{\Delta t}$, or at the limit by $\frac{dx}{dt}$.

Again, the degree of painfulness of labour would be
$\frac{l}{t}$ if it remained invariable; but as it is highly variable, we must again compare small increments, and
$\frac{\Delta l}{\Delta t}$, or, at the limit, $\frac{dl}{dt}$ correctly represents the *degree
of painfulness of labour*.   But we must also take
into account the fact that the utility of commodity
is not constant.   If a man works regularly twelve
hours a day, he will produce more commodity than
in ten hours; therefore the final degree of utility of
his commodity, whether he consume it himself or

whether he exchange it, will not be quite so high as when he produced less. This degree of utility is denoted, as before, by $\dfrac{du}{dx}$, the ratio of the increment of utility to the increment of commodity.

The amount of reward of labour can now be expressed; for it is $\dfrac{dx}{dt} \cdot \dfrac{du}{dx}$; that is to say, it is the product of the ratio of the commodity produced to the time, multiplied by the ratio of the utility to the amount of produce. Thus, the last two hours of work in the day generally gives less reward, both because less produce is then created in proportion to the time spent, and because that produce is less necessary and useful to one who makes enough to support himself in the other ten hours.

We can now ascertain the length of time which should be selected as the most advantageous term of labour. A free labourer endures the irksomeness of work because the pleasure he expects to receive, or the pain he expects to ward off, by means of the produce, exceeds the pain of exertion. When labour itself is a worse evil than that which it saves him from, there can be no motive for further exertion, and he ceases. Therefore he will cease to labour just at the point when the pain becomes equal to the corresponding pleasure gained; and we thus have t defined by the equation

$$\frac{dl}{dt} = \frac{dx}{dt} \cdot \frac{du}{dx}.$$

In this, as in the other questions of Economics, all
depends upon the final increments, and we have
expressed in the above formula *the final equivalence
of labour and utility.*   A man must be regarded as
earning all through his hours of labour an excess of
utility; what he produces must be considered not
merely the exact equivalent of the labour he gives
for it, for it would be, in that case, a matter of
indifference whether he laboured or not.   As long
as he gains, he labours, and when he ceases to gain,
he ceases to labour.

In some cases, as in some kinds of machine labour,
the rate of production is uniform, or nearly so, and
by choice of suitable units may be made equal to
unity; the result may then be put more simply in
this way.   Labour may be considered as expended
in successive small quantities, Δl, each lasting, for
instance, for a quarter of an hour; the corresponding
benefit derived from the labour will then be denoted
by Δu.   Now, so long as Δu exceeds in amount of
pleasure the negative quantity or pain of Δl, the
difference of sign being disregarded, there will be
gain inducing to continued labour.   Were Δu to fall
below Δl, there would be more harm than good in
labouring; therefore, the boundary between labour
and inactivity will be defined by the equality of
Δu and Δl, and at the limit we have the equation

$$\frac{du}{dx} = \frac{dl}{dx}.$$

Dimensions of Labour

If I have correctly laid down, in preceding chapters, the Theory of Dimensions of Utility and Value, there ought not to be much difficulty in stating the similar theory as regards Labour. We might in fact treat labour as simply one case of *disutility* or negative utility, that is as pain, or at any rate as a generally painful balance of pleasure and pain, endured in the action of acquiring commodity. Thus its dimensions might be described as identical with those of utility; U would then denote intensity of labour, or degree of labour, just as it was used to denote degree of utility. If we measure labour with respect to the quantity of commodity produced, that is, if we make commodity the variable, then total amount of labour will be the integral of $U d M$, and the dimensions of amount of labour will be MU, identical with those of total utility.

If for any reasons of convenience we prefer to substitute a new symbol, specially appropriated to express the dimensions of labour, and say that *intensity of labour* is represented by E (Endurance), and *total quantity of labour* incurred in the production of certain commodity by ME, it must be remembered that the change is one of convenience only; U and E are essentially quantities of the same nature, and the difference, so far as there is any, arises from the fact that quantities symbolised by E will

usually be negative as compared with those symbolised
by U. Labour, however, is often measured and
bought and sold by *time*, instead of by piecework or
commodity produced ; in this case, while E continues
to express intensity of labour, ET will express the
dimensions of amount of labour.

Rate of production will obviously possess the
same dimensions as rate of consumption (p. 64),
namely, MT^{-1}, and this quantity forms a link
between labour as measured by time and by produce ;
for $ET \times MT^{-1} = ME$. It would be possible to
invent various other economic quantities, such as
acceleration of production, with the dimensions
MT^{-2} ; but, until it is apparent how such quantities
enter into economic theorems, it seems needless to
consider them further.

Balance between Need and Labour

In considering this Theory of Labour an interesting question presents itself. Supposing that circumstances alter the relation of produce to labour, what
effect will this have upon the amount of labour which
will be exerted ? There are two effects to be considered. When labour produces more commodity,
there is more reward, and therefore more inducement
to labour. If a workman can earn ninepence an hour
instead of sixpence, may he not be induced to extend
his hours of labour by this increased result ? This
would doubtless be the case were it not that the very

fact of getting half as much more than he did before, lowers the utility to him of any further addition. By the produce of the same number of hours he can satisfy his desires more completely ; and if the irksomeness of labour has reached at all a high point, he may gain more pleasure by relaxing that labour than by consuming more products. The question thus depends upon the direction in which the balance between the utility of further commodity and the painfulness of prolonged labour turns.

In our ignorance of the exact form of the functions either of utility or of labour, it will be impossible to decide this question in an *à priori* manner ; but there are a few facts which indicate in which direction the balance does usually turn. Statements are given by Porter, in his *Progress of the Nation*,[1] which show that when a sudden rise took place in the prices of provisions in the early part of this century, workmen increased their hours of labour, or, as it is said, worked double time, if they could obtain adequate employment. Now, a rise in the price of food is really the same as a decrease of the produce of labour, since less of the necessaries of life can be acquired in exchange for the same money wages. We may conclude, then, that English labourers enjoying little more than the necessaries of life, will work harder the less the produce ; or, which comes to the same thing, will work less hard as the produce increases.

Evidence to the like effect is found in the general

[1] Edition of 1847, pp. 454, 455.

tendency to reduce the hours of labour at the present day, owing to the improved real wages now enjoyed by those employed in mills and factories. Artisans, mill-hands, and others, seem generally to prefer greater ease to greater wealth, thus proving that the painfulness of labour varies so rapidly as easily to overbalance the gain of utility. The same rule seems to hold throughout the mercantile employments. The richer a man becomes, the less does he devote himself to business. A successful merchant is generally willing to give a considerable share of his profits to a partner, or to a staff of managers and clerks, rather than bear the constant labour of superintendence himself. There is also a general tendency to reduce the hours of labour in mercantile offices, due to increased comfort and opulence.

It is obvious, however, that there are many intricacies in a matter of this sort. It is not always possible to graduate work to the worker's liking; in some businesses a man who insisted on working only a few hours a day would soon have no work to do. In the professions of law, medicine, and the like, it is the reputation of enjoying a large practice which attracts new clients. Thus a successful barrister or physician generally labours more severely as his success increases. This result partly depends upon the fact that the work is not easily capable of being performed by deputy. A successful barrister, too, soon begins to look forward to the extrinsic rewards of a high judicial or parliamentary position. But the case of an eminent solicitor, architect, or engineer is one where the work is to a great extent done by employees, and done without reference to social or political rewards, and where yet the most successful man endures the most labour, or rather is most constantly at work. This indicates that the irksomeness of the labour does not increase so as to overbalance the utility of the increment of reward. In some characters and in some occupations, in short, success of labour only excites to new exertions, the work itself being of an interesting and stimulating nature. But the general rule is to the contrary effect, namely, that a certain success disinclines a man to increased labour. It may be added that in the highest kinds of labour, such as those of the philosopher, scientific discoverer, artist, etc., it is questionable how far great success is compatible with ease; the mental powers must be kept in perfect training by constant exertion, just as a racehorse or an oarsman needs to be constantly exercised.

It is evident that questions of this kind depend greatly upon the character of the race. Persons of an energetic disposition feel labour less painfully than their fellow-men, and, if they happen to be endowed with various and acute sensibilities, their desire of further acquisition never ceases. A man of lower race, a negro for instance, enjoys possession less, and loathes labour more; his exertions, therefore, soon stop. A poor savage would be content to gather the almost gratuitous fruits of nature, if they were suffi-

cient to give sustenance; it is only physical want
which drives him to exertion. The rich man in
modern society is supplied apparently with all he can
desire, and yet he often labours unceasingly for more.
Bishop Berkeley, in his *Querist*,[1] has very well asked,
" Whether the creating of wants be not the likeliest
way to produce industry in a people ? And whether,
if our (Irish) peasants were accustomed to eat beef
and wear shoes, they would not be more industrious ? "

Distribution of Labour

We now come to consider the conditions which
regulate the comparative amounts of different commodities produced in a country. Theoretically speaking,
we might regard each person as capable of producing various commodities, and dividing his labour
according to certain rules between the different employments; it would not be impossible, too, to mention
cases where such division does take place. But the
result of commerce and the division of labour is
usually to make a man find his advantage in perform-
ing one trade only; and I give the formulæ as they
would apply to an individual, only because they are
identical in general character with those which apply
to a whole nation.

Suppose that an individual is capable of producing
two kinds of commodity. His sole object, of course,
is to produce the greatest amount of utility; but this

[1] Query No. 20.

will depend partly upon the comparative degrees of
utility of the commodities, and partly on his comparative facilities for producing them. Let x and y be
the respective quantities of the commodities already
produced, and suppose that he is about to apply more
labour ; on which commodity shall he spend the next
increment of labour ?—Plainly, on that which will
yield most utility. Now, if an increment of labour, Δl,
will yield either of the increments of commodity Δx
and Δy, the ratios of produce to labour, namely,

$$\frac{\Delta x}{\Delta l} \text{ and } \frac{\Delta y}{\Delta l}$$

will form one element in the problem. But to obtain
the comparative utilities of these commodities, we
must multiply respectively by

$$\frac{\Delta u_1}{\Delta x} \text{ and } \frac{\Delta u_2}{\Delta y}.$$

For instance,

$$\frac{\Delta u_1}{\Delta x} \cdot \frac{\Delta x}{\Delta l_1}$$

expresses the amount of utility which can be obtained
by producing a little more of the first commodity ; if
this be greater than the same expression for the other
commodity, it would evidently be best to make more
of the first commodity until it ceased to yield any
excess of utility. When the labour is finally distributed, we must have the increments of utility from
the several employments equal, and at the limit we
have the equation—

$$\frac{du_1}{dx} \cdot \frac{dx}{dl_1} = \frac{du_2}{dy} \cdot \frac{dy}{dl_2}.$$

When this equation holds, there can be no motive for altering or regretting the distribution of labour, and the utility produced is at its maximum.

There are in this problem two unknown quantities, namely, the two portions of labour appropriated to the two commodities. To determine them, we require one other equation in addition to the above. If we put

$$l = l_1 + l_2,$$

we have still an unknown quantity to determine, namely, l ; but the principles of labour (pp. 172-7) now give us an equation. Labour will be carried on until the increment of utility from any of the employments just balances the increment of pain. This amounts to saying that du_1, the increment of utility derived from the first employment of labour, is equal in amount of feeling to dl_1, the increment of labour by which it is obtained. This gives us then the further equation—

$$\frac{du_1}{dx} \cdot \frac{dx}{dl_1} = 1.$$

If we pay regard to sign, indeed, we must remember that dl is, when measured in the same scale as du, intrinsically negative, but inasmuch as it is given in exchange for du, which is received, it will in this respect be taken negatively, and thus the above equation holds true.[1]

---

[1] While revising this edition it seems to me probable that this, as well as some other parts of the theory, might be more simply and generally stated, but what is given is substantially true and correct, and it must stand for the present.

Relation of the Theories of Labour and Exchange

It may tend to give the reader confidence in the preceding theories when he finds that they lead directly to the well-known law, as stated in the ordinary language of economists, that value is proportional to the cost of production. As I prefer to state the same law, it is to the effect that the ratio of exchange of commodities will conform in the long run to the *ratio of productiveness*, which is the reciprocal of the ratio of the costs of production. The somewhat perplexing relations of these quantities will be fully explained in the next section, but we may now proceed to prove the above result symbolically.

To simplify our expressions, let us substitute for the *rate of production* [1] $\dfrac{dx}{dl}$ the symbol ϖ. Then ϖ_1, ϖ_2, express the relative quantities of two different commodities produced by an increment of labour, and we have the following equation, identical with that on page 184,

$$\phi x . \varpi_1 = \psi y . \varpi_2.$$

Let us suppose that the person to whom it applies is in a position to exchange with other persons. The conditions of production will now, in all probability, be modified. For x the quantity of our commodity may perhaps be increased to $x + x_1$, and y diminished to $y - y_1$, by an exchange of the quantities x_1 and y_1.

---

[1] That is, the *productiveness* of labour for *one* commodity.—[Ed.]

If this be so, we shall, as shown in the Theory of Exchange, have the equation

$$\frac{\phi(x + x_1)}{\psi(y - y_1)} = \frac{y_1}{x_1}.$$

Our equation of production will now be modified, and become

$$\phi(x + x_1) \cdot \varpi_1 = \psi(y - y_1)\varpi_2 \, ;$$

or $$\frac{\phi(x + x_1)}{\psi(y - y_1)} = \frac{\varpi_2}{\varpi_1}.$$

But this equation has its first member identical with the first member of the equation of exchange given above, so that we may at once deduce the all-important equation

$$\frac{\varpi_2}{\varpi_1} = \frac{y_1}{x_1}.$$

The reader will remember that ϖ expresses the ratio of produce to labour; thus we have proved that commodities will exchange in any market in the ratio of the quantities produced by the same quantity of labour. But as the increment of labour considered is always the final one, our equation also expresses the truth, that *articles will exchange in quantities inversely as the costs of production of the most costly portions, i.e. the last portions added.* This result will prove of great importance in the theory of Rent.

Let it be observed that, in uniting the theories of exchange and production, a complicated double adjustment takes place in the quantities of commodity involved. Each party adjusts not only its consumption of articles in accordance with their ratio of exchange, but it also adjusts its production of them. The ratio of exchange governs the production as much as the production governs the ratio of exchange. For instance, since the Corn Laws have been abolished in England, the effect has been, not to destroy the culture of wheat, but to lessen it. The land less suitable to the growth of wheat has been turned to grazing or other purposes more profitable comparatively speaking. Similarly the importation of hops or eggs or any other article of food does not even reduce the quantity raised here, but prevents the necessity for resorting to more expensive modes of increasing the supply. It is not easy to express in words how the ratios of exchange are finally determined. They depend upon a general balance of producing power and of demand as measured by the final degree of utility. Every additional supply tends to lower the degree of utility ; but whether that supply will be forthcoming from any country depends upon its comparative powers of producing different commodities.

Any very small tract of country cannot appreciably affect the comparative supply of commodities : it must therefore adjust its productions in accordance with the general state of the market. The county of Bedford, for instance, would not appreciably affect the markets for corn, cheese, or cattle, whether it devoted every acre to corn or to grazing. Therefore the agriculture of Bedfordshire will have to be adapted to circumstances, and each field will be employed for arable or grazing land according as prevailing prices render one employment or the other more profitable. But any large country will affect the markets as well as be affected. If the whole habitable surface of Australia, instead of producing wool, could be turned to the cultivation of wine, the wool market would rise, and the wine market fall. If the Southern States of America abandoned cotton in favour of sugar, there would be a revolution in these markets. It would be inevitable for Australia to return to wool and the American States to cotton. These are illustrations of the reciprocal relation of exchange and production.

Relations of Economic Quantities

I hope that I may sometime be able, in a future and much larger work, to explain in detail the results which can be derived from the mathematical theory expounded in the previous pages. This essay gives them only in an implicit manner. But, before leaving the subject of exchange, it may be well without delay to point out how the results so far set forth connect themselves with the recognised doctrines of political economy. For the sake of accuracy I have avoided the use of the word *value*; the expression *cost of production*, so continually recurring in most economical treatises, is also here conspicuous by its absence. The reader then, unless he be very careful, may be thrown into some perplexity, when he proceeds to compare my results with those familiar to him elsewhere.

I will therefore proceed to trace out the connections between the several quantitative expressions, which most commonly occur in discussions concerning value, exchange, and production.

In the first place, the ratio of exchange is the actual numerical ratio of the quantities given and received. Let X and Y be the names of the commodities : x and y the quantities of them respectively exchanged. Then the ratio of exchange is that of y to x. But the value of a commodity in exchange is greater as the quantity received is less, so that the ratio of the quantities dealt with must be the reciprocal of the ratio of the values of the substances, meaning by value the value per unit of the commodity. Thus we may say

$$\frac{y}{x} = \frac{\text{Value of X per unit}}{\text{Value of Y per unit.}}$$

Value is of course very frequently estimated by *price*, that is, by the quantity of legal money for which the commodity may be exchanged. Price is indeed ambiguous in the same way as value ; it means either the *price of the whole quantity*, or the *price per unit of the quantity*. Let p_1 be the price per unit of X, and p_2 the similar price of Y. Then it is apparent that $y \times p_2$ will be the whole price of y, and $x \times p_1$ will be the whole price of x. These two must be equal to each other, so that we get

$$\frac{y}{x} = \frac{p_1}{p_2}.$$

Thus we find that, when price means price per unit, the quantities exchanged are reciprocally as the prices. When price means price of the whole quantity, the quantities given and received are always of equal price.

Turning now to the production of commodity, it is sufficiently obvious that the cost of production, so far as this expression can be accurately interpreted, varies as the reciprocal of the degree of productiveness. The rate of wages remaining constant, the cost per unit of commodity must of course be lower as the quantity produced in return for a certain amount of wages is greater. Thus we may lay down the equation

$$\frac{\text{Degree of productiveness of Y [1]}}{\text{Degree of productiveness of X}} = \frac{\text{Cost of production of X}}{\text{Cost of production of Y.}}$$

Now, it was shown in pp. 186-7 that the quantities exchanged are directly proportional to the degrees of productiveness,

$$\text{or} \quad \frac{y}{x} = \frac{\text{Degree of productiveness of Y}}{\text{Degree of productiveness of X.}}$$

But the ratio of the values is the reciprocal of $\frac{y}{x}$, and the ratio of the costs of production is the reciprocal of the other member of the above equation. Thus it follows that

$$\frac{\text{Value per unit of X}}{\text{Value per unit of Y}} = \frac{\text{Cost of production per unit of X}}{\text{Cost of production per unit of Y,}}$$

---

[1] " Degree of productiveness of Y " is to be understood as meaning "degree of productiveness of labour in producing Y," and similarly for X.—[Ed.]

or, in other words, *value is proportional to cost of production.* As, moreover, the final degrees of utility of commodities are inversely as the quantities exchanged, it follows that the values per unit are directly proportional to the final degrees of utility.

As it is quite indispensable that the student of political economy should keep the relations of these quantities before his mind with perfect clearness, I repeat the results in several forms of statement. Thus we may group the ratios together—

$$\text{Ratio of exchange} = \frac{y}{x} = \frac{\text{Quantity of Y given or received}}{\text{Quantity of X received or given}}$$

$$= \frac{\text{Value per unit of X}}{\text{Value per unit of Y}} = \frac{\text{Price per unit of X}}{\text{Price per unit of Y}}$$

$$= \frac{\text{Final degree of utility of X}}{\text{Final degree of utility of Y}}$$

$$= \frac{\text{Cost of production per unit of X}}{\text{Cost of production per unit of Y}}$$

$$= \frac{\text{Degree of productiveness of Y}}{\text{Degree of productiveness of X}}.$$

We may state the matter more briefly in the following words :—*The quantities of commodity given or received in exchange are directly proportional to the degrees of productiveness of labour applied to their production, and inversely proportional to the values and prices of those commodities and to their costs of production per unit, as well as to their final*

degrees of utility.   I will even repeat the same statements once more in the form of a diagram—

Quantities of Commodity exchanged vary

directly as the quantities produced by the same labour.	inversely as their
	(1) Values
	(2) Prices
	(3) Costs of production
	(4) Final degrees of utility.

Various Cases of the Theory

As we have now reached the principal question in
Economics, it will be well to consider the meaning
and results of our equations in some detail.

It will, in the first place, be apparent that the
absolute facility of producing commodities will not
determine the character and amount of trade.   The
ratio of exchange $\frac{y_1}{x_1}$ is not determined by ϖ_1, nor by
ϖ_2 separately, but by their comparative magnitudes.
If the producing power of a country were doubled,
no direct effect would be produced upon the terms of
its commerce provided that the increase were equal
in all branches of production.   This is a point of
great importance, which was correctly conceived by
Ricardo, and has been fully explained by J. S. Mill.

But though there is no such direct effect, it may
happen that there will be an indirect effect through the
variation in the degree of utility of different articles.
When an increased amount of every commodity can

be produced, it is not likely that the increase will be equally desired in each branch of consumption. Hence the degree of utility will fall in some cases more than in others. An alteration of the ratios of exchange must result, and the production of the less needed commodities will not be extended so much as in the case of the more needed ones. We might find in such instances new proofs that value depends not upon labour but upon the degree of utility.

It will also be apparent that nations possessing exactly similar powers of production cannot gain by mutual commerce, and consequently will not have any such commerce, however free from artificial restrictions. We get this result as follows :—Taking $\varpi_1 \varpi_2$, as before, to be the final ratios of productiveness[1] in one country, and $\mu_1 \mu_2$ in a second, then, if the conditions of production are exactly similar, we have

$$\frac{\varpi_2}{\varpi_1} = \frac{\mu_2}{\mu_1}.$$

But when a country does not trade at all, its labour and consumption are distributed according to the condition

$$\frac{\phi x}{\psi y} = \frac{\varpi_2}{\varpi_1}.$$

Now, from these equations, it follows necessarily that

$$\frac{\phi x}{\psi y} = \frac{\mu_2}{\mu_1};$$

that is to say, the production and consumption already

---

[1] Rather, *final productivenesses*, or *rates of production*, to be consistent with the nomenclature adopted on p. 186.—[Ed.]

conform to the conditions of production of the second country, and will not undergo any alteration when trade with this country becomes possible.

This is the doctrine usually stated in works on Political Economy, and for which there are good grounds. But I do not think the statement will hold true if the conditions of consumption be very different in two countries. There might be two countries exactly similar in regard to their powers of producing beef and corn, and if their habits of consumption were also exactly similar, there would be no trade in these articles. But suppose that the first country consumed proportionally more beef, and the second more corn ; then, if there were no trade, the powers of the soil would be differently taxed, and different ratios of exchange would prevail. Freedom of trade would cause an interchange of corn for beef. Thus I conclude that it is only where the habits of consumption, as well as the powers of production, are alike, that trade brings no advantage.

The general effect of foreign commerce is to disturb, to the advantage of a country, the mode in which it distributes its labour. Excluding from view the cost of carriage, and the other expenses of commerce, we must always have true

$$\frac{\varpi_2}{\varpi_1} = \frac{y_1}{x_1} = \frac{\mu_2}{\mu_1}.$$

If, then, ϖ_2 was originally less in proportion to ϖ_1 than is in accordance with these equations, some labour will be transferred from the production of y to that of x until, by the increased magnitude of ϖ_2, and the lessened magnitude of ϖ_1, equality is brought about.

As in the theory of exchange, so in the theory of production, any of the equations may fail, and the meaning is capable of interpretation. Thus, if the equation

$$\frac{\varpi_2}{\varpi_1} = \frac{y_1}{x_1}$$

cannot be established, it is impossible that the production of both commodities, y and x, can go on. One of them will be produced at an expenditure of labour constantly out of proportion to that at which it may be had by exchange. If we could not, for instance, import oranges from abroad, part of the labour of the country would probably be diverted from its present employment to raise them; but the cost of production would be always above that of getting them indirectly by exchange, so that free trade necessarily destroys such a wasteful branch of industry. It is on this principle that we import the whole of our wines, teas, sugar, coffee, spices, and many other articles from abroad.

The ratio of exchange of any two commodities will be determined by a kind of struggle between the conditions of consumption and production; but here again failure of the equations may take place. In the all-important equations

$$\frac{\phi(x + x_1)}{\psi(y - y_1)} = \frac{\varpi_2}{\varpi_1} = \frac{y_1}{x_1},$$

ϖ_2 expresses the ease with which we may make additions to y. If we find any means, by machinery or otherwise, of increasing y without limit, and with the same ease as before, we must, in all probability, alter the ratio of exchange $\dfrac{y_1}{x_1}$ in a corresponding degree. But if we could imagine the existence of a large population, within reach of the supposed country, whose desire to consume the quantity y_1 never decreased, however large was the quantity available, then we should never have $\dfrac{y_1}{x_1}$ equal to $\dfrac{\varpi_2}{\varpi_1}$, and the producers of y would make large gains of the nature of rent.

Joint Production

In one of the most interesting chapters of his *Principles of Political Economy*, Book III., chap. xvi., John Stuart Mill has treated of what he calls "Some peculiar Cases of Value." Under this title he refers to those commodities which are not produced by separate processes, but are the concurrent or joint results of the same operations. "It sometimes happens," he says, "that two different commodities have what may be termed a joint cost of production. They are both products of the same operation, or set of operations, and the outlay is incurred for the sake of both together, not part for one and part for the other. The same outlay would have to be incurred for either of the two, if the other were not wanted or used at all. There are not a few instances of commodities thus associated in their production. For example, coke and coal-gas are both produced from the same material, and by the same operation. In a more partial sense, mutton and wool are an example ; beef, hides, and tallow ; calves and dairy produce ; chickens and eggs. Cost of production can have nothing to do with deciding the values of the associated commodities relatively to each other. It only decides their joint value. . . . A principle is wanting to apportion the expenses of production between the two." He goes on to explain that, since the cost of production principle fails us, we must revert to a law of value anterior to cost of production, and more fundamental, namely, the law of supply and demand.

On some other occasion I may perhaps more fully point out the fallacy involved in Mill's idea that he is reverting to *an anterior law of value*, the law of supply and demand, the fact being that in introducing the cost of production principle, he had never quitted the laws of supply and demand at all. The cost of production is only one circumstance which governs supply, and thus indirectly influences values.

Again, I shall point out that these cases of joint production, far from being "some peculiar cases," form the general rule, to which it is difficult to point out any clear or important exceptions. All the great staple commodities at any rate are produced jointly with minor commodities. In the case of corn, for instance, there are the straw, the chaff, the bran, and

the different qualities of flour or meal, which are products of the same operations.   In the case of cotton,
there are the seed, the oil, the cotton waste, the
refuse, in addition to the cotton itself.   When beer is
brewed the grains regularly return a certain price.
Trees felled for timber yield not only the timber, but
the loppings, the bark, the outside cuts, the chips, etc.
No doubt the secondary products are often nearly
valueless, as in the case of cinders, slag from blast
furnaces, etc.   But even these cases go to show all the
more impressively that it is not cost of production
which rules values, but the demand and supply of
the products.

The great importance of these cases of joint production renders it necessary for us to consider how
they can be brought under our theory.   Let us suppose
that there are two commodities, X and Y, yielded by
one same operation, which always produces them in
the same ratio, say of m of X to n of Y.   It might
seem at first sight as if this ratio would correspond to
the ratio of the degrees of productiveness, as shown a
few pages above, that we might say

$$\frac{m}{n} = \frac{\varpi_2}{\varpi_1} = \frac{y_1}{x_1},$$

and thus arrive at the conclusion that things jointly
produced would always exchange in the ratio of productiveness.   But this would be entirely false, because
*that equation can only be established when there is
freedom of producing one or the other*, at each appli-

cation of a new increment of labour. It is the freedom of varying the quantities of each that allows of the produce being accommodated to the need of it, so that the ratio of the degrees of utility, of the degrees of productiveness, and of the quantities exchanged are brought to equality. But in cases of joint production there is no such freedom; the one substance cannot be made without making a certain fixed proportion of the other, which may have little or no utility.

It will easily be seen, however, that such cases are brought under our theory by simply aggregating together the utilities of the increments of the joint products. If dx cannot be produced without dy, these being the products of the same increment of labour, dl, then the ratio of produce to labour cannot be written otherwise than as

$$\frac{dx + dy}{dl}.$$

It is impossible to divide up the labour and say that so much is expended on producing X, and so much on Y. But we must estimate separately the utilities of dx and dy, by multiplying by their degrees of utility $\frac{du_1}{dx}$ and $\frac{du_2}{dy}$, and we then have the aggregate ratio of utility to labour as

$$\frac{du_1}{dx} \cdot \frac{dx}{dl} + \frac{du_2}{dy} \cdot \frac{dy}{dl}.$$

It is plain that we have no equation arising out of these conditions of production, so that the ratio of exchange of X and Y will be governed only by the

degrees of utility. But if we compare X and Y with
a third commodity Z, as regards its production, we
shall arrive at the equation

$$\frac{du_1}{dx} \cdot \frac{dx}{dl} + \frac{du_2}{dy} \cdot \frac{dy}{dl} = \frac{du_3}{dz} \cdot \frac{dz}{dl}.$$

In other words, the increment of utility obtained
by applying an increment of labour to the production
of Z, must equal the sum of the increments of utility
which would be obtained if the same increment of
labour were applied to the joint production of X and Y.
It is evident that the above equation taken alone
gives us no information as to the ratios existing between
the quantities dx, dy, and dz. Before we can obtain
any ratios of exchange we must have the further
equation between the degrees of utility of X and Y,
namely,

$$\frac{du_1}{du_2} = \frac{dy}{dx}.$$

As a general rule, however, any two processes of
production will both yield joint products, so that the
equation of productiveness will take the form of a sum
of increments of utility on both sides, which we may
thus write briefly—

$$du_1 + du_2 + \dots = du_n + du_{n+1} + \dots.$$

Such an equation becomes then a kind of equation of
condition of which the influence may be very slight
regarding the ratio of exchange of any two of the
commodities concerned. And if in some cases the
terms on one side of such an equation are reduced to

one or two, it is probably because the other increments
of produce are nearly or quite devoid of utility.   As
in the cases of cinders, chips, sawdust, spent dyes,
potato stalks, chaff, etc. etc., almost every process of
industry yields refuse results, of which the utility is
zero or nearly so.   To solve the subject fully, however,
we should have to admit negative utilities, as elsewhere explained, so that the increment of utility
from any increment dl of labour would really take
the form

$$du_1 \pm du_2 \pm du_3 \pm. \ldots$$

The waste products of a chemical works, for instance,
will sometimes have a low value ; at other times it
will be difficult to get rid of them without fouling the
rivers and injuring the neighbouring estates ; in this
case they are discommodities and take the negative
sign in the equations.

Over-production

The theory of the distribution of labour enables us
to perceive clearly the meaning of *over-production* in
trade.   Early writers on Economics were always in
fear of a supposed *glut*, arising from the powers of
production surpassing the needs of consumers, so that
industry would be stopped, employment fail, and all
but the rich would be starved by the superfluity of
commodities.   The doctrine is evidently absurd and
self-contradictory.   As the acquirement of suitable
commodities is the whole purpose of industry and

trade, the greater the supplies obtained the more perfectly industry fulfils its purpose. To bring about a universal glut would be to accomplish completely the aim of the economist, which is to maximise the products of labour. But the supplies must be *suitable* —that is, they must be in proportion to the needs of the population. Over-production is not possible in all branches of industry at once, but it is possible in some as compared with others. If, by miscalculation, too much labour is spent in producing one commodity, say silk goods, our equations will not hold true. People will be more satiated with silk goods than cotton, woollen, or other goods. They will refuse, therefore, to purchase them at ratios of exchange corresponding to the labour expended. The producers will thus receive in exchange goods of less utility than they might have acquired by a better distribution of their labour.

In extending industry, therefore, we must be careful to extend it proportionally to all the requirements of the population. The more we can lower the degree of utility of all goods by satiating the desires of the purchasers the better; but we must lower the degrees of utility of different goods in a corresponding manner, otherwise there is an apparent glut and a real loss of labour.

Limits to the Intensity of Labour

I have mentioned (p. 170) that labour may vary either in duration or intensity, but have yet paid little attention to the latter circumstance. We may approximately measure the intensity of labour by the amount of physical force undergone in a certain time, although it is the pain attending that exertion of force which is the all-important element in Economics. Interesting laws have been or may be detected connecting the amount of work done with the intensity of labour. Even where these laws have not been ascertained, long experience has led men, by a sort of unconscious process of experimentation and inductive reasoning, to select that rate of work which is most advantageous.

Let us take such a simple kind of work as digging. A spade may be made of any size, and if the same number of strokes be made in the hour, the requisite exertion will vary nearly as the cube of the length of the blade. If the spade be small the fatigue will be slight, but the work done will also be slight. A very large spade, on the other hand, will do a great quantity of work at each stroke, but the fatigue will be so great that the labourer cannot long continue at his work. Accordingly, a certain medium-sized spade is adopted, which does not overtax a labourer and prevent him doing a full day's work, but enables him to accomplish as much as possible. The size of a spade should depend partly upon the tenacity and weight of the material, and partly upon the strength of the labourer. It may be observed that, in excavating stiff clay, navvies use a small strong spade; for ordinary garden purposes a larger spade is

employed; for shovelling loose sand or coals a broad
capacious shovel is used; and a still larger instrument
is employed for removing corn, malt, or any loose
light powder.

In most cases of muscular exertion the weight of
the body or of some limb is of great importance.   If
a man be employed to carry a single letter, he really
moves a weight of say a hundred and sixty pounds
for the purpose of conveying a letter weighing perhaps half an ounce.   There will be no appreciable
increase of labour if he carries twenty letters, so that
his efficiency will be multiplied twenty times.   A
hundred letters would probably prove a slight burden,
but there would still be a vast gain in the work done.
It is obvious, however, that we might go on loading
a postman with letters until the fatigue became excessive; the maximum useful result would be obtained
with the largest load which does not severely fatigue
the man, and trial soon decides the weight with considerable accuracy.

The most favourable load for a porter was investigated by Coulomb, and he found that most work
could be done by a man walking upstairs without any
load, and raising his burden by means of his own
weight in descending.   A man could thus raise four
times as much in a day as by carrying bags on his
back with the most favourable load.   This great
difference doubtless arises from the muscles being
perfectly adapted to raising the human body, whereas
any additional weight throws irregular or undue stress

upon them. Charles Babbage, also, in his admirable *Economy of Manufactures*, has remarked on this subject, and has pointed out that the weight of some limb of the body is an element in all calculations of human labour.

"The fatigue produced on the muscles of the human frame," says Babbage, "does not altogether depend on the actual force employed in each effort, but partly on the frequency with which it is exerted. The exertion necessary to accomplish every operation consists of two parts : one of these is the expenditure of force which is necessary to drive the tool or instrument; and the other is the effort required for the motion of some limb of the animal producing the action.   In driving a nail into a piece of wood, one of these is lifting the hammer, and *propelling* its head against the nail; the other is *raising* the arm itself, and moving it in order to use the hammer.   If the weight of the hammer is considerable, the former part will cause the greatest portion of the exertion. If the hammer is light, the exertion of *raising* the arm will produce the greatest part of the fatigue.   It does therefore happen that operations requiring very trifling force, if frequently repeated, will tire more effectually than more laborious work.   There is also a degree of rapidity beyond which the action of the muscles cannot be pressed." [1]

It occurred to me, some time since, that this was

---

[1] Babbage, *On the Economy of Machinery and Manufactures*, sec. 32, p. 30.

a subject admitting of interesting inquiry, and I tried to determine, by several series of experiments, the relation between the amount of work done by certain muscles and the rate of fatigue. One series consisted in holding weights varying from one pound to eighteen pounds in the hand while the arm was stretched out at its full length. The trials were two hundred and thirty-eight in number, and were made at intervals of at least one hour, so that the fatigue of one trial should not derange the next. The average number of seconds during which each weight could be sustained was found to be as follows :—

Weight in pounds . .	18	14	10	7	4	2	1
Time in seconds . . .	15	32	60	87	148	219	321.

If the arm had been thus employed in any kind of useful work, we should have estimated the useful effect by the product of the weight sustained and the time. The results would be as follows, in pound-seconds :—

Weight	18	14	10	7	4	2	1
Useful effect. . . .	266	455	603	612	592	438	321.

The maximum of useful effect would here appear to be about seven pounds, which is about the weight usually chosen for dumb-bells and other gymnastic instruments. Details of the other series of experiments are described in an article in *Nature* (30th June 1870, vol. ii. p. 158).

I undertook these experiments as a mere illustration of the mode in which some of the laws forming the physical basis of Economics might be ascertained. I was unaware that Professor S. Haughton had already, by experiment, arrived at a theory of muscular action, communicated to the Royal Society in 1862. I was gratified to find that my entirely independent results proved to be in striking agreement with his principles, as was pointed out by Professor Haughton in two articles in *Nature*.[1]

I am not aware that any exact experiments upon walking or marching have been made, but, as Professor Haughton has remarked to me, they might easily be carried out in the movements of an army. It would only be necessary, on each march which is carried up to the limits of endurance, to register the time and distance passed over. Had we a determination of the exact relations of time, space, and fatigue, it would be possible to solve many interesting problems. For instance, if one person has to overtake another, what should be their comparative rates of walking? Assuming the fatigue to increase as the square of the velocity multiplied by the time, we easily obtain an exact solution, showing that the total fatigue will be least when one person walks twice as quickly as he whom he wishes to overtake.

In different cases of muscular exertion we shall

[1] Vol. ii. p. 324 ; vol. iii. p. 289. See also Haughton's *Principles of Animal Mechanics*, 1873, pp. 444-450. The subject has since been followed up with much care and ability by Professor Francis E. Nipher, of the Washington University, St. Louis, Missouri, U.S.A. Details of his experiments will be found in the *American Journal of Science*, vol. ix. pp. 130-7 ; vol. x., etc. ; *Nature*, vol. xi. pp. 256, 276, etc.

find different problems to solve. The most advantageous rate of marching will greatly depend upon whether the loss of time or the fatigue is the most important. To march at the rate of four miles an hour would soon occasion enormous fatigue, and could only be resorted to under circumstances of great urgency. The distance passed over would bear a much higher ratio to the fatigue at the rate of three, or even two and a half miles an hour. But, if the speed were still further reduced, a loss of strength would again arise, owing to that expended in merely sustaining the body, as distinguished from that of moving it forward.

The Economics of Labour will constantly involve questions of this kind. When a work has to be completed in a brief space of time, workmen may be incited by unusual reward to do far more than their usual amount of work ; but so high a rate would not be profitable in other circumstances. The fatigue always rapidly increases when the speed of work passes a certain point, so that the extra result is far more costly in reality. In a regular and constant employment the greatest result will always be gained by such a rate as allows a workman each day, or each week at the most, to recover all fatigue and recommence with an undiminished store of energy.

CHAPTER VI

THEORY OF RENT

Accepted Opinions concerning Rent

THE general correctness of the views put forth in preceding chapters derives great probability from their close resemblance to the Theory of Rent, as it has been accepted by English writers for nearly a century. It has not been usual to state this theory in mathematical symbols, and clumsy arithmetical illustrations have been employed instead; but it is easy to show that the fluxional calculus is the branch of mathematics which most correctly applies to the subject.

The Theory of Rent was first discovered and clearly stated by James Anderson in a tract published in 1777, and called *An Inquiry into the Nature of the Corn Laws, with a view to the Corn Bill proposed for Scotland*. An extract from this work may be found in MacCulloch's edition of the *Wealth of Nations*, p. 453, giving a most clear explanation of the effect of the various fertility of land,

and showing that it is not the rent of land which determines the price of its produce, but the price of the produce which determines the rent of the land. The following passage must be given in Anderson's own words :—[1]

". . . In every country there is a variety of soils, differing considerably from one another in point of fertility. These we shall at present suppose arranged into different classes, which we shall denote by the letters A, B, C, D, E, F, etc., the class A comprehending the soils of the greatest fertility, and the other letters expressing different classes of soils, gradually decreasing in fertility as you recede from the first. Now, as the expense of cultivating the least fertile soil is as great or greater than that of the most fertile field, it necessarily follows that if an equal quantity of corn, the produce of each field, can be sold at the same price, the profit on cultivating the most fertile soil must be much greater than that of cultivating the others ; and as this continues to decrease as the sterility increases, it must at length happen that the expense of cultivating some of the inferior soils will equal the value of the whole produce."

The theory really rests upon the principle, which I have called the Law of Indifference, that for the same commodity in the same market there can only be one price or ratio of exchange. Hence, if different qualities of land yield different amounts of produce to the same labour, there must be an excess of profit

[1] *Inquiry*, etc., p. 45, note.

in some over others.   There will be some land which will not yield the ordinary wages of labour, and which will, therefore, not be taken into cultivation, or if, by mistake, it is cultivated, will be abandoned. Some land will just pay the ordinary wages; better land will yield an excess, so that the possession of such land will become a matter of competition, and the owner will be able to exact as rent from the cultivators the whole excess above what is sufficient to pay the ordinary wages of labour.

There is a secondary origin for rent in the fact, that if more or less labour and capital be applied to the same portion of land, the produce will not increase proportionally to the amount of labour.   It is quite impossible that we could go on constantly increasing the yield of one farm without limit, otherwise we might feed the whole country upon a single farm.   Yet there is no definite limit; for, by better and better culture, we may always seem able to raise a little more.   But the last increment of produce will come to bear a smaller and smaller ratio to the labour required to produce it, so that it soon becomes, in the case of all land, undesirable to apply more labour.

MacCulloch has given, in his edition of the *Wealth of Nations*,[1] a supplementary note, in which he explains, with the utmost clearness and scientific accuracy, the nature of the theory.   This note contains by far the best statement of the theory, as it

[1] New edition, 1839, p. 444.

seems to me, and I will therefore quote his recapitulation of the principles which he establishes.

> " 1. That if the produce of land could always be increased in proportion to the outlay on it, there would be no such thing as rent.

> " 2. That the produce of land cannot, at an average, be increased in proportion to the outlay, but may be indefinitely increased in a less proportion.

> " 3. That the least productive portion of the outlay, which, speaking generally, is the last, must yield the ordinary profits of stock. And

> " 4. That all which the other portions yield more than this, being above ordinary profits, is rent."

A most satisfactory account of the theory is also given in James Mill's *Elements of Political Economy*, a work which I never read without admiring its brief, clear, and powerful style. James Mill constantly uses the expression *dose of capital*. "The time comes," he says, " at which it is necessary either to have recourse to land of the second quality, or to apply a second dose of capital less productively upon land of the first quality." He evidently means by a *dose of capital* a little more capital, and though the name is peculiar, the meaning is simply that of an *increment of capital*. The number of doses or increments mentioned is only three, but this is clearly to avoid prolixity of explanation. There is no reason why we should not consider the whole capital divided into many more doses. The same general law which makes the second dose less productive than the first, will make a hundredth dose, speaking generally, less productive than the preceding ninety-ninth dose. Theoretically speaking, there is no need or possibility of stopping at any limit. A mathematical law is in theory always continuous, so that the *doses* considered are indefinitely small and indefinitely numerous. I consider, then, that James Mill's mode of expression is exactly equivalent to that which I have adopted in earlier parts of this book. As mathematicians have invented a precise and fully recognised mode of expressing *doses* or *increments*, I know not why we should exclude language from Economics which is found convenient in all other sciences. It is mere pedantry to insist upon calling that a *dose* in Economics, which in all the other sciences is called by the perfectly established and expressive term *increment*.

The following are James Mill's general conclusions as to the nature of Rent.[1] "In applying capital, either to lands of various degrees of fertility, or in successive doses to the same land, some portions of the capital so employed are attended with a greater produce, some with a less. That which yields the least yields all that is necessary for reimbursing and rewarding the capitalist. The capitalist will receive no more than this remuneration for any portion

[1] *Elements*, p. 17.

of the capital which he employs, because the competition of others will prevent him. All that is yielded above this remuneration the landlord will be able to appropriate. Rent, therefore, is the difference between the return yielded to that portion of the capital which is employed upon the land with the least effect, and that which is yielded to all the other portions employed upon it with a greater effect."

Symbolic Statement of the Theory

The accepted Theory of Rent, as given above, needs little or no alteration to adapt it to expression in mathematical symbols. For doses or increments of capital I shall substitute increments of labour, partly because the functions of capital remain to be considered in the next chapter, and partly because James Mill, J. S. Mill, and MacCulloch hold the application of capital to be synonymous with the application of labour. This assumption is implied in James Mill's statement (p. 13); it is expressly stated in J. S. Mill's *First Fundamental Proposition concerning the Nature of Capital* ;[1] and MacCulloch adds a footnote[2] to make it clear, that as all capital was originally produced by labour, the application of additional capital is the application of additional labour. "Either the one phrase or the other may be used indiscriminately." This doctrine is in itself altogether erroneous, but it will not be erroneous to assume as a mode of

---

[1] Book i., chap. v. sec. 1.   [2] *Wealth of Nations*, p. 445.

simplifying the problem that the increments of labour applied are equally assisted by capital. It is a separate and subsequent problem to determine how rent or interest arises when the same labour is assisted by different quantities of capital.

I shall suppose that a certain labourer, or, what comes to exactly the same thing, a body of labourers, expend labour on several different pieces of ground. On what principle will they distribute their labour between the several pieces? Let us imagine that a certain amount has been spent upon each, and that another small portion, Δl, is going to be applied. Let there be two pieces of land, and let Δx_1, Δx_2, be the increments of produce to be expected from the pieces respectively. They will naturally apply the labour to the land which yields the greatest result. So long as there is any advantage in one use of labour over another, the most advantageous will certainly be adopted. Therefore, when they are perfectly satisfied with the distribution made, the increment of produce to the same labour will be equal in each case ; or we have

$$\Delta x_1 = \Delta x_2.$$

To attain scientific accuracy, we must decrease the increments infinitely, and then we obtain the equation—

$$\frac{dx_1}{dl} = \frac{dx_2}{dl}.$$

Now $\frac{dx}{dl}$ represents the ratio of produce, or the productiveness of labour, as regards the last increment of labour applied. We may say, then, that whenever a labourer or body of labourers distribute their labour over pieces of land with perfect economy, the *final ratios of produce to labour will be equal*.

We may now take into account the general law, that when more and more labour is applied to the same piece of land, the produce ultimately does not increase proportionately to the labour. This means that the function $\dfrac{dx}{dl}$ diminishes without limit towards zero after x has passed a certain quantity. The whole produce of a piece of land is x, the whole labour spent upon it is l; and x varies in some way as l varies, never decreasing when l increases. We may say, then, that x is a function of l; let us call it Pl. When a little more labour is expended, the increment of produce dx is dPl, and $\dfrac{dPl}{dl}$ is the final rate of production, the same as was previously denoted by $\dfrac{dx}{dl}$.[1]

In the Theory of Labour it was shown that no increment of labour would be expended unless there was sufficient recompense in the produce, but that labour would be expended up to the point at which the increment of utility exactly equals the increment of pain incurred in acquiring it. Here we find an exact definition of the amount of labour which will be profitably applied.

---

[1] The final rate of production $\dfrac{dx}{dl}$ is now generally known as *marginal productiveness* or *productivity*.—[Ed.]

It was also shown that the last increment of labour is the most painful, so that if a person is recompensed for the last increment of labour which he applies to land by the rate of production $\dfrac{dx}{dl}$, it follows that all the labour he applies might be recompensed sufficiently at the same rate. The whole labour is l, so that if the recompense were equal over the whole, the result would be $l \cdot \dfrac{dx}{dl}$. Consequently, he obtains more than the necessary return to labour by the amount

$$Pl - l \cdot \frac{dx}{dl}\,;$$

or, as we may write it,

$$Pl - l \cdot P'l,$$

in which $P'l$ is the differential coefficient of Pl, or the final rate of production. This expression represents the advantage he derives from the possession of land in affording him more profit than other methods of employing his labour. It is therefore the rent which he would ask before yielding it up to another person, or equally the rent which he would be able and willing to pay if hiring it from another.

The same considerations apply to every piece of land cultivated. When the same person or body of labourers cultivate several pieces, $P'l$ will be of the same magnitude in each case, but the quantities of labour, and possibly the functions of labour, will be

different.   Thus with two pieces of land the rent may
be represented as

$$P_1 l_1 + P_2 l_2' - (l_1 + l_2) P_1' l_1 ;$$

or, speaking generally of any number of pieces, it is
the sum of the quantities of the form Pl, *minus* the
sum of the quantities of the form $l \cdot P'l$.

Illustrations of the Theory

It is very easy to illustrate the Theory of Rent by
diagrams.   For, let distances along the line ox denote

Fig. 10.

quantities of labour, and let the curve apc represent
the variation of the rate of production, so that the
area of the curve will be the measure of the produce.
Thus when labour has been applied to the amount om,
the produce will correspond to the area $apmo$.   Let a
small new increment of labour, mm', be applied, and
suppose the rate of production equal over the whole
of the increment.   Then the small parallelogram,

$pp'm'm$, will be the produce. This will be proportional in quantity to pm, so that the height of any point of the curve perpendicularly above a point of the line ox represents the rate of production at that point in the application of labour.

If we further suppose that the labourer considers his labour, mm', repaid by the produce pm', there is no reason why any other part of his labour should not be repaid at the same rate. Drawing, then, a horizontal line, rpq, through the point p, his whole labour, om, will be repaid by the produce represented by the area $orpm$. Consequently, the overlying area, rap, is the excess of produce which can be exacted from him as rent, if he be not himself the owner of the land.

Imagining the same person to cultivate another piece of land, we might take the curve, bqc, to represent its productiveness. The same rate of production will repay the labourer in this case as in the last, so that the intersection of the same horizontal line, rpq, with the curve, will determine the final point of labour, n. The area, rn, will be the measure of the sufficient recompense to the whole labour, on, spent upon the land; and the excess of produce, or rent, will be the area, rbq. In a similar manner, any number of pieces of land might be considered. The figure might have been drawn so that the curves would rise on leaving the initial line oy, indicating that a very little labour will have a poor rate of production; and that a certain amount of labour is requisite to develop the fertility of the soil. This may often or always be the case, as a considerable quantity of labour is generally requisite in first bringing land into cultivation, or merely keeping it in a fit state for use. The laws of rent depend on the undoubted principle, that the curves always *ultimately* decline towards the base line *ox*, that is, the final rate of production always *ultimately* sinks towards zero.

CHAPTER VII

THEORY OF CAPITAL

The Function of Capital

In considering the nature and principles of Capital, we enter a distinct branch of our subject. There is no close or necessary connection between the employment of capital and the processes of exchange. Both by the use of capital and by exchange we are enabled vastly to increase the sum of utility which we enjoy; but it is conceivable that we might have the advantages of capital without those of exchange. An isolated man like Alexander Selkirk might feel the benefit of a stock of provisions, tools, and other means of facilitating industry, although cut off from traffic with other men. Economics, then, is not solely the science of Exchange or Value: it is also the science of Capitalisation.

The views which I shall endeavour to establish on this subject are in fundamental agreement with those adopted by Ricardo; but I shall try to put the Theory of Capital in a more simple and consistent

manner than has been the case with some later
economists. We are told, with perfect truth, that
capital consists of wealth employed to facilitate production ; but when economists proceed to enumerate
the articles of wealth constituting capital, they obscure
the subject. "The capital of a country," says Mac-
Culloch,[1] "consists of those portions of the produce
of industry existing in it which may be directly
employed either to support human beings, or to
facilitate production." Professor Fawcett again says :[2]
" Capital is not confined to the food which feeds the
labourers, but includes machinery, buildings, and, in
fact, every product due to man's labour which can be
applied to assist his industry ; but capital which is in
the form of food does not perform its functions in the
same way as capital that is in the form of machinery :
the one is termed circulating capital, the other fixed
capital."

The notion of capital assumes a new degree of
simplicity as soon as we recognise that what has been
called a part is really the whole. Capital, as I regard
it, consists merely in the *aggregate of those commodities
which are required for sustaining labourers of any
kind or class engaged in work.* A stock of food is
the main element of capital ; but supplies of clothes,
furniture, and all the other articles in common daily
use are also necessary parts of capital. The *current
means of sustenance constitute capital in its free*

[1] *Principles of Political Economy*, p. 100.
[2] *Manual of Political Economy*, 2nd ed., p. 47.

or uninvested form. The single and all-important function of capital is to enable the labourer to await the result of any long-lasting work,—to put an interval between the beginning and the end of an enterprise.

Not only can we, by the aid of capital, erect large works which would otherwise have been impossible, but the production of articles which would have been very costly in labour may be rendered far more easy. Capital enables us to make a great outlay in providing tools, machines, or other preliminary works, which have for their sole object the production of some important commodity, and which will greatly facilitate production when we enter upon it.

Capital is concerned with Time

Several economists have clearly perceived that the time elapsing between the beginning and end of a work is the difficulty which capital assists us to surmount. Thus James Mill has said : " If the man who subsists on animals cannot make sure of his prey in less than a day, he cannot have less than a whole day's subsistence in advance. If hunting excursions are undertaken which occupy a week or a month, subsistence for several days may be required. It is evident, when men come to live upon those productions which their labour raises from the soil, and which can be brought to maturity only once in the year, that subsistence for a whole year must be laid up in advance." [1]

---

[1] *Elements of Political Economy*, 3rd ed., 1826, p. 9.

Much more recently, Professor Hearn has said, in his admirable work entitled *Plutology* :[1] "The first and most obvious mode in which capital directly operates as an auxiliary of industry is to render possible the performance of work which requires for its completion some considerable time. In the simplest agricultural operations there is the seed-time and the harvest. A vineyard is unproductive for at least three years before it is thoroughly fit for use. In gold mining there is often a long delay, sometimes even of five or six years, before the gold is reached. Such mines could not be worked by poor men unless the storekeepers gave the miners credit, or, in other words, supplied capital for the adventure. But, in addition to this great result, capital also implies other consequences which are hardly less momentous. One of these is the steadiness and continuity that labour thus acquires. A man, when aided by capital, can afford to remain at his work until it is finished, and is not compelled to leave it incomplete while he searches for the necessary means of subsistence. If there were no accumulated fund upon which the labourer could rely, no man could remain for a single day exclusively engaged in any other occupation than those which relate to the supply of his primary wants. Besides these wants, he should also from time to time search for the materials on which he was to work."

These passages imply, as it seems to me, a clear

---

[1] *Plutology; or The Theory of the Efforts to Satisfy Human Wants,* 1864 (Macmillan), p. 139.

insight into the nature and purposes of capital, except that the writers have not with sufficient boldness followed out the consequences of their notion. If we take a comprehensive view of the subject, it will be seen that not only the chief but the sole purpose of capital is as above described. Capital simply allows us *to expend labour in advance.* Thus, to raise corn we need to turn over the surface of the soil. If we proceed straight to the work, and use the implements with which nature has furnished us—our fingers—we should spend an enormous amount of painful labour with very little result. It is far better, therefore, to spend the first part of our labour in making a spade or other implement to assist the rest of our labour. This spade represents so much labour which has been invested, and so far spent; but if it lasts three years, its cost may be considered as repaid gradually during those three years. This labour, like that of digging, has for its object the raising of corn, and the only essential difference is that it has to precede the production of corn by a longer interval. The average interval of time for which labour will remain invested in the spade is half of the three years. Similarly, if we possess a larger capital, and expend it in making a plough, which will last for twenty years, we invest at the beginning a great deal of labour which is only gradually repaid during those twenty years, and which is therefore, on the average, invested for about ten years.

It is true that in modern industry we should

seldom or never find the same man making the spade
or plough, and afterwards using the implement. The
division of labour enables me, with much advantage,
to expend a portion of my capital in purchasing the
implement from some one who devotes his attention
to the manufacture, and probably expends capital
previously in facilitating the work. But this does
not alter the principles of the matter. What capital
I give for the spade merely replaces what the manufacturer had already invested in the expectation that
the spade would be needed. Exactly the same considerations may be applied to much more complicated
applications of capital. The ultimate object of all
industry engaged with cotton is the production of
cotton goods. But the complete process of producing
those goods is divided into many parts; and it is
necessary to begin the spending of labour a long time
before any goods can be finished.

In the first place, labour will be required to till
the land which is to bear the cotton plants, and probably two years at least will elapse between the time
when the ground is first broken and the time when
the cotton reaches the mills. A cotton mill, again,
must be a very strong and durable structure, and
must contain machinery of a very costly character,
which can only repay its owner by a long course of
use. We might spin and weave cotton goods as in
former times, or as it is done in Cashmere, with a very
small use of capital; but then the labour required
would be enormously greater in proportion to the

produce. It is far more economical in the end to spend a vast amount of labour and capital in building a substantial mill and filling it with the best machinery, which will then go on working with unimpaired efficiency for thirty years or more. This means that, in addition to the labour spent in superintending the machines at the moment when goods are produced, a great quantity of labour has been spent from one to thirty years in advance, or, on the average, fifteen years in advance. This expenditure is repaid by an annuity of profit extending over those thirty years.

The interval elapsing between the first exertion of labour and the enjoyment of the result is further increased by any time during which the raw material may lie in warehouses before reaching the machines ; and by the time employed in distributing the goods to retail dealers, and through them to the consumers. It may even happen that the consumer finds it desirable to keep a certain stock on hand, so that the time when the real object of the goods is fulfilled becomes still further deferred. During this time, also, capital seems to me to be invested, and only as actual utilisation takes place is expenditure repaid by corresponding utility enjoyed.

I would say, then, in the most general manner, that *whatever improvements in the supply of commodities lengthen* [1] *the average interval between the moment when labour is exerted and its ultimate result*

---

[1] Meaning *involve a lengthening of.*—[Ed.]

or purpose accomplished, such improvements depend upon the use of capital. And I would add that this is the sole use of capital. Whenever we overlook the irrelevant complications introduced by the division of labour and the frequency of exchange, all employments of capital resolve themselves into the fact of time elapsing between the beginning and the end of industry.

Quantitative Notions concerning Capital

One main point which has to be clearly brought before the mind in this subject is the difference between the *amount of capital invested* and the *amount of investment of capital.* The first is a quantity of one dimension only—the quantity of capital; the second is a quantity of two dimensions, namely, the quantity of capital, and the length of time during which it remains invested. If one day's labour remains invested for two years, the capital is only that equivalent to one day; but it is locked up twice as long as if it were invested for only one year. Now all questions in which we consider the most advantageous employment of capital turn upon the length of investment quite as much as upon the amount. The same capital will serve for twice as much industry if it be absorbed or invested for only half the time.

The amount of investment of capital will evidently be determined by multiplying each portion of capital invested at any moment by the length of time for

which it remains invested. One pound invested for
five years gives the same result as five pounds invested for one year, the product being *five pound-
years*. Most commonly, however, investment proceeds continuously or at intervals, and we must form
clear notions on the subject. Thus, if a workman be
employed during one year on any work, the result of
which is complete, and enjoyed at the end of that
time, the absorption of capital will be found by multiplying each day's wages by the days remaining till
the end of the year, and adding all the results
together. If the daily wages be four shillings, then
we have

$$4 \times 364 + 4 \times 363 + 4 \times 362 \ldots \ldots + 4 \times 1 ;$$

or, $4 \times \dfrac{365 \times 364}{2}$, or 265,720 *shilling-days*.

We may also represent the investment by a diagram such as fig. 11. The length along the line *ox*

Fig. 11.

indicates the duration of investment, and the height
attained at any point, *a*, is the amount of capital
invested. But it is the whole area of the rectangles
up to any point, *a*, which measures the amount of
investment during the time *oa*.

The whole result of continued labour is not often consumed and enjoyed in a moment; the result generally lasts for a certain length of time. We must then conceive the capital as being progressively *uninvested*. Let us, for sake of simple illustration, imagine the labour of producing the harvest to be continuously and equally expended between the first of September in one year and the same day in the next. Let the harvest be then completely gathered, and its consumption begin immediately and continue equally during the succeeding twelve months. Then

FIG. 12.

the amount of investment of capital will be represented by the area of an isosceles triangle, as in fig. 12, the base of which corresponds to two years of duration. Now the area of a triangle is equal to the height multiplied by half the base; and as the height represents the greatest amount invested, that upon the first of September, when the harvest is gathered; half the base, or one year, is the *average time of investment of the whole amount*.

In the 37th proposition of the first book of Euclid it is proved that all triangles upon the same base and between the same parallels are equal in area. Hence we may draw the conclusion that, provided capital be

invested and uninvested continuously and in simple
proportion to the time, we need only regard the
greatest amount invested and the greatest time of
investment. Whether it be all invested suddenly,
and then gradually withdrawn ; or gradually invested
and suddenly withdrawn ; or gradually invested and
gradually withdrawn ; the amount of investment will
be in every case the greatest amount of capital multiplied by half the time elapsing from the beginning to
the end of the investment.

Expression for Amount of Investment

To render our notions of the subject still more
exact and general, let us resort once more to mathematical symbols.

Let Δp = amount of capital supposed to be invested in the time Δt ; let t = time elapsing before its
result is enjoyed, the enjoyment taking place in an
interval of time Δt, which may be disregarded in
comparison with t. Then $t . \Delta p$ is the amount of
investment ; and if the investment is repeated, the
sum of the quantities of the nature of $t . \Delta p$, or, in
the customary mode of expression, $\Sigma t . \Delta p$ is the
total amount of investment. But it will seldom be
possible to assign each portion of result to an exactly
corresponding portion of labour. Cotton goods are
due to the aggregate industry of those who tilled the
ground, grew the cotton, plucked, transported, cleaned,
spun, wove, and dyed it ; we cannot distinguish the

moment when each labourer's work is separately repaid. To avoid this difficulty, we must fix on some moment of time when the whole transaction is closed, all labour upon the ground repaid, the mill and machinery worn out and sold, and the cotton goods consumed. Let t now denote the time elapsing from any moment up to this final moment of closing the accounts. Let Δp be as before an increment of capital invested, and let Δq be an increment of capital uninvested by the sale of the products and their enjoyment by the consumer. Thus it will be pretty obvious that the sum of the quantities $t \cdot \Delta p$, less by the sum of the quantities $t \cdot \Delta q$, will be the total investment of capital, or expressed in symbols $\Sigma t \cdot \Delta p - \Sigma t \cdot \Delta q$.

Dimensions of Capital, Credit and Debit

As the subject presents itself to me at present, I apprehend that capital is to be regarded simply as commodity. If so, the dimension of capital will be represented by M, and the *amount of investment of capital*, possessing the additional dimension of time, will have the symbol MT. How then are we to determine the quantitative nature of what Senior called *Abstinence*, that temporary sacrifice of enjoyment which is essential to the existence of capital? Senior thus explicitly defined what he meant by the word:[1] " By the word Abstinence, we wish to express that

[1] *Political Economy*, by Nassau W. Senior, 5th ed., 1863, p. 59.

agent, distinct from labour and the agency of nature, the concurrence of which is necessary to the existence of capital, and which stands in the same relation to profit as labour does to wages." He goes on to explain that abstinence, though usually accompanying labour, is distinct from it. A careful consideration of Senior's remarks shows that in reality abstinence is the endurance of want, the abstaining from the enjoyment of utility which might be enjoyed. Now the degree or intensity of want is measured by the degree of utility of commodity if it were consumed. Great degree of utility simply means great want, so that one dimension of abstinence must be U, and time being also obviously an element of abstinence, the required symbolic statement of its dimensions will be UT. This result satisfactorily corresponds with Senior's definition, for he says that abstinence is to profit as labour is to wages. Now profit or interest is clearly symbolised by M, and wages also by M, both consisting simply of quantities of commodity. Thus UT bears just the same relation to M that ET does to M, for E signifies the degree of painfulness of labour, and can barely be distinguished from U, except in sign.

The relation of abstinence, UT, to total utility, MU, also confirms our result. For if we convert *abstinence* into *satisfaction*, by giving a supply of commodity for consumption, this action is symbolically represented by multiplying UT into MT^{-1}, which yields MU, or utility.

It will need no argument to show that the dimension of *debit* and *credit*, having regard only to what is borrowed and owed, will be the dimension of commodity simply, or M.   According to the practice of commerce, a contract of debt is a contract to return a certain physically defined quantity of a specified substance, such as an ounce of gold, a ton of pig-iron, a hogshead of palm oil.   No attempt is made to define quantities of utility, so that the debt when repaid shall yield utility equal to what it possessed when lent.   The borrower and lender either take their chance about this, or provide for it in the rate of interest to be paid.   It is equally obvious that in another sense the *amount of credit or debit* will be proportional to the duration of the operation, and will have the dimensions MT.

Effect of the Duration of Work

Perhaps the most interesting point in the Theory of Capital is the advantage arising from the rapid performance of work, if it is capable of being done with convenience and with the same ultimate result. To investigate this point, suppose that $w =$ the whole amount of wages which it is requisite to pay in building a house, and that this does not alter when we vary, within certain limits, the time employed in the work, denoted by t.   If the work goes on continuously, we shall, during each unit of time, have an amount invested equal to the tth part of w.   The whole amount of investment of capital will therefore be represented by the area of a triangle whose base is t and height w; that is, the investment is $\frac{1}{2}tw$. Thus when the whole expenditure is ultimately the same, the amount of investment is simply proportional to the time. The result would be more serious if the accumulation of compound interest during the time were taken into account; but the consideration of compound interest would render the formulæ very complex, and is not requisite for the purpose in view.

We must clearly distinguish the case treated above, in which the amount of labour is the same, but spread over a longer time, from other cases where the labour increases in proportion to the time. The investment of capital, then, grows in an exceedingly rapid manner. Neglecting the first cost of tools, materials, and other preparations, let the first day's labour cost a; during the second day this remains invested, and the amount of capital a is added; on each following day a like addition is made. The amount of capital invested is evidently

At beginning of second day . . a,
  „   „   third „   . . $a + a$,
  „   „   fourth „   . . $a + a + a$;

and so on. If the work lasts during $n + 1$ days, the total amount of investment of capital will be

$$a + 2a + 3a + 4a + \ldots \ldots na.$$

The sum of the series is

$$a\left(\frac{n}{2}+\frac{n^2}{2}\right),$$

which increases by a term involving the square of the time. The employment of capital thus grows in proportion to the triangular numbers

1, 3, 6, 10, 15, 21, etc.

If we regard the investment as taking place continuously, the whole absorption of capital is repre-

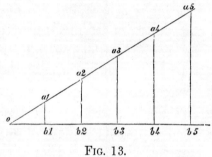

FIG. 13.

sented by the area of a right-angled triangle (fig. 13), in which ob_1, b_1b_2, b_2b_3, etc., are the successive units of time. The heights of the lines a_1b_1, a_2b_2 represent the amounts invested at the ends of the times. The daily investment being a, the total amount of investment will be $a\dfrac{n^2}{2}$, increasing as the square of the time.

Cases of this kind continually occur, as in sinking a deep mine, of which the requisite depth cannot be previously known with accuracy. Any large work,

such as a breakwater, an embankment, the foundations of a great bridge, a dock, a long tunnel, the
dredging of a channel, involves a problem of a similar
nature; for it is seldom known what amount of labour
and capital will be required; and if the work lasts
much longer than was expected, the result is usually
a financial disaster.

Illustrations of the Investment of Capital

The time during which capital remains invested,
and the circumstances of its investment and repro-
duction, are exceedingly various in different employments. If a person plants cabbages, they will be
ready in the course of a few months, and the labour
of planting and tending them, together with a part
of the labour of preparing and manuring the soil,
yields its results with very little delay. In planting
a forest tree, however, a certain amount of labour is
expended, and no result obtained until after the lapse
of thirty, forty, or fifty years. The first cost of
enclosing, preparing, and planting a plantation is
considerable; and though, after a time, the loppings
and thinnings of the trees repay the cost of superintendence and repairs, yet the absorption of capital is
great, and we may thus account for the small amount
of planting which goes on. The ageing of wine is a
somewhat similar case. A certain amount of labour
is expended without result for ten or fifteen years,
and the cost of storage is incurred during the whole

time. To estimate the real cost of the articles at
the end of the time, we must, in all such cases,
add compound interest, and this grows in a rapid
manner. Every pound invested at the commencement of a business becomes 1·63 pounds at the end
of ten years, 11·47 pounds at the end of fifty years,
and no less than 131·50 pounds at the end of a
century, the rate of interest being taken at five per
cent. Thus it cannot be profitable to store wine for
fifty years, unless it become about twelve times as
valuable as it was when new. It cannot pay to plant
an oak and let it live a century, unless the timber
then repays the cost of planting 132 times.

If an annual charge, however small, has to be
incurred (for instance, the cost of storage and superintendence), the expense mounts up in a still more
alarming manner. Thus, if the cost of any investment is one pound per annum, the amount invested,
with compound interest at five per cent, becomes
12·58 pounds at the end of ten years, 209·35 pounds
at the end of fifty years, and the enormous amount
of 2610·03 at the end of a century. We shall almost
always have to take into account both the original
and continuous cost of an investment. Thus if a
stock of wine worth £100 be laid by for fifty years,
and the cost of storage be £1 per annum, the total
cost at the end of the time will be £1147·0 on
account of original cost, and £209·35 for storage, or
in all £1356·35.

It is to be feared that the rapid accumulation of

compound interest is often overlooked in estimating
the cost of public works and other undertakings of
considerable duration. A great fort, breakwater, or
canal (the Caledonian Canal, for instance) is often
not completed for twenty years after its commencement, and in the meantime it may be of little or no
use. Suppose that its cost has been £10,000 each
year; then the aggregate cost would seem to be
£200,000, but allowing for interest at five per cent
it is really £330,000. The French engineer and
economist, Minard,[1] fully understood this point of
finance, and showed that in the case of some public
works, such as the great *digue* of Cherbourg harbour,
and canals, the execution of which is allowed sometimes to drag on for half a century before any adequate
result is returned, the real cost is incomparably greater
than it is represented to be by merely stating the
sums of money expended. In some cases, such as
the first canal of Saint Quentin, a work, after being
long prosecuted, is abandoned, and the loss by first
cost and interest becomes enormous. The Guernsey
Harbour is a case in point, and the English dockyards
would supply abundance of similar facts.

An interesting example of the investment of
capital occurs in the case of gold and silver, a large
stock of which is maintained either in the form of
money, or plate and jewellery. Labour is spent in
the digging or mining of the metals, which is gradu-

[1] Minard, *Annales des Ponts et Chaussées*, 1850, 1er Semestre,
p. 57.

ally repaid by the use or satisfaction arising from the possession of the metals during the whole time for which they continue in use. Hence the investment of capital extends over the average duration of the metals. Now, if the stock of gold requires one per cent of its amount to maintain it undiminished, it will be apparent that each particle of gold remains in use 100 years on the average; if $\frac{1}{2}$ per cent is sufficient, the average duration will be 200 years. We may state the result thus:

Loss of gold or silver annually					Average duration of each particle in use
1 per cent	.	.	.	.	100 years
$\frac{1}{2}$,,	.	.	.	.	200 ,,
$\frac{1}{4}$,,	.	.	.	.	400 ,,
$\frac{1}{10}$,,	.	.	.	.	1000 ,,

The wear and loss of the precious metals in a civilised country is probably not more than $\frac{1}{200}$ part annually, including plate, jewellery, and money in the estimate, so that the average investment will be for 200 years. It is curious that, if we regard a quantity of gold as wearing away annually by a fixed percentage of what remains, the duration of some part is infinite, and yet the average duration is finite. Some of the gold possessed by the Romans is doubtless mixed with what we now possess; and some small part of it will be handed down as long as the human race exists.

Fixed and Circulating Capital

Economists have long been accustomed to distinguish capital into the two kinds, fixed and circulating. Adam Smith called that circulating which passes from hand to hand, and yields a revenue by being parted with. The fact of being frequently exchanged is, however, an accidental circumstance which leads to no results of importance. Ricardo altered the use of the terms, applying the name *circulating* to that which is frequently destroyed and has to be reproduced. He says unequivocally :[1] " In proportion as fixed capital is less durable, it approaches to the nature of circulating capital. It will be consumed, and its value reproduced in a shorter time, in order to preserve the capital of the manufacturer." Accepting this doctrine, and carrying it out to the full extent, we must say that no precise line can be drawn between the two kinds. The difference is one of amount and degree. The duration of capital may vary from a day to several hundred years ; the most circulating is the least durable ; the most fixed the most durable.

Free and Invested Capital

I believe that the clear explanation of the doctrine of capital requires the use of a term *free capital,*

[1] *On the Principles of Political Economy and Taxation*, chap. i., sec. 5, 3rd ed., p. 36.

which has not been hitherto recognised by economists.   By free capital I mean the wages of labour,
either in its transitory form of money, or its real
form of food and other necessaries of life.   The
ordinary sustenance requisite to support labourers
of all ranks when engaged upon their work is really
the true form of capital.   It is quite in agreement
with the ordinary language of commercial men to
say, not that a factory, or dock, or railway, or ship,
is capital, but that *it represents so much capital sunk
in the enterprise.*   To invest capital is to spend
money, or the food and maintenance which money
purchases, upon the completion of some work.   The
capital remains invested or sunk until the work has
returned profit, equivalent to the first cost, with
interest.

Much clearness would result from making the
language of Economics more nearly coincident with
that of commerce.   Accordingly, I would not say
that a railway *is fixed capital*, but that *capital is
fixed in the railway.*   The capital is not the railway,
but the food of those who made the railway.
Abundance of free capital in a country means that
there are copious stocks of food, clothing, and every
article which people insist upon having—that, in
short, everything is so arranged that abundant
subsistence and conveniences of every kind are forthcoming without the labour of the country being
much taxed to provide them.   In such circumstances it is possible that a part of the labourers

of the country can be employed on works of which the utility is distant, and yet no one will feel scarcity in the present.

Uniformity of the Rate of Interest

A most important principle of this subject is, that *free capital can be indifferently employed in any branch or kind of industry.*   Free capital, as we have just seen, consists of a suitable assortment of all kinds of food, clothing, utensils, furniture, and other articles which a community requires for its ordinary sustenance.   Men and families consume much the same kind of commodities, whatever may be the branch of manufacture or trade by which they earn a living.   Hence there is nothing in the nature of free capital to determine its employment to one kind of industry rather than another.   The very same wages, whether we regard the money wages, or the real wages purchased with the money, will support a man whether he be a mechanic, a weaver, a coal miner, a carpenter, a mason, or any other kind of labourer.

The necessary result is, that the rate of interest for free capital will tend to and closely attain uniformity in all employments.   The market for capital is like all other markets : *there can be but one price for one article at one time.*   It is a case of the Law of Indifference (p. 90).   Now the article in question is the same, so that its price must be the same. Accordingly, as is well known, the rate of interest, when freed from considerations of risk, trouble, and other interfering causes, is the same in all trades; and every trade will employ capital up to the point at which it just yields the current interest. If any manufacturer or trader employs so much capital in supporting a certain amount of labour that the return is less than in other trades, he will lose; for he might have obtained the current rate by lending it to other traders.

General Expression for the Rate of Interest

We may obtain a general expression for the rate of interest yielded by capital in any employment provided that we may suppose the produce for the same amount of labour to vary as some continuous function of the time elapsing between the expenditure of the labour and the enjoyment of the result. Let the time in question be t, and the produce for the same amount of labour the function of t denoted by Ft, which may be supposed always to increase with t. If we now extend the time to $t + \Delta t$, the produce will be $F(t + \Delta t)$, and the increment of produce $F(t + \Delta t) - Ft$. The ratio which this increment bears to the increment of investment of capital will determine the rate of interest. Now, at the end of the time t, we might receive the product Ft, and this

is the amount of capital which remains invested when
we extend the time by Δt. Hence the amount of
increased investment of capital is $\Delta t \cdot Ft$; and,
dividing the increment of produce by this last
expression, we have

$$\frac{F(t + \Delta t) - Ft}{\Delta t} \times \frac{1}{Ft}.$$

When we reduce the magnitude of Δt infinitely, the
limit of the first factor of the above expression is the
differential coefficient of Ft, so that we find the rate
of interest to be represented by

$$\frac{dFt}{dt} \cdot \frac{1}{Ft} \quad \text{or} \quad \frac{F't}{Ft}.$$

The interest of capital is, in other words, *the rate of
increase of the produce divided by the whole produce*; but this is a quantity which must rapidly
approach to zero, unless means can be found of continually maintaining the rate of increase. Unless
a body moves with a rapidly increasing speed, the
space it moves over in any unit of time must ultimately become inconsiderable compared with the
whole space passed over from the commencement.
There is no reason to suppose that industry, generally speaking, is capable of returning any such
vastly increasing produce from the greater application of capital. Every new machine or other great
invention will usually require a fixation of capital for
a certain average time, and may be capable of paying
interest upon it; but when this average time is

reached, it fails to afford a return to more prolonged investments.[1]

To take an instance, let us suppose that the produce of labour in some case is proportional to the interval of abstinence t; then we have say $Ft = a \cdot t$, in which a is an unknown constant. The differential coefficient $F't$ is now a; and the rate of interest $\frac{a}{Ft}$ or $\frac{a}{at}$ or $\frac{1}{t}$; or the rate of interest varies inversely as the time of investment.

Dimension of Interest

The formula which we obtained in the preceding section has been subjected to close criticism by an eminent mathematician, who proposed several alternative formulæ, but finally accepted my solution of the question as correct. As Professor Adamson, however, has also raised some objections to the formula, it seems desirable to explain its meaning and mode of derivation more fully than was done in the first edition.

In the first place, as regards the theory of dimensions the formula is clearly correct. The rate of interest expresses the ratio which the sum paid per annum for the loan of capital bears to the

---

[1] The truth of the formula here given for rate of interest—or better, for the productivity of capital—is evident if it be stated in the more familiar modern terminology. An explanation and discussion of this difficult section will be found in Appendix I.—[Ed.]

capital. The interest and the capital are quantities of the same nature, their ratio being an abstract number. Dividing by length of time *rate of interest* will have the dimension T^{-1}.

Or we may put it in this way—Interest is paid per annum, or per month, or per other unit of time, and the less the magnitude of this unit, the less must be the numerical expression of the rate of interest. Simple interest at five per cent per annum is 0·416 . . . . per cent per month, and so on. Hence time enters negatively, and the dimension of the rate of interest will be T^{-1}. Or, again, we may state it thus symbolically—The capital advanced may be taken as having the dimension M; the annual return has the dimensions MT. Dividing the former by the latter we obtain [1]

$$\frac{M}{MT} = T^{-1}.$$

Now the formula $\dfrac{F't}{Ft}$ clearly agrees with this result; for the denominator is a certain unknown function of the time of advance of the capital t. We may assume that it can be expressed in a finite series of the powers of t, and the numerator, being the differential coefficient of the same function, will be of one degree

---

[1] The text is printed here as it stands in the second edition, but a little consideration shows that it should read : Capital advanced has the dimension M; the annual return has the dimensions MT^{-1}. Dividing the *latter* by the *former* we have $\dfrac{M}{MT} = T^{-1}$.—[Ed.]

of power less than Ft.   Hence the dimensions of the
formula will be

$$\frac{T^{n-1}}{T^n}, \text{ or } \frac{1}{T}, \text{ or } T^{-1}.$$

It must be carefully remembered that it is the *rate of
interest* which has the dimension T^{-1}, not interest
itself, which, being simply commodity of some kind,
has the dimension of commodity, namely M, of the
same nature, and having the same dimensions.

The function of capital is simply this, that labour
which would produce certain commodity m_1, if that
commodity were needed immediately for the satisfaction of wants, is applied so as to produce m_2 after the
lapse of the time t.   The reason for this deferment
is that m_2 usually exceeds m_1, and the difference
or *interest* $m_2 - m_1$ is commodity having the same
dimensions as m_1.   Hence the *rate of interest*, apart
from the question of time, would be $m_2 - m_1$ divided
by m_1, and the quantities being of the same nature,
the ratio will be an abstract number devoid of dimensions.   But the time for which the results of labour
are foregone is as important a matter as the quantity
of commodity.   The amount of deferment is $m_1 t$, so
that the rate of interest is $m_2 - m_1$ divided by $m_1 t$,
which will have the dimension T^{-1}.

Exactly the same result would be obtained, however, if we regarded the use of capital from a different
point of view.   Capital and deferment of consumption
are not needed only in order to increase production,
that is to say, the manufacture of goods; they are

needed also to equalise consumption, and to allow commodity to be consumed when its utility is at the highest point. Now, when certain commodity is consumed within an interval of time, the utility produced will, as we have seen, possess the dimensions $MUT^{-1}T$, or MU. Suppose that instead of being consumed within that interval, the commodity is held in hand for a time before being consumed at all. Then the amount of deferment of utility will be proportional both to the interval of time over which it is deferred, and to the utility which is deferred. Thus the amount of deferment will have the dimensions MUT. The increase of utility due to deferment will clearly have the same dimensions as were previously determined, namely MU. Hence the ratio of this increase to the amount of deferment will have the dimensions $\dfrac{MU}{MUT}$ or T^{-1}, and this result corresponds with the dimension of the rate of interest as otherwise reached.

Peacock on the Dimensions of Interest

The need of some care in forming our conceptions of these quantities is strikingly illustrated by the fact that not quite fifty years ago so profound and philosophic a mathematician as the late Dean Peacock completely misapprehended the matter. In the first edition of his celebrated and invaluable *Treatise on Algebra*, published in 1830, he gives (§ 111, p. 91) the interest of money as an example of a quantity of *three dimensions*, and one which may be represented by a solid. He says : " If p represent the principal or sum of money lent or forborne, r the rate of interest (of £1 for one year), and t the number of years, then the interest accumulated or due will be represented by prt ; for if r be the interest of £1 for one year, pr will be the interest of a sum of money denoted by p for one year, and therefore prt will be the amount of this interest in t years, no interest being reckoned upon interest due : such would be the result according to the principles of Arithmetical Algebra.

" If we now suppose prt represented respectively by lines which form the adjacent edges of a parallelopipedon, the solid thus formed will represent the interest accumulated or due : in other words, it will represent whatever is represented by the general formula prt when specific values and significations are given to its symbols : for in whatever manner we may suppose any one of the symbols of prt to vary, the solid will vary in the same proportion.

" The lines which we assume to represent units of p, r, and t, are perfectly arbitrary, whether they are made equal to each other or not : this is clearly the case with p and t, which are quantities of a different nature : and the third quantity is likewise different from the other two, being an abstract numerical quantity : for it expresses the relation between the interest of £1 and £1, or between the interest of £100 and £100, which is the quotient of the division of one quantity by another of the same nature : thus, if the interest be five per cent, then $r = \frac{5}{100}$ or $\frac{1}{20}$: if four per cent, then $r = \frac{4}{100}$ or $\frac{1}{25}$: and similarly in other cases : the line, therefore, which is assumed to represent the abstract unit to which r is referred, is independent of the lines which represent units of p and of t, and may therefore be assumed at pleasure, equally with those lines.

" The lines which represent p and t form a rectangular area, which is the geometrical representation of their product : the third quantity r, being merely numerical, may either be represented by a line, as in the case just considered, when a solid parallelopipedon is made the representative of prt : or we may consider the area pt as representing the product prt when $r = 1$, and that this product in any other case is represented by a rectangle which bears to the rectangle pt the ratio of r to 1 : this may be effected by increasing or diminishing one of the sides of the rectangle in the required ratio : the product prt may therefore be correctly represented either by a solid or an area, when one of the factors is an abstract number."

The conclusion at which he arrives is a lame one, for he thinks that the same kind of quantity may be represented indifferently by a solid or an area.   The fact is that Peacock confused a product of three factors with a quantity of three dimensions.   He took these dimensions as if they were, say $M = $ money, $R = $ rate of interest, and $T = $ time.   If we simply multiply these together, as Peacock first does, we get a quantity apparently of three dimensions, MRT. If, according to Peacock's subsequent idea, we take R to be an abstract numerical quantity, then we have two dimensions left, namely, MT.   He overlooks the fact that the rate of interest involves time negatively, although he describes r as "the rate of interest (of £1 for one year)."   Correctly stated, the dimensions of prt, the quantity of *interest* are $M \times T^{-1} \times T$ or M,   that is simply the dimension of the money advanced.

If you say, for instance, that the simple interest of £300 at five per cent per annum for five years is £75, there remains no reference in this result to time : £75 is simply £75, and is of exactly the same nature as the £300 which bore the interest.

That Peacock subsequently discovered error, or at least difficulty, in this section, is rendered probable by the fact that he omitted the illustration altogether in his second edition ; but he does not, so far as I have observed, give any explanation.

Tendency of Profits to a Minimum

It is one of the favourite doctrines of economists since the time of Adam Smith, that as society progresses and capital accumulates, the rate of profit, or more strictly speaking, the rate of interest, tends to fall.   The rate will always ultimately sink so low, they think, that the inducements to further accumulation will cease.   This doctrine is in striking agreement with the result of the somewhat abstract analytical investigation given above. Our formula for the rate of interest shows that unless there be constant progress in the arts, the rate must tend to sink towards zero, supposing accumulation of capital to go on. There are sufficient statistical facts, too, to confirm this conclusion historically. The only question that can arise is as to the actual cause of this tendency.

Adam Smith vaguely attributed it to the competition of capitalists, saying: "The increase of stock which raises wages, tends to lower profit. When the stocks of many rich merchants are turned into the same trade, their mutual competition naturally tends to lower its profit; and when there is a like increase of stock in all the different trades carried on in the same society, the same competition must produce the same effect in them all." [1]

Later economists have entertained different views. They attributed the fall of interest to the rise in the cost of labour. The produce of labour, they said, is divided between capitalists and labourers, and if it is necessary to give more to labour, there must be less left to capital, and the rate of profit will fall. I shall discuss the validity of this theory in the final chapter, and will only remark here, that it is not in agreement with the view which I have ventured to take concerning the origin of interest. I consider that interest is determined by the increment of produce which it enables a labourer to obtain, and is altogether inde-

[1] *Wealth of Nations*, book i., chap. ix., second paragraph.

pendent of the total return which he receives for this labour. Our formula (p. 246) shows that the rate of interest will be greater as the whole produce Ft is less, if the advantage of more capital, measured by $F't$, remains unchanged. In many ill-governed countries, where the land is wretchedly tilled, the average produce is small, and yet the rate of interest is high, simply because the want of security prevents the due supply of capital : hence more capital is urgently needed, and its price is high. In America and the British Colonies the produce is often high, and yet interest is high, because there is not sufficient capital accumulated to meet all the demands. In England and other old countries the rate of interest is generally lower because there is an abundance of capital, and the urgent need of more is not actually felt.

I conceive that the returns to capital and labour are independent of each other. If the soil yields little, and capital will not make it yield more, then both wages and interest will be low, provided that the capital be not attracted away to more profitable employment. If the soil yields much, and capital will make it yield more, then both wages and interest will be high ; if the soil yields much, and capital will not make it yield more, then wages will be high and interest low, unless the capital finds other investments. But the subject is much complicated by the interference of rent. When we speak of the soil yielding much, we must distinguish between the *whole yield* and the

final rate of yield. In the Western States of America
the land yields a large total, and all at a high final
rate, so that the labourer enjoys the result. In
England there is a large total yield, but a small
final yield, so that the landowner receives a large rent
and the labourer small wages. The more fertile land
having here been long in cultivation, the wages of
the labourer are measured by what he can earn by
cultivating sterile land which it only just pays to
take into cultivation.

Advantage of Capital to Industry

We must take great care not to confuse the rate
of interest on capital with the whole advantage which
it confers on industry. The rate of interest depends
on the advantage of the last increment of capital, and
the advantages of previous increments may be greater
in almost any ratio. In considering the laws of
utility, we found that an article possessing an immensely great total utility, for instance corn or water,
might have a very low final degree of utility, because
our need of it was almost entirely satisfied; yet the
ratio of exchange always depends upon the final, not
the previous degree of utility. The case is the same
with capital. Some capital may be indispensable to
a manufacture; hence the benefit conferred by the
capital is indefinitely great, and were there no more
capital to be had, the rate of interest which could be
demanded, assuming the article manufactured to be

necessary, would be almost unlimited. But as soon
as ever a larger supply of capital becomes available,
the prior benefit of capital is overlooked. As free
capital is always the same in quality, the second
portion may be made to replace the first if needful :
hence capitalists can never exact from labourers the
whole advantages which their capital confers—they
can exact only a rate determined by the advantage
of the last increment. A lender of capital cannot say
to a borrower who wants £3000 : " I know that £1000
is indispensable to your business, and therefore will
charge you 100 per cent interest upon it ; for the
second £1000, which is less necessary, I will charge
twenty per cent ; and as upon the third £1000 you can
only earn the common profit, I will only ask five per
cent." The answer would be, that there are many
people only earning five per cent on their capital who
would be glad to lend enough at a small advance of
interest ; and it is a matter of indifference who is the
lender.

The general result of the tendency to uniformity
of interest is, that employers of capital always get it
at the lowest prevailing rate ; they always borrow
the capital which is least necessary to others, and
either the labourers themselves, or the public generally as consumers, gather all the excess of advantage.
To illustrate this result, let distances along the line
ox, in fig. 14, mark quantities of capital employing in any branch of industry a fixed number of
labourers. Let the area of the curve denote the whole

produce of labour and capital. Thus to the capital, on, results a produce measured by the area of the curvilinear figure between the upright lines oy and qn. But the amount of increased produce which would be due to an increment of capital would be measured by the line qn, so that this will represent $F't$ (p. 246). The interest of the capital will be its amount, on, multiplied by the rate qn, or the area of

FIG. 14.

the rectangle oq. The remainder of the produce, $pqry$, will belong to the labourer. But had less capital been available, say not more than om, its rate of interest would have been measured by pm, the amount of interest by the rectangle op, while the labourer must have remained contented with the smaller share, psy. I will not say that the above diagram represents with strict accuracy the relations of capital, produce, wages, rate of interest, and amount of interest ; but it may serve roughly to illustrate

their relations.   I see no way of representing exactly
the theory of capital in the form of a diagram.[1]

Are Articles in the Consumers' hands Capital?

The views of the nature of capital expressed in
this chapter generally agree with those entertained
by Ricardo and various other economists ; but there
is one point in which the theory leads me to a result
at variance with the opinions of almost all writers.
I feel quite unable to adopt the opinion that the
moment goods pass into the possession of the consumer they cease altogether to have the attributes of
capital.   This doctrine descends to us from the time
of Adam Smith, and has generally received the
undoubting assent of his followers.   The latter,
indeed, have generally omitted all notice of such
goods, treating them as if no longer under the view
of the economist.   Adam Smith, although he denied
the possessions of a consumer the name of capital,
took care to enumerate them as part of the *stock* of
the community.   He divides into three portions the
general stock of a country, and while the second and
third portions are fixed and circulating capital, the
first is described as follows :—[2]

" The first is that portion which is reserved for
immediate consumption, and of which the character-
istic is, that it affords no revenue or profit.   It con-

---

[1] Some remarks on this section and the preceding one will be
found in Appendix I.—[Ed.]

[2] *Wealth of Nations*, book ii., chap. i., twelfth paragraph.

sists in the stock of food, clothes, household furniture, etc., which have been purchased by their proper consumers, but which are not yet entirely consumed. The whole stock of mere dwelling-houses too subsisting at any one time in the country make a part of this first portion. The stock that is laid out in a house, if it is to be the dwelling-house of the proprietor, ceases from that moment to serve in the function of a capital, or to afford any revenue to its owner. A dwelling-house, as such, contributes nothing to the revenue of its inhabitant ; and though it is, no doubt, extremely useful to him, it is as his clothes and household furniture are useful to him, which, however, make a part of his expense, and not of his revenue."

MacCulloch, indeed, in his edition of the *Wealth of Nations*, p. 121, has remarked upon this passage, that " the capital laid out in building houses for such persons is employed as much for the public advantage as if it were vested in the tools or instruments they make use of in their respective businesses." He appears, in fact, to reject the doctrine, and it is surprising that economists have generally acquiesced in Adam Smith's view, though it leads to manifest contradictions. It leads to the absurd conclusion that the very same thing fulfilling the very same purposes will be capital or not according to its accidental ownership. To procure good port wine it is necessary to keep it for a number of years, and Adam Smith would not deny that a stock of wine kept in the wine merchant's possession for this purpose is capital, because it yields him revenue. If a consumer buys it when new, and keeps it to improve, it will not be capital, although it is evident that he gains the same profit as the merchant by buying it at a lower price. If a coal merchant lays in a stock of coal when cheap, to sell when dear, it is capital; but if a consumer lays in a stock, it is not.

Adam Smith's views seem to be founded upon a notion that capital ought to give an annual revenue or increase of wealth like a field yields a crop of corn or grass. Speaking of a dwelling-house, he says: " If it is to be let to a tenant for rent, as the house itself can produce nothing, the tenant must always pay the rent out of some other revenue, which he derives either from labour, or stock, or land. Though a house, therefore, may yield a revenue to its proprietor, and thereby serve in the function of a capital to him, it cannot yield any to the public, nor serve in the function of a capital to it, and the revenue of the whole body of the people can never be in the smallest degree increased by it. Clothes and household furniture, in the same manner, sometimes yield a revenue, and thereby serve in the function of a capital to particular persons. In countries where masquerades are common, it is a trade to let out masquerade dresses for a night. Upholsterers frequently let furniture by the month or by the year. Undertakers let the furniture of funerals by the day and by the week. Many people let furnished houses, and get a rent, not only for the use of the house, but for that of the furniture. The revenue, however, which is derived from such things, must always be ultimately drawn from some other source of revenue." [1]

This notion that people live upon a kind of net revenue flowing in to them appears to be derived from the old French economists, and plays no part in modern Economics. Nothing is more requisite than a dwelling-house, and if a person cannot hire a house at the required spot, he must find capital to build it. I think that no economist would refuse to count among the fixed capital of the country that which is sunk in dwelling-houses. Capital is sunk in farming that we may have bread, in cotton mills that we may be clothed, and why not in houses that we may be lodged? If land yields an annual revenue of corn and wool, milk, beef, and other necessaries, houses yield a revenue of shelter and comfort. The sole end of all industry is to satisfy our wants; and if capital is requisite to supply shelter, and furniture and useful utensils, as it undoubtedly is, why refuse it the name which it bears in all other employments?

Can we deny that the property of a hotel-keeper is capital and yields a revenue to its owner? Yet it is invested in pots and pans, and beds, and all kinds of common furniture. In America it is not uncommon for people to live all their lives in hotels or boarding-houses; and we might readily conceive the system to advance until no one would undertake housekeeping

---

[1] *Wealth of Nations*, book ii., chap. i., twelfth paragraph continued.

except as a profession. Now if we allow to what is invested in hotels, hired furnished houses, lodgings, and the like, the nature of capital, I do not see how we can refuse it to common houses. We should thus be led into all kinds of absurdities.

For instance, if two people live in their own houses, these are not, according to present opinion, capital; if they find it convenient to exchange houses and pay rent each to the other, the houses are capital. At great watering-places like Brighton it is a regular business to lease houses, fill them with furniture, and then let them for short periods as furnished houses : surely it is capital which is embarked in the trade. If a private individual happens to own a furnished house which he does not at the time want, and lets it, can we refuse to regard his house and furniture as capital? Whenever one person provides the articles and another uses them and pays rent, there is capital. Surely, then, if the same person uses and owns them, the nature of the things is not fundamentally different. There is no need for a money payment to pass ; but every person who keeps accurate accounts should debit those accounts with an annual charge for interest and depreciation on what he has invested in house and furniture. House-keeping is an occupation involving wages, capital and interest, like any other business, except that the owner consumes the whole result.

By accepting this view of the subject, we shall avoid endless difficulties. What, for instance, shall

we say to a theatre ?   Is it not the product of capital ?
Can it be erected without capital ?   Does it not return
interest, if successful, like any cotton mill or steam
vessel ?   If the economist agrees to this, he must
allow, on similar grounds, that a very large part of
the aggregate capital of the country is invested in
theatres, hotels, schools, lecture rooms, and institu-
tions of various kinds which do not belong to the
industry of the country, taken in a narrow sense, but
which none the less. contribute to the wants of its
inhabitants, which is the sole object of all industry.

I may add that even the food, clothes, and many
other possessions of extensive classes are often in-
dubitable capital ; they are bought upon credit, and
interest is undoubtedly paid for the capital sunk in
them by the dealers.   There is hardly, I suppose, a
man of fashion in London who walks in his own
clothes ; and the tailors find in the practice of giving
credit a very profitable investment for capital.   Except
among the poorer classes, and often among them, food
is seldom paid for until after it is consumed.   Interest
must be paid one way or another upon the capital
thus absorbed.   Whether or not these articles in the
consumers' hands are *capital*, at any rate they have
capital invested in them—that is, labour has been
spent upon them of which the whole benefit is not
enjoyed at once.

I might also point out at almost any length, that
the stock of food, clothing, and other requisite articles
of subsistence in the country are a main part of capital

according to the statements of J. S. Mill, Professor Fawcett, and most other economists. Now what does it really matter if these articles happen to lie in the warehouses of traders or in private houses, so long as there is a stock? At present it is the practice for farmers and corn merchants to hold the produce of the harvest until the public buys and consumes it. Surely the stock of corn is capital. But if it were the practice of every housekeeper to buy up corn in the autumn and keep it in a private granary, would it not serve in exactly the same way to subsist the population? Would not everything go on exactly the same, except that every one would be his own capitalist in regard to corn in place of paying farmers and corn merchants for doing the business?

CHAPTER VIII

The Doctrine of Population

IT is no part of my purpose in this work to attempt
to trace out, with any approach to completeness, the
results of the theory given in the preceding chapters.
When the views of the nature of Value, and the
general method of treating the subject by the application of the fluxional calculus, have received some
recognition and acceptance, it will be time to think
of results. I shall therefore only occupy a few more
pages in pointing out the branches of economic
doctrine which have been passed over, and in indicating their connection with the theory.

The doctrine of population has been conspicuously
absent, not because I doubt in the least its truth and
vast importance, but because it forms no part of the
direct problem of Economics. I do not remember to
have seen it remarked that it is an inversion of the
problem to treat labour as a varying quantity, when
we originally start with labour as the first element of

production, and aim at the most economical employment of that labour. The problem of Economics may, as it seems to me, be stated thus :—*Given, a certain population, with various needs and powers of production, in possession of certain lands and other sources of material : required, the mode of employing their labour which will maximise the utility of the produce.* It is what mathematicians would call a change of the variable, afterwards to treat that labour as variable which was originally a fixed quantity. It really amounts to altering the conditions of the problem so as to create at each change a new problem. The same results, however, would generally be obtained by supposing the other conditions to vary. Given, a certain population, we may imagine the land and capital at their disposal to be greater or less, and may then trace out the results which will, in many respects, be applicable respectively to a less or greater population with the original land and capital.

Relation of Wages and Profit

There is another inversion of the problem of Economics which is generally made in works upon the subject. Although labour is the starting-point in production, and the interests of the labourer the very subject of the science, yet economists do not progress far before they suddenly turn round and treat labour as a commodity which is bought up by capitalists. Labour becomes itself the object of the laws of supply and demand, instead of those laws acting in the distribution of the products of labour.   Economists have invented, too, a very simple theory to determine the rate at which capital can buy up labour.   The average rate of wages, they say, is found by dividing the whole amount of capital appropriated to the payment of wages by the number of the labourers paid; and they wish us to believe that this settles the question. But a little consideration shows that this proposition is simply a *truism.   The average rate of wages must be equal to what is appropriated to the purpose divided by the number who share it.*   The whole question will consist in determining how much is appropriated for the purpose; for it certainly need not be the whole existing amount of circulating capital.   Mill distinctly says, that because industry is limited by capital, we are not to infer that it always reaches that limit;[1] and, as a matter of fact, we often observe that there is abundance of capital to be had at low rates of interest, while there are also large numbers of artisans starving for want of employment.   The wage-fund theory is therefore illusory as a real solution of the problem, though I do not deny that it may have a certain limited and truthful application, to be shortly considered.

Another part of the current doctrines of Economics determines the rate of profit of capitalists in a very simple manner.   The whole produce of industry must be divided into the portions paid as rent, taxes,

---

[1] *Principles of Political Economy*, book i., chap. v., sec. 2.

profits, and wages. We may exclude taxes as exceptional, and not very important. Rent also may be eliminated, for it is essentially variable, and is reduced to zero in the case of the poorest land cultivated. We thus arrive at the simple equation—

$$\text{Produce} = \text{profit} + \text{wages}.$$

A plain result also is drawn from the formula; for we are told that if wages rise profits must fall, and *vice versâ*. But such a doctrine is radically fallacious; *it involves the attempt to determine two unknown quantities from one equation.* I grant that if the produce be a fixed amount, then if wages rise profits must fall, and *vice versâ*. Something might perhaps be made of this doctrine if Ricardo's theory of a natural rate of wages, that which is just sufficient to support the labourer, held true. But I altogether question the existence of any such rate.

The wages of working men in this kingdom vary from perhaps ten shillings a week up to forty shillings or more; the minimum in one part of the country is not the minimum in another. It is utterly impossible, too, to define exactly what are the necessaries of life. I am inclined, therefore, to reject altogether the current doctrines as to the rate of wages; and even if the theory held true of any one class of labourers separately, there is the additional difficulty that we have to account for the very different rates which prevail in different trades. It is impossible that we should accept for ever Ricardo's sweeping simplification of the subject, involved in his assumption, that there is a natural ordinary rate of wages for common labour, and that all higher rates are merely exceptional instances, to be explained away on other grounds.

The view which I accept concerning the rate of wages is not more difficult to comprehend than the current one. It is that *the wages of a working man are ultimately coincident with what he produces, after the deduction of rent, taxes, and the interest of capital.* I think that in the equation

$$\text{Produce} = \text{profit} + \text{wages},$$

the quantity of produce is essentially variable, and that profit is the part to be first determined. If we resolve profit into wages of superintendence, insurance against risk, and interest, the first part is really wages itself; the second equalises the result in different employments; and the interest is, I believe, determined as stated in the last chapter. The reader will observe the important qualification that wages are only *ultimately* thus determined—that is, in the long run, and on the average of any one branch of employment.

The fact that workmen are not their own capitalists introduces complexity into the problem. The capitalists, or *entrepreneurs*, enter as a distinct interest. It is they who project and manage a branch of production, and form estimates as to the expected produce. It is the amount of this produce which incites them to invest capital and buy up labour. They pay the lowest current rates for the kind of labour required; and if the produce exceeds the average, those who are first in the field make large profits. This soon induces competition on the part of other capitalists, who, in trying to obtain good workmen, will raise the rate of wages. Competition will proceed until the point is reached at which only the market rate of interest is obtained for the capital invested. At the same time wages will have been so raised that the workmen reap the whole excess of produce, unless indeed the price of the produce has fallen, and the public, as consumers, have the benefit. Whether this latter result will follow or not depends upon the number of labourers who are fitted for the work. Where much skill and education is required, extensive competition will be impossible, and a permanently high rate of wages will exist. But if only common labour is requisite, the price of the goods cannot be maintained, wages will fall to their former point, and the public will gain the advantage of cheaper supplies.

It will be observed that this account of the matter involves the temporary application of the wage-fund theory. It is the proper function of capitalists to sustain labour before the result is accomplished, and as many branches of industry require a large outlay long previous to any definite result being arrived at, it follows that capitalists must undertake the risk of any branch of industry where the ultimate profits are not accurately known. But we now have some clue as to the amount of capital which will be appropriated to the payment of wages in any trade. The amount of capital will depend upon the amount of anticipated profits, and the competition to obtain proper workmen will strongly tend to secure to the latter all their legitimate share in the ultimate produce.

For instance, let a number of schemes be set on foot for laying telegraphic cables. The ultimate profits are very uncertain, depending upon the utility of the cables as compared with their cost. If capitalists make a large estimate of those profits, they will apply much capital to the immediate manufacture of the cables. All workmen competent at the moment to be employed will be hired, and high wages paid if necessary. Every man who has peculiar skill, knowledge, or experience, rendering his assistance valuable, will be hired at any requisite cost. At this point it is the wage-fund theory that is in operation. But, after a certain number of years, the condition of affairs will be totally different. Capitalists will learn, by experience, exactly what the profits of cables may be ; that amount of capital will be thrown into the work which finds the average amount of profits, and neither more nor less. The cost of transmitting messages will be reduced by competition, so that no excessive profits will be made by any of the parties concerned ; the rate of wages, therefore, of every species of labour will be reduced to the average proper to labour of that degree of skill. But if there be required in any branch of the work a very special kind of skilled and experienced labour, it will not be affected by competition in the same way, and the wages or salary will remain high.

I think that it is in this way quite possible to reconcile theories which are at first sight so different. The wage-fund theory acts in a wholly temporary manner. Every labourer ultimately receives the due value of his produce after paying a proper fraction to the capitalist for the remuneration of abstinence and risk. At the same time workers of different degrees of skill receive very different shares according as they contribute a common or a scarce kind of labour to the result.

Professor Hearn's Views

I have the more pleasure and confidence in putting forward these somewhat heretical views concerning the general problem of Economics, inasmuch as they are nearly identical with those arrived at by Professor Hearn, of Melbourne University. It would be a somewhat long task to trace out exactly the coincidence of opinions between us, but he certainly adopts the notion that the capitalist merely buys up temporarily the prospects of the concern he manages and the labourers he employs. Thus he says : " In place of having a share in the undertaking, the co-operator sells for a stipulated price his labour or the use of his capital. The case therefore comes within the ordinary conditions of exchange; and the price of labour and the price of capital are determined in the same manner as all other questions of price are determined. Yet the general character of the partnership is not destroyed. Although each particular transaction amounts to a sale, yet for the continuance of the business a nearer connection arises. Although the whole loss of the undertaking, if the undertaking be unfortunate, falls upon the last proprietor, and the interests of the other parties have been previously secured, yet each such loss prevents a repetition of the transaction from which it arose. The capital which ought to have been replaced, and which if replaced would have afforded the means of employing labour and of defraying the interest upon other capital, has disappeared; and thus the market for labour and for capital is by so much diminished. Both the labourer and the intermediate capitalist are therefore directly concerned in the success of every enterprise towards which they have contributed. If it be successful, they feel the advantage; if it be not successful, they feel in like manner the loss. But this community of interest is no longer direct, but is indirect merely; and it arises not from the gains or the losses of partners, but from the increased ability, or the diminished demands, of customers." [1]

---

[1] *Plutology: or The Theory of the Efforts to satisfy Human Wants.* By William Edward Hearn, LL.D., Professor of History and Political Economy in the University of Melbourne. London (Macmillan and Co.), 1864, p. 329.

This passage really contains a statement of the views which I am inclined wholly to accept; but no passages which I can select will convey an adequate notion of the enlightened view which Professor Hearn takes of the industrial structure of society in his admirable work on *Plutology*.

The Noxious Influence of Authority

I have but a few lines more to add. I have ventured in the preceding pages to call in question not a few of the favourite doctrines of economists. To me it is far more pleasant to agree than to differ; but it is impossible that one who has any regard for truth can long avoid protesting against doctrines which seem to him to be erroneous. There is ever a tendency of the most hurtful kind to allow opinions to crystallise into creeds. Especially does this tendency manifest itself when some eminent author, enjoying power of clear and comprehensive exposition, becomes recognised as an authority. His works may perhaps be the best which are extant upon the subject in question; they may combine more truth with less error than we can elsewhere meet. But "to err is human," and the best works should ever be open to criticism. If, instead of welcoming inquiry and criticism, the admirers of a great author accept his writings as authoritative, both in their excellences and in their defects, the most serious injury is done to truth. In matters of philosophy and science authority has ever been the

great opponent of truth.   A despotic calm is usually
the triumph of error.   In the republic of the sciences
sedition and even anarchy are beneficial in the
long run to the greatest happiness of the greatest
number.

In the physical sciences authority has greatly lost
its noxious influence.   Chemistry, in its brief existence
of a century, has undergone three or four complete
revolutions of theory.   In the science of light, Newton's
own authority was decisively set aside, though not
until after it had retarded for nearly a century the
progress of inquiry.   Astronomers have not hesitated,
within the last few years, to alter their estimates of
all the dimensions of the planetary system, and of the
universe, because good reasons have been shown for
calling in question the real coincidence of previous
measurements.   In science and philosophy nothing
must be held sacred.   Truth indeed is sacred ; but, as
Pilate said, "What is truth?"   Show us the undoubted
infallible criterion of absolute truth, and we will hold
it as a sacred inviolable thing.   But in the absence of
that infallible criterion, we have all an equal right to
grope about in our search of it, and no body and no
school nor clique must be allowed to set up a standard
of orthodoxy which shall bar the freedom of scientific
inquiry.

I have added these words because I think there is
some fear of the too great influence of authoritative
writers in Political Economy.   I protest against
deference for any man, whether John Stuart Mill, or

Adam Smith, or Aristotle, being allowed to check inquiry. Our science has become far too much a stagnant one, in which opinions rather than experience and reason are appealed to.

There are valuable suggestions towards the improvement of the science contained in the works of such writers as Senior, Cairnes, Macleod, Cliffe-Leslie, Hearn, Shadwell, not to mention a long series of French economists from Baudeau and Le Trosne down to Bastiat and Courcelle-Seneuil; but they are neglected in England, because the excellence of their works was not comprehended by David Ricardo, the two Mills, Professor Fawcett, and others who have made the orthodox Ricardian school what it is. Under these circumstances it is a positive service to break the monotonous repetition of current questionable doctrines, even at the risk of new error. I trust that the theory now given may prove accurate; but, however this may be, it will not be useless if it cause inquiry to be directed into the true basis and form of a science which touches so directly the material welfare of the human race.

APPENDIX I

IT will be my endeavour to show in this note that
the theory of interest presented by the author in
Chapter VII. (pp. 244-259) is true, so far as it goes ;
and that, if interpreted in the way probably intended
by him, it is in agreement with the modern theory of
marginal productivity. The concise and abstract
handling of the subject in the section on a *General
Expression for the Rate of Interest* has led to its
being misunderstood ; and an attempt at amplifica-
tion of the author's statement, in the sense which,
after repeated consideration, it appears to me to
bear, may not be out of place. I may add that I
have been disappointed in the outcome of searching
my father's manuscript notes with the object of
finding any which might throw further light on his
opinions regarding the theory of interest. He does
not seem to have followed the subject further.

In writing of Interest, my father has followed
the unfortunate practice of the Ricardian school by
abstracting for treatment certain ideas, and assuming

that his readers are familiar with their relations, and take his point of view. He undoubtedly wrote, not for the general public, but for students already familiar with the current economic doctrines. I think a study of his examples, especially in the sections on the *Tendency of Profits to a Minimum* and on the *Advantage of Capital to Industry* (pp. 253-259), makes it clear that he well understood that his formula for "rate of interest" may also be taken as an expression for the *final rate of yield*, or *marginal productivity*, of capital, a quantity which, in practice, is adjusted to the rate of interest at which capital can be obtained. The examples on p. 255 alone seem to me sufficient to show that he did not, as seems to be suggested by Marshall,[1] overlook the importance of supply in determining market rate of interest. He did not attempt to give a complete account of the causes determining the rate of interest, but was concerned to show that it is much more intimately connected with the quantity of capital in proportion to labour which a community possesses than with rate of wages (p. 254). Probably he tacitly assumed that supply of capital remained constant; and thus it is possible that, whilst not misunderstanding the theory of the causes which determine rate of interest, he failed to give adequate weight to the growth of the means of

[1] See Review of the *Theory of Political Economy* by Marshall in the *Academy* for April 1, 1872 ; quoted in Marshall's *Principles of Economics*, 5th edition (1907), p. 521 : 4th edition (1898), p. 591.

saving as a factor in causing the historic fall in the rate of interest.

A point which is sometimes lost sight of is that it is not capital itself which is productive, but the investment of capital over a certain length of time. Using the term adopted by the author in the second appendix of this volume, namely, *capitalisation*, which is to be taken to have the same meaning as *amount of investment*, we may say that a certain quantity of produce results from a given amount of capitalisation. Capitalisation is a quantity of two dimensions, represented by CT; and an increment of capitalisation may be made either by increasing the capital or the time. In either case an increment of produce results. Hence, if we are thinking of the produce simply as a quantity, not as an income, or as a rate of production, we can only conceive a marginal productivity of capitalisation, not of capital. In the theory of distribution, however, it is correct to treat of the marginal productivity of *capital* as such ; for the shares of the other factors of production must be of the nature of income, and if the produce of capital be treated as income derived in a certain time from a certain amount of investment of capital, time cancels out. But marginal productivity of capital is a derived idea. In investigating the fundamental properties of capital the view of a certain lot of produce resulting from a given capitalisation is more helpful, because we find in practice that an increase of capitalisation means a

greater *duration of investment* in an individual
commodity or machine quite as frequently as an
increase of the capital invested in it.

Bearing in mind that the *General Expression for
the Rate of Interest* should be *General Expression
for Marginal Productivity of Capitalisation*, we
may now proceed to investigate the conditions to
which the formula given by the author in this
difficult section is directly applicable, and may note
those which he probably had in mind. The first
case to be considered is the one to which the formula
most obviously applies—quite possibly that which
suggested this particular formula to the author:
namely, when by the expenditure of a certain amount
of labour a natural process is started which yields a
commodity continually increasing in utility with the
time for which the process is allowed to act. When
wine is allowed to mature, or forest trees are planted,
as mentioned by the author on p. 238, the market
value of the produce constantly grows as time
elapses (assuming the price realisable to remain
constant) until a certain ultimate limit is reached.
Before this limit is reached, however, the rate of
increase of value diminishes; and the length of
investment which may be profitable is determined
by the current rate of interest. In this case Ft is
the value of the wine or trees at any moment, and
$F't$ is the rate of increase of that value at that
moment, due to allowing the produce to remain
invested a little longer. The increment of capitalisa-

tion is obtained by varying the time. The most convenient symbolic expression for the marginal productivity of capitalisation in this case would seem to be $\dfrac{\delta p}{c \cdot \delta t}$, where c is capital in terms of money, t is time, and p is produce in money.

In the second case the produce of a certain amount of labour does not mature merely by the operation of a natural process, but requires the application of further labour, with the assistance of machines and tools, to bring it to the condition of a finished commodity. In other words, the produce of the initial labour, that is the capital, forms the raw material of an industry; as, for instance, the wool, etc., which are ultimately moulded into felt hats, to quote the example suggested by Marshall.[1] A number of different processes or arrangements in a factory can be imagined, each requiring different lengths of time for converting the raw material into finished hats, but involving the same charges for labour and capital. If a process taking a long time is to exist in competition with one taking less time, it must produce from the same quantity of raw material so many more hats than the quicker process as to pay at least the current rate of interest during the necessary extension of time on the value of the hats produced by the quicker process. In practice, a longer process more often produces a better quality than a larger quantity,

[1] In his Review, quoted in the *Principles*, *ibid.*

but we may correctly pay regard only to the value
of the produce. The processes of varying duration
yield at their conclusion produce of differing value ;
and the value may be regarded as a function of the
duration of the process—in symbols the value is the
Ft of the author's formula, whilst $F't$ is the ratio of
the additional value obtained by adopting a slightly
longer process to the necessary extension of time
carried to the limit. In deciding which of two processes to adopt, an intending manufacturer should
estimate the productivity of an increment of capitalisation obtained by an extension of time. The funding
of the capital which turns an extension of time into
an increase of capital invested in raw material does
not alter the fundamental principle.

Passing now from capital invested in raw material
—Professor Clark's passive goods—to the case of
that which is invested in machines and other instruments of production, we encounter an inversion of
the problem. There is not an investment of capital
which by lapse of time increases, but the invested
capital at once begins to evest itself, and the evest-
ment continues steadily until the tool is worn out.[1]
Yet the same relations of quantities may be traced
here as in the preceding cases ; the chief difference
being that the capital invested, as well as the time,
is here deliberately increased to obtain an increment

[1] I venture to use the term *to evest* as being more euphonious than
the author's *to uninvest*, with which it corresponds exactly in meaning.
It also seems to me preferable etymologically.

of capitalisation. The life of a machine can be lengthened by the investment in it of extra capital in more careful construction. To bring this case into line with the others, however, we must assume that an increase of the life of the machine does not affect its rate of production of the goods manufactured—in fact, that it remains the same machine in every way, but lasts longer. If an increase of capital invested always produced a *proportional* increase in the life of a machine there would be no advantage in making machines durable; though there would be a tendency to invest in durability when capital was plentiful.

In this case of investment in a machine, the productivity of capitalisation is represented by the ratio of the increment of the money produce obtained from the machine during the extension of its life to the increment of capitalisation (capital × time) resulting from the increase both of the capital and of the average duration of its investment. Symbolically stated, and ignoring the product of the differences, the productivity of capitalisation in the case of the machine is

$$\frac{\delta p}{\frac{1}{2}(\kappa \,.\, \delta t + \tau \,.\, \delta c)},$$

where κ represents the whole capital invested and τ the life of the machine. Assuming conditions parallel with the first case, namely, that *all* the capital remains invested for the *whole* time t, or that we are dealing with the average amount of capital invested c, and the average time of its investment t, the formula is simply

$$\frac{\delta p}{c \,.\, \delta t + t \,.\, \delta c}.$$

In the third case the increase of capitalisation is obtained by increasing the capital only, as when a machine or building destined to last only for a known period is improved solely to increase the value of its product during that period. The symbolic expression is then $\dfrac{\delta p}{t \,.\, \delta c}$ in all forms of investment, where t is the *average* duration of the investment.

Individual investments of capital represented by each of these cases can be " integrated " into a continuously existing fund of capital which produces a steady flow of money produce (quasi-rent), besides keeping itself intact. The idea of productivity of capitalisation applies, as in the third of the cases just considered; but to make the expression of it accord with the idea of an income arising from a fund of capital, we may write it $\dfrac{1}{\delta c} \,.\, \delta\!\left(\dfrac{\delta p}{\delta t}\right)$, which, in the limit, is the same as $\dfrac{d_2 p}{dc \,.\, dt}$.

The assumption which appears to underlie the argument of the author's section on a *General Expression for the Rate of Interest* is akin to the first of the above three cases, but in an " integrated " form. Capital invested and maintained in all manner of physical forms appears collectively as a constantly growing fund. The product which is essentially due to the first investment of capital—or, in the author's words, due to the labour which the capital supported —is not enjoyed by consumption, but is continually reinvested. It is as though a man put some money into his business and arranged to leave it there to multiply at compound interest, supposing him able to earmark that part of his profit resulting from the investment of his capital, and constantly to reinvest it.[1] As in the cases of maturing wine, and growing forest trees, the ratio of the rate of increase of the capital to the whole capital accumulated ultimately becomes very small as the amount of capital invested becomes very great. In his discussion on the tendency of profits to a minimum, mentioned in the section under notice, but discussed more fully on p. 254, the author is evidently extending his assumption to include the reinvestment by the whole community of the whole of the specific produce of capital, or at least of an annual sum equivalent to the annual produce of all capital invested, a rate of saving which probably exceeds the reality. His theory remains true, however, on the assumption that a certain fraction of the annual produce of capital is consumed; and the greater this fraction the slower would be the fall in the rate of interest. In reality, of course, the rate of interest is maintained by inventions, and by the development of new wants

---

[1] Rather, at compound productivity, for the productivity may be variable.

by education, as well as by the flow of capital to new countries.

The symbolic statement of the author's theory may be interpreted with the aid of the diagram (Fig. 14) on p. 258, which I reproduce here (Fig. 15), with the slight difference of showing the intersection of the curve pq with the axis oy at h, because

FIG. 15.

the intersection must occur at finite distance. The independent variable is the amount of capital invested, and it is taken as abscissa. Presumably, the quantities of labour, and of the other factors of production with which it is invested, are assumed to remain invariable, and in constant proportion to one another. The ordinates represent the marginal productivity (the author's final rate of yield) of additional units of capital; and a rectangle, such as $omps$, therefore, represents the total income which is the specific produce of the capital *om*, that is, the total interest.

Bearing in mind the idea of a fund of capital growing with lapse of time, let us assume time to be measured along an axis *oz* perpendicular to the plane of the paper. During a small interval of time the rectangle *omps* moves forward from the plane of the paper towards the reader, and as the capital increases

Fig. 16.

mp shortens slightly, thus lowering the line *sp* a little. Reducing the interval of time to the limit, however, the figure becomes practically a rectangular parallelopiped, as in Fig. 16.

In this thin solid figure *ov* represents δt; *om* represents *c*, the fund of capital actually invested at the moment; the rectangle *omps* represents $\dfrac{\delta c}{\delta t}$, or the total interest from capital which is supposed to be added to the capital, and may, therefore, be regarded as the rate of growth of the capital fund. Then os represents $\frac{1}{c} \cdot \frac{\delta c}{\delta t}$. But the line mp, which is equal to os, may be regarded in another way. The area $ohpm$ represents the whole income from industry (which we may write $\frac{\delta p}{\delta t}$)—that is to say, the shares of all the agents of production, of which the income of the capitalist ($omps$) is but one. Differentiating this total rate of production of money by industry ($ohpm$) with regard to capital (om) we get the marginal productivity of capital, which we may write

$$\frac{\delta\left(\frac{\delta p}{\delta t}\right)}{\delta c},$$

and this is represented by mp. Hence we have the equation :

$$\frac{1}{c} \cdot \frac{\delta c}{\delta t} = \frac{\delta\left(\frac{\delta p}{\delta t}\right)}{\delta c}.$$

This equation can be derived easily from another consideration. The adjustment of marginal productivity and rate of interest to one another being assumed, the right-hand term of the last equation if multiplied by c, the total capital, gives the total annual interest paid. But, on the assumption made by the author that the total interest is continually added to the capital, we can write

$$\frac{\delta c}{\delta t} = c \cdot \frac{\delta\left(\frac{\delta p}{\delta t}\right)}{\delta c},$$

which becomes, on transposing the c, identical with the former equation.

Since $\frac{1}{c} \cdot \frac{\delta c}{\delta t}$ is merely the author's expression $\frac{F't}{Ft}$ in other symbols, we can now see clearly the connection between the different quantitative relations of interest with capital, as expressed by Marshall and later writers, and by our author. The latter's formula does not explain how interest is determined. It is only a symbolic statement of a well-known relation. But the text following makes it abundantly clear, I think, that the author had reached the conception of marginal productivity of capital, which he called final rate of yield, and had realised the all-important part which it plays in determining the demand for capital. The phrase "urgency of the need for more capital" used frequently in the third paragraph of the section on the *Tendency of Profits to a Minimum* (see p. 255) can mean nothing but marginal productivity; and clearly he is referring to the demand, because he speaks separately of the supply, as being restricted for want of security in one case, and as being abundant in another.[1] Numerous passages show that the author

[1] It may be suggested that the sentence at the bottom of page 254, if it had been more carefully written, would have read thus: "I consider that interest is determined by the increment of produce which an increment of capital enables a labourer to obtain. . . ." This certainly is a one-sided statement; but the author is here mainly

well understood also the causes which lead to the decline of marginal productivity with an increase of the capital at the disposal of the community.

A slip, or unconscious error, in the author's explanation of Fig. 14 should be noticed. On p. 258, lines 5 to 7, he says that the increased produce "due to an increment of capital would be measured by the line qn, so that this will represent $F't$." He must have intended to write "will represent $\dfrac{F't}{Ft}$," instead of "$F't$," for a few lines further on he says clearly that when the capital is om the *rate of interest* is "measured by pm," which equals qn, and in a previous section (p. 245), he has most clearly stated that the rate of interest is represented by $\dfrac{F't}{Ft}$.

In the above explanation of the sections on the theory of interest I do not think I have been guilty of unconsciously reading into the author's words the results of later discoveries. I admit that the first paragraph of the section on a *General Expression for the Rate of Interest* (p. 245) is capable of being interpreted on other assumptions than the one I have stated here as being probably the one the author had in mind, but his argument and formula apply equally well whatever the actual conditions assumed; and it may well be that the author intentionally left his

engaged in rebutting the wage-fund doctrine; and in advocating in its place the productivity idea he does so with his customary verve, and without the manifold reservations in which Marshall rightly rejoices.

statement in a perfectly general form, because he knew that whatever conditions lead to capital being invested for an additional interval of time, the productivity of that capital during that time is measured as stated in his formula.

I believe that any one who carefully compares his section on the *Advantage of Capital to Industry* (p. 256) with the difficult section on a *General Expression for the Rate of Interest* will admit that, though he did not state it clearly, Professor Jevons discovered, and completely anticipated, the modern theory of the approximation of interest to the marginal productivity of capital. This view is borne out by the concise but lucid statement of his theory of interest in section 24 of his *Brief Account of a General Mathematical Theory of Political Economy*, read before the British Association in 1862 and published in the journal of the Statistical Society for 1866. I may refer the reader to p. 303 in Appendix III. of this volume, in which this paper is reprinted in full.

It is interesting to note that the author's view as to the determining cause of wages is also in exact accord with the modern theory of marginal productivity, as shown by numerous passages in the chapters on Labour and Rent. He does not seem, however, to have realised that the same principle governs rent; and, as Mr. Wicksteed has remarked, there is no evidence that he conceived the idea of a general theory of distribution by marginal productivity.

APPENDIX II

A FRAGMENT ON CAPITAL
INTENDED TO FORM PART OF CHAPTER XXV. OF THE
AUTHOR'S *PRINCIPLES OF ECONOMICS*

Capitalisation

THERE is no part of the subject of economics which
is at once so important and so difficult to comprehend
precisely and correctly as that of capital. Difficult
as it may be to trace the intricacies of the theory
of value and avoid confusion of ideas, an even greater
intricacy and confusion of ideas besets us here.

It is usual to commence the subject by saying
that capital is the third requisite of labour—that
it consists of an accumulated stock of the produce
of past labour applied to promote the production of
more wealth. Capital, it has been said by Senior,
proceeds from abstinence; and by this word he
expresses " that agent, distinct from labour and
the agency of Nature, the concurrence of which is
necessary to the existence of capital, and which
stands in the same relation to profit as labour does
to wages." [1] But according to the view and nomen-

---

[1] *Encycl. Metropolitana*, 1836 ; separately printed, *Political
Economy*, 5th ed., 1863, p. 59.

clature here adopted it would be said that abstinence is capitalisation and capitalisation is abstinence. If there is any enjoyment which we could procure by present labour, but we abstain from enjoyment and use the labour for a distant but greater end, here is proper capitalisation.

A little consideration will show that to avoid confusion of ideas we ought not to speak of capital but of capitalisation. Capital, if it consists of concrete wealth, is simply a thing, and involves no idea of time; whereas we can have no reference to the use of capital without introducing time as the essence of the matter. It is, in fact, impossible to say what capital is—it is not literally any article or thing, no more than credit is a thing. We ought indeed to use capital in the abstract like credit. The last necessarily involves time; so capital necessarily involves time. It is measured by the utility which certain labour might possess now multiplied by the time of abstinence from its enjoyment. *Credit* is an intangible abstract thing—the power of obtaining loans of property. So *capital* is the power and will of granting loans, also an intangible abstract idea.

It will be apparent after a little reflection that there is really nothing which marks off certain commodities as being by nature capital as compared with other commodities which are not capital. The very same bag of flour may have to change its character according to the mental changes of its owner. Capital is the power of *deferring the fruition of labour results* (Laing)—anything which satisfies the labourer in the present instead of leading him to produce for momentary wants. There is hardly any part of the property of society which may not then contribute towards capitalisation. Little consideration is needed to show that we cannot possibly point to any part of the wealth of the nation and say it is capital. Capital, say [the classical economists], is wealth employed in the production of further wealth. Such is the loaf, they would add, which is given to the productive labourer. But then until it is actually given we cannot be certain what will be the destination of the loaf. Bread from the same baker's shop may go to feed the hardworking navvy, the idle beggar, the well-to-do annuitant. The bread is the same—the use of it different. It is, then, to its employment, not to the thing itself, that we must apply the idea of capital or capitalisation.

How are we to discriminate between what is capital and what is not? To make a thing before it is wanted and simply keep it on hand involves no advantage of capital. Labour has been sunk in it which might have been otherwise used to facilitate production. To be enabled to work before the result is needed and enjoyed is advantageous because the things can be much more easily and abundantly made, and it is capital which enables this to be done. The aggregate of the capital of the country thus consists of the aggregate of the things which satisfy the wants of individuals. . . . There is no need to say that capital is the produce of past labour. It is simply wealth employed in a particular manner, or with a particular object. It matters not whether it comes from a bread-fruit tree or a well-stocked river.

.   .   .   .   .   .

It is obvious that if each portion of commodity as it came into possession were immediately consumed, there would never be more than an infinitely small quantity in use at any moment. . . . It does not matter so far as we are concerned whether the commodity is in or out of the stomach. Even in the duration of the effect of a meal there is a small capitalisation.

Advantages of Capitalisation

It is not difficult to see that any advance, even the simplest, in the arts of industry necessitates capitalisation. In the rudest state of society a rude savage supplies each want as it arises. When he is hungry he goes to the forest and catches an animal, or collects grass seeds like the natives of Australia. But unless the savage can count securely on immediate success, he may need capitalisation in its simplest form.

The need of capitalisation arises in many ways only partly related to each other. The rhythmical recurrence of the seasons renders it practically indispensable in the temperate regions which produce a harvest but once a year. Hence a nation in order to be agricultural in such regions must have such a stock of food as will carry it over the interval between one year and the next. As the proverb says—" While the grain groweth the horse starveth," a contingency which must be provided against. Otherwise recourse must be had to inferior and more laborious modes of gaining food.

There are, however, many ways of employing labour with advantage which involve capitalisation. All use of tools comes under this head, for a tool is some instrument made to assist further operations. The labour spent upon the tools did not give immediate good, but only conduced to a greater future good. Many tools last for weeks, months, or years; so that the total labour spent upon them is not repaid till after that interval of time.

Let us now analyse the motives which may lead to the storing up of wealth :—

(1) The greater advantage to be derived from future consumption;

(2) The continuous utility arising from possession in the meantime;

(3) The interest to be gained by investment.

A surplus of corn in a year of good harvest is naturally laid by to be consumed when the supply is less abundant. The stock may be held either by the producer and consumer or by speculators. In a simple state of society like that of Norway the farmer stores his own grain in his own granary, and eats it as needed.

.　　　.　　　.　　　.　　　.　　　.

It ought to be clearly understood that capitalisation in the sense of long duration of work is never a purpose in itself. It is only a condition which must usually be borne with. Accordingly every improvement which lessens the average interval between labour and utilisation is good as liberating capital for other purposes. For instance, rapid conveyance of goods by railways avoids the long delay of goods which attended their conveyance by road or canal, and saves the investment of capital in the meantime. The manufacturer or dealer can turn over his stock so many more times in the year. As this applies to a large part of the whole floating wealth of the country an equal amount of capital renders more effective services to industry.

.　　　.　　　.　　　.　　　.　　　.

There is a general presumption in favour of producing permanent objects; but then these must be objects not merely permanent in form, but *permanent in utility.* To build in a very costly and substantial manner a structure which is only needed for a certain series of years is not only a loss of labour, but it may even occasion labour in removal. It is on this principle that we may somewhat excuse the light building of speculators. Neighbourhoods change, and a house which suits very well now may have to be pulled down fifty years hence. Suppose a house to last fifty years can be built for £3000, but in order to make it last a hundred years an additional £1000 must be spent at first. But had this £1000 been laid by and invested at compound interest at 4 per cent it would at the end of fifty years have become £7107 ; and even at the end of twenty-eight years it would yield enough to rebuild the house in the same manner as before. There must, therefore, be a large gain of comfort, health, beauty, etc., in the costly house in order to repay the superior cost.

Capital Invested in Education

Nothing is more important than to obtain clear ideas of the investment of capital throughout the course of life. How far, for instance, is capital invested in the course of education—a child at an infant school, a boy at a boarding school, a young man at college or reading for the law? Adhering, however, to our principle that deference of enjoyment is the fundamental idea there is no real difficulty.

The sustenance and education of a young child does not return investment because the child is not capable of earning anything. No labour, therefore, is devoted to the future which might be devoted to the present. As to the food and other articles necessary to the subsistence of the child, they are simply so much commodity which the parents are bound to supply. Whether the child is intended to labour in the future or not, the law requires that he shall be maintained, and will in the last resort provide his maintenance in the workhouse.

Mr. Shadwell has very soundly and acutely pointed out that " if we are to suppose that the common rate of wages is the return for the capital expended in maintaining children before they are able to work, we must suppose that parents bring up children with no other object than to secure them a certain position in the world, and that they are not influenced by the pleasure which they themselves derive from the possession of a family." [1] Against the cost of any process we must set all advantage or pleasure derived in the course of the process. Now if a considerable part of the parents' pleasure of life arise from the family circle, the expenditure on children repays itself at the moment. The child entering on work is started free from capital liabilities, as it were.

But it is another matter when we come to an age at which earnings may be made. Thus a young man between twenty-one and twenty-five years of age might be earning a salary of, say, £75 a year. If, then, he prefers to read for the law, he forgoes present in favour of greater future earnings. This is the measure of capitalisation. It is true that he will need maintenance which will probably be £150 a year. This we must suppose he gets from friends, or from previous resources. But although £150 a year be spent, this is not necessarily the measure of capitalisation. A portion may be spent on needless amusements, etc., and is simply expenditure. Another portion, however,

---

[1] *A System of Political Economy,* by J. L. Shadwell, 1877, p. 140.

spent on fees, books, and necessary expenses is truly capitalised. Is not the measure of capitalisation the difference between what he would spend if not reading and that which he does spend ? Thus :—

Reading.	Not Reading.
£75 private income.	£75 earnings.
£75 lent by friends.	£75 private income.

Here there is clearly capitalisation to the extent of £75 lent by friends. He is expending that now with the necessity of repaying it in the future, and is forgoing possible immediate earnings of labour.

An artisan employed during the day works also during his evening or leisure hours at making a machine. The measure of capitalisation is simply what he could have earned of immediate wages in those same hours had he not spent the labour on the machine. What is ordinarily called his capital is simply the ordinary wages which he is living upon.

It seems obvious that what is spent upon a man's education ceases to be capital, because it is gone and the result is subject to the *laws of wages.* It is not what has been, but what is. So capital expended in a fixed form ceases to be subject to the laws of interest. It is *free capital* which we have to treat as distinct in its nature, and as *capital* properly speaking. The other things pay rent or wages.

APPENDIX III

BRIEF ACCOUNT OF A GENERAL MATHEMATICAL
THEORY OF POLITICAL ECONOMY

[*A Reprint of a Paper read before Section F of the British
Association at Cambridge in 1862 (see Report of the Association for
1862, " Transactions of Sections," pp. 157-8) ; and first printed in
extenso in the " Journal of the Statistical Society of London," vol.
xxix. (1866), p. 283.*]

1. The following paper briefly describes the nature
of a Theory of Economy which will reduce the main
problem of this science to a mathematical form.
Economy, indeed, being concerned with quantities,
has always of necessity been mathematical in its
subject, but the strict and general statement, and the
easy comprehension of its quantitative laws has been
prevented by a neglect of those powerful methods of
expression which have been applied to most other
sciences with so much success. It is not to be
supposed, however, that because economy becomes
mathematical in form, it will, therefore, become a
matter of rigorous calculation. Its mathematical

principles may become formal and certain, while its individual data remain as inexact as ever.

2. A true theory of economy can only be attained by going back to the great springs of human action —*the feelings of pleasure and pain.* A large part of such feelings arise periodically from the ordinary wants and desires of body or mind, and from the painful exertion we are continually prompted to undergo that we may satisfy our wants.

Economy investigates the relations of ordinary pleasures and pains thus arising, and it has a wide enough field of inquiry. But economy does not treat of all human motives. There are motives nearly always present with us, arising from conscience, compassion, or from some moral or religious source, which economy cannot and does not pretend to treat. These will remain to us as outstanding and disturbing forces; they must be treated, if at all, by other appropriate branches of knowledge.

3. We always treat feelings as being capable of *more or less,* and I now hold that they are quantities capable of scientific treatment.

Our estimation of the comparative amounts of feeling is performed in the act of choice or volition. Our choice of one course out of two or more proves that, in our estimation, this course promises the greatest balance of pleasure. When there is a large overbalancing force on one side, indeed, the estimation of the amount of this balance is no doubt very rude; but all the critical points of the theory will depend on that nice estimation of the opposing motives which we make when these are nearly equal, and we hesitate between them.

4. As several writers have previously remarked, feelings have two dimensions, *intensity* and *duration*. A pleasure or a pain may be either weak or intense in any indivisible moment; it may also last a long or a short time. If the intensity remain uniform, the quantity of feeling generated is found by multiplying the units of intensity into the units of duration. But if the intensity, as is usually the case, varies as some function of the time, the quantity of feeling is got by infinitesimal summation or *integration*.

Thus, if the duration of a feeling be represented by the abscissa of a curve, the intensity will be the ordinate, and the quantity of feeling will be the area.

5. Pleasure and pain, of course, are opposed as positive and negative quantities.

6. A principle of the mind which any true theory must take into account is that of *foresight*. Every expected future pleasure or pain affects us with similar feelings in the present time, but with an intensity diminished in some proportion to its uncertainty and its remoteness in time. But the effects of *foresight* merely complicate without altering the other parts of the theory.

7. Such are the main principles of feeling on which economy is founded. A second part of the

theory proceeds from feelings to the *useful objects* or *utilities* by which pleasurable feeling is increased or pain removed.

An object is useful when it either affects the senses pleasurably in the present moment, or when, by foresight, it is expected that it will do so at some future time. Thus we must carefully distinguish *actual utility* in present use from *estimated future utility*, which yet, by allowing for the imperfect force of anticipation, and for the uncertainty of future events, gives a certain present utility.

8. *Amount of utility* corresponds to amount of pleasure produced. But the continued uniform application of an useful object to the senses or the desires, will not commonly produce uniform amounts of pleasure. Every appetite or sense is more or less rapidly satiated. A certain quantity of an object received, a further quantity is indifferent to us, or may even excite disgust. Every successive application will commonly excite the feelings less intensely than the previous application. The utility of the last supply of an object, then, usually decreases in some proportion, or as some function of the whole quantity received. This variation theoretically existing even in the smallest quantities, we must recede to infinitesimals, and what we shall call the *coefficient of utility*, is the ratio between the last increment or infinitely small supply of the object, and the increment of pleasure which it occasions, both, of course, estimated in their appropriate units.

9. The coefficient of utility is, then, some generally diminishing function of the whole quantity of the object consumed. Here is the most important law of the whole theory.

This function of utility is peculiar to each kind of object, and more or less to each individual. Thus the appetite for dry bread is much more rapidly satisfied than that for wine, for clothes, for handsome furniture, for works of art, or, finally, for money. And every one has his own peculiar tastes in which he is nearly insatiable.

10. A third part of the theory now treats of *labour*; which, although the means by which we seek pleasure, is always accompanied by a certain painful exertion, rapidly increasing as some function of the intensity or the duration of the labour. Thus, labour will be exerted both in intensity and duration until a further increment will be more painful than the increment of produce thereby obtained is pleasurable. Here labour will stop, but up to this point it will always be accompanied by an excess of pleasure.

It is obvious that the final point of labour will depend upon the final ratio of utility of the object produced.

11. I assume, as obviously true, that the abilities of men are infinitely varied, whether by nature or by education, so that both the same person may vary in his power of producing different objects, and any two persons may vary in respect of the same object.

This, indeed, is in direct opposition to the erroneous simplification of the science effected by Ricardo, when he assumed that all labourers have a certain uniform power; the higher classes of mechanics and other skilled or learned producers being treated as mere exceptions to the rule.

12. The theory of rent, which here comes in, is not materially different from that of Dr. Anderson and later writers.

13. We now arrive at the *theory of exchange*, which is a deduction from the laws of utility.

If a person has any useful object, but an object belonging to another person would have greater utility, he will be glad to give the one in return for the other. But it is a necessary condition that the other person will likewise gain, or at least not lose by the exchange.

Whether the exchange will take place or not can only be ascertained by estimating the utility of the objects on either side, which is done by integrating the appropriate functions of utility up to the quantity of each object as limits. A balance of utility on both sides will lead to an exchange.

14. Suppose, however, that the useful objects on either side are commodities of which more or less may be given, and this even down to infinitely small quantities. Such is substantially the case in ordinary commercial sales. There are now no definite amounts of utility to be balanced against each other, but the one person will now give to the other so much of his

commodity, and at such a ratio of exchange, that if he gave an infinitely small quantity, either more or less, but at the same rate, he would not gain in utility by it. The increments of utility lost and gained at the limits of the quantities exchanged must be equal, otherwise further exchange would take place.

The ratio of the increments of the commodities, however, would be indeterminate but for the existence of a law that all quantities of the same commodity, being uniform in kind, must be exchanged at the same rate. The last increments, then, must be exchanged, in the ratio of the whole quantities exchanged. To explain in ordinary words how the adjustment takes place under this condition is almost impossible. But light is at once thrown on the whole matter by stating that in every such exchange we have two *unknown quantities* and two equations by which to determine them. The *unknown quantities* are the quantities of commodity given and received. The known quantities are those of the commodities previously possessed. We have also the functions of utility of the commodities with respect to the persons. An equation may thus be established on either side between the utility gained and sacrificed at the ratio of exchange of the whole commodities, upon the last increments exchanged.

15. When the useful object on one side only is infinitely divisible, we shall have only one unknown quantity, namely, that of the divisible commodity

given for the indivisible object, and also one equation to determine it by, namely, that on the part of the person holding the divisible commodity, and able to give more or less for it.   But this does not apply to unique objects, like a statue, a rare book, or gem, which do not admit of the conception of more or less.

When both commodities are indivisible as first supposed (section 13), we have neither unknown quantities nor equations.

16. The equations in an exchange may prove impossible, or without solutions.   This will indicate either that no exchange of commodity can take place at all, or that at least one of the parties to the exchange is not satisfied even with the whole of the commodity formerly belonging to the other.

17. The principle of exchange thus deduced in the case of two persons and two commodities, applies to any number of persons and commodities.   It, therefore, applies not only to the general inland trade of a country, but to the trade between aggregates of men or nations—international trade.

The number of equations is very rapidly increased according to the simple law of combinations.

18. Of course such equations as are here spoken of are merely theoretical.   Such complicated laws as those of economy cannot be accurately traced in individual cases.   Their operation can only be detected in aggregates and by the method of averages.   *We must think under the forms of these laws in their theoretic perfection and complication;*

in practice we must be content with approximate and empirical laws.

19. Let it be remarked, that though the exchanges be regulated by equations, there cannot be equality in the whole utilities gained and lost, which are found by integrating the functions of utility of the respective commodities before and after exchange. The balance is the gain of utility, and from the nature of exchange there must be a gain on one side at least.

20. Combining the theory of exchanges with that of labour and production, the quantity which each person produces will be dependent upon the result of the exchanges; for this may greatly modify the conditions of utility.

A new set of unknown quantities are thus introduced; but it will be found that just as many new equations to determine them may be established. Each such equation is between the utility of the last increment of produce and the increment of labour necessary to produce it.

21. The only further part of the theory which I will here at all attempt to explain is that referring to capital. I shall give a definition of capital different from the established one, and much simpler. Mr. J. S. Mill says (*Principles*, 3rd edition, vol. i. p. 67), "What capital does for production is to afford the shelter, protection, tools and materials which the work requires, and to feed and otherwise maintain the labourers during the process."

To understand capital properly, we must omit all but the last enumerated part. Thus, I define capital as consisting of *all useful objects which, in supplying a labourer's ordinary wants and desires, enable him to undertake works of which the result will be deferred for a greater or less space of time.* Capital, in short, is nothing but *maintenance of labourers.*

It is, of course, perfectly true that buildings, tools, materials, etc., are a necessary means of production; but they are already the product of labour assisted by capital or maintenance. They are the results of the application of capital to labour at an imperfect stage.

Without capital a person must have immediate returns, or else he perishes. With capital he may sow in the spring that he may reap in the autumn; or he may undertake labour-saving enterprises, such as roads and railways, which will not make a full return for many years. Most improved modes of applying labour require that the enjoyment of the result shall be deferred.

22. While amount of capital is estimated by the amount of utility of which the enjoyment is deferred, *amount of employment of capital* is the amount of utility multiplied by the number of units of time during which its enjoyment is deferred.

23. The interest of all capital in a market is of one rate only, and that, therefore, the lowest rate; because capital consists only in maintenance, and may therefore be applied indifferently to any branch

of industry. Buildings, tools, etc., which have
hitherto been classed with capital, are, on the
contrary, usually applicable only to the single
purpose for which they were designed. The profit
they bring, therefore, in no way follows the laws of
the interest of capital, but rather those of rent, or
the produce of natural agents. This has been already
remarked by Professor Newman, in his *Lectures on
Political Economy*, and by other writers.

24. As labour must be supposed to be aided with
some capital, the rate of interest is always determined
by the *ratio which a new increment of produce bears
to the increment of capital by which it was produced.*
As the interest of all capital must be uniform, the
benefit which the mass of capital already available
confers upon the labourer goes for nothing in
determining the rate of interest, which depends
solely upon the portion last added, or which may be
added.

25. We can now easily explain the known fact,
that the interest of capital always tends to fall very
rapidly as its amount increases, in proportion to the
labour it supports. It is because for equal increments
of time the necessary increments of capital increase
with the time. Thus, if I undertake a work which
I can finish in one year, I have to await the result
on an average only half a year. If, however, I work
a second year before getting the result, I wait a
whole year for the former year's work and half a year
for the second year's work. Thus I employ at least

three times as much capital in the second year as in the first. In the third year I should employ at least five times as much capital, in the fourth year at least seven times, and so on. Unless, then, the advantages of the successive deferments increase in the arithmetical series 3, 5, 7, 9, etc., the proportional profit from the new additions must fall, and, as was said before, the lowest rate for which capital may be had governs the rate of all other capital.

26. It is the accepted opinion of writers of the present day, that the rate of interest tends to fall because the soil does not yield proportionate returns as its cultivation is pushed. But I must hold that this decrease in the proportionate returns would chiefly fall upon the wages of the labourer. The interest of capital has no relation to the absolute returns to labour, but only to the increased return which the last increment of capital allows.

27. Having thus explained some of the principal features of the theory, I shall close without venturing into the higher complications of the subject, where the effects of money, of credit, of combination of labour, of the risk or uncertainty of undertakings, and of bankruptcy, are taken into account.

The last result of the theory will be to give a determination of the rate of wages, or the produce of labour after deduction of rent, interest, profit, insurance and taxation, which are so many payments which the labourer makes for advantages enjoyed.

APPENDIX IV

LIST OF WORKS AND PAPERS UPON ECONOMICAL SUB-
JECTS BY THE AUTHOR OF THE PRESENT BOOK

1857. Comparison of the Land and Railway Policy of New
South Wales. The Public Lands of New South Wales.
Articles in the *Empire* newspaper, April 7th and June 23rd.
Sydney, New South Wales.

1862. Diagram, showing all the Weekly Accounts of the Bank
of England, since the passing of the Bank Act of 1844, with
the Amount of Bank of England, Private, and Joint Stock
Bank Promissory Notes in Circulation during each week,
and the Bank Minimum Rate of Discount. *London*. Sheet,
20 × 30 inches, coloured.

This Diagram represents to the eye all the useful results
of tables, containing about 113,000 figures.

1862. Diagram, showing the Price of the English Funds, the
Price of Wheat, the Number of Bankruptcies, and the Rate
of Discount, monthly, since 1731 ; so far as the same have
been ascertained. *London*. Sheet, 20 × 30 inches, coloured.

This Diagram is drawn from tables carefully compiled for
the purpose, and containing more than 12,000 figures.
Explanatory Notes and References are appended to each
Diagram.

1862. (1) On the Study of Periodic Commercial Fluctuations.
With five diagrams. (2) Notice of a general Mathematical
Theory of Political Economy. Papers read in the F section
of the British Association at the Cambridge Meeting.
Report. Proceedings of Sections, pp. 157-8—(1) Reprinted

in *Investigations*, (2) subsequently published in full, see 1866, and reprinted in the present volume, Appendix III.

1863. A Serious Fall in the Value of Gold Ascertained, and its social effects set forth. With two diagrams. *London* : Edward Stanford, Charing Cross. 8vo. 73 pp. Reprinted in *Investigations*.

1865. The Coal Question ; an Inquiry concerning the Progress of the Nation, and the Probable Exhaustion of our Coal Mines. *London and Cambridge* : Macmillan & Co. 8vo. xix, 349 pp.

1865. On the Variation of Prices, and the Value of the Currency since 1782. Paper read before the London Statistical Society, May 1865. Journal of the Statistical Society, vol. xxviii., pp. 294-320. With four diagrams. Reprinted in *Investigations*.

1866. On the frequent Autumnal Pressure in the Money Market, and the Action of the Bank of England. Paper read before the Statistical Society, April 1866. Journal of the Statistical Society of London, vol. xxix., pp. 235-53. Reprinted in *Investigations*.

1866. Brief Account of a General Mathematical Theory of Political Economy. (Read at the British Association, 1862.) Journal of the Statistical Society of London, vol. xxix., pp. 282-87. Reprinted in the present volume.

1866. The Coal Question, etc. Second edition. *London*. 8vo. xxvi, 383 pp.

1866. An Introductory Lecture on the Importance of diffusing a Knowledge of Political Economy. Delivered in Owens College, Manchester, at the opening of the Session of Evening Classes, on October 12. *Manchester*. 12mo. 35 pp.

1867. Science Lectures for the People. Lecture IX. On Coal : its importance in manufactures and trade. Delivered in the Carpenters' Hall, Manchester, January 16, 1867. (Science Lectures, vol. i., pp. 128-40.)

1867. On the Analogy between the Post-Office, Telegraphs and other systems of Conveyance of the United Kingdom, as regards Government Control. Paper read before the

Manchester Statistical Society, April 1867. Transactions, 1866-67, pp. 89-104. Reprinted in *Methods*.

1868. A Lecture on Trades' Societies : their Objects and Policy. Delivered by request of the Trades Unionists' Political Association, March 31st. *Manchester*. 8vo. 16 pp. Reprinted in *Methods*.

1868. Lecture on the Probable Exhaustion of our Coal Mines. Royal Institution of Great Britain. Friday Evening, March 13th. 8vo. 7 pp.

1868. On the International Monetary Convention, and the Introduction of an International Currency into this kingdom. Paper read before the Manchester Statistical Society, May 13th. Transactions, 1867-68, pp. 79-92.

1868. On the Condition of the Metallic Currency of the United Kingdom, with reference to the Question of International Coinage. Paper read before the Statistical Society of London, November. Journal of the Statistical Society of London, vol. xxxi., pp. 426-64. Reprinted in *Investigations*.

1869. The Pressure of Taxation (a Report to the Chancellor of the Exchequer). Printed officially, but not published. Reprinted in *Principles*, 1905. (The statement "now first printed" in the preface to the author's *Principles of Economics*, p. xiv, is erroneous.)

1869. The Value of Gold. Letter to *The Economist* newspaper, May 8th. Reprinted in the Journal of the Statistical Society of London, December, vol. xxxii., p. 445. Reprinted in *Investigations*.

1869. On the Work of the Society in connection with the Questions of the Day. Inaugural Address read before the Manchester Statistical Society, November 10th, 1869. Transactions, 1869-70, pp. 1-14. Reprinted in *Methods*.

1870. Opening Address of the President of Section F (Economic Science and Statistics) of the British Association for the Advancement of Science at the Fortieth Meeting, at Liverpool, September 1870. Report. Transactions of the Sections, pp. 178-87. Journal of the Statistical Society of London, vol. xxxiii., pp. 309-26. Reprinted in *Methods*.

1870. On Industrial Partnerships. A Lecture delivered under

the auspices of the National Association for the Promotion of Social Science, April 5th, 1870. *London* : 1 Adam Street, Adelphi. 12mo. 39 pp. Reprinted in *Methods*.

1871. The Match Tax : a Problem in Finance. *London.* 8vo. 66 pp. Reprinted in *Principles*.

1871. The Theory of Political Economy. *London and New York* : Macmillan & Co. 8vo. xvi, 267 pp. Translated into Italian (1875) and French (1909).

1874. The Progress of the Mathematical Theory of Political Economy, with an explanation of the Principles of the Theory. Paper read before the Manchester Statistical Society, November 11th. Transactions, 1874-75, pp. 1-19, with a diagram. Reprinted in the Journal of the Statistical Society of London, vol. xxxvii., p. 478.

1874. Railways and the State. Essays and Addresses by Professors and Lecturers, Owens College. Reprinted in *Methods*.

1874. Théorie mathématique de l'échange. Question de priorité. Correspondance entre M. Jevons, Professeur à Manchester, et M. Walras, Professeur à Lausanne. Journal des économistes, t. xxxiv.

1875. On the Progress of the Coal Question. British Association, Bristol, 1875. Transactions of Sections, p. 216.

1875. The Post-Office Telegraphs and their Financial Results. *Fortnightly Review*, December 1st, vol. xviii., N.S., pp. 826-35. Reprinted in *Methods*.

1875. La Teorica dell' economia politica, esposta da W. Stanley Jevons. Biblioteca dell' Economista. 3ª serie, tome ii, pp. 175-311. (Translated under the superintendence of Professor Gerolamo Boccardo.)

1875. Money and the Mechanism of Exchange (International Scientific Series, vol. xvii.). *London* : H. S. King & Co. ; *New York* : D. Appleton & Co. Post 8vo. xviii, 349 pp. Reprinted frequently, 1878, etc.

1876. La Monnaie et le mécanisme de l'échange. *Paris* : Librairie Germer Baillière et Cie. (Bibliothèque Scientifique Internationale, vol. xx.). 8vo. viii, 288 pp.

1876. Geld und Geldverkehr. *Leipzig* : F. A. Brockhaus (Internationale wissenschaftliche Bibliothek, Band xxi.). 8vo. xvi, 359 pp.

1876. La Moneta ed il mecanismo dello scambio. *Milano*: Fratelli Dumolard. (Biblioteca Scientifica Internazionale, vol. vi.) 8vo. xxix, 319 pp.

1876. On the United Kingdom Alliance and its Prospects of Success. Paper read before the Manchester Statistical Society, March 8th. Transactions, pp. 127-42. Reprinted in *Methods*.

1876. On the Frequent Autumnal Pressure in the Money Market, and the action of the Bank of England. Paper reprinted from the Journal of the Statistical Society of London, 1866, in the Transactions of the Manchester Statistical Society. Appendix, pp. 17-41. Reprinted in *Investigations*.

1876. The Future of Political Economy. Introductory Lecture at the Opening of the Session, 1876-77, at University College, London, Faculty of Arts and Laws. *Fortnightly Review*, December, vol. xx., pp. 617-31. (See also next entry, 1877.) Reprinted in *Principles*.

1877. Le Passé et l'avenir de l'économie politique. Les Méthodes. Les Économistes contemporains. Le Political Economy Club. Journal des économistes. Mars, 1877. 3ᵉ série, tome xlv., pp. 325-42.

1877. The Silver Question : A Paper read by Hamilton A. Hill, of Boston, before the American Social Science Association at Saratoga, September 5th. *Boston* : Published for the Association by A. Williams & Co., pp. 26-32. Reprinted in the *London Bankers' Magazine*, December, 7 pp. ; and in *Investigations*.

1878. Science Primers—Primer of Political Economy. *London* : Macmillan & Co. 18mo. 134 pp. Reprinted frequently.

1878. L'Économie politique, par W. Stanley Jevons, traduite par Henri Gravez, ingénieur. *Paris* : Librairie Germer Baillière et Cie. (Bibliothèque Utile, vol. xliv.) 18mo. 184 pp.

1878. The Periodicity of Commercial Crises and its Physical Explanation. Paper read before the F Section of the British

Association at the Dublin Meeting, August 19th.   Report,
Transactions of Section F, p. 666.   Published in the Journal
of the Statistical and Social Inquiry Society of Ireland,
August 1878.   Vol. vii., pp. 334-42.   Reprinted in
Investigations.

1878. Commercial Crises and Sun-spots.   Article printed in
Nature of November 14, vol. xix., pp. 33-7.   Reprinted in
Investigations.

1878. Remarks on the Statistical use of the Arithmometer.
Journal of the Statistical Society of London, vol. xli., pp.
597-601.

1879. Methods of Social Reform, No. II.   A State Parcel Post.
Article in the *Contemporary Review* of January ; vol. xxxiv.,
pp. 209-29.   Reprinted in *Methods*.

1879. Sun-spots and Commercial Crises.   *Nature*, April 24, vol.
xix., pp. 588-90.   Reprinted in *Investigations*.

1879. The Theory of Political Economy.   Second edition,
revised and enlarged, with new preface and appendixes.
London : Macmillan & Co.   8vo.   lxiii, 315 pp.

1880. Postal Notes, Money Orders, and Bank Cheques.   *Contemporary Review*, July; vol. xxxviii., pp. 150-61.   Reprinted
in *Methods*.

1880. Preface to the English Translation of the Guide to the
Study of Political Economy by Luigi Cossa.   *London* :
Macmillan & Co.   Cr. 8vo.   pp. vii-xii.

1881. Richard Cautillon and the Nationality of Political
Economy.   *Contemporary Review*, January, vol. xxxix., pp.
61-80.   Reprinted in *Principles*.

1881. Bimetallism.   Article in *Contemporary Review*, May, vol.
xxxix., pp. 750-57.   Reprinted in *Investigations*.

1882. The Solar Commercial Cycle.   *Nature*, July 6 ; vol. xxvi.,
pp. 226-8.

1882. The State in Relation to Labour.   (The English Citizen
Series.)   *London* : Macmillan & Co.   Cr. 8vo.   vii, 166 pp.

1883. Methods of Social Reform, and other papers.   (A collection
mostly on social, economic, and educational subjects.)
London : Macmillan & Co.   8vo.   viii, 383 pp.

1884. Investigations in Currency and Finance.   Edited, with

Introduction, by H. S. Foxwell, M.A. *London* : Macmillan
& Co. 8vo. xliv, 414 pp. .

1886. Letters and Journal of W. Stanley Jevons. Edited by
his wife, with complete bibliography of his works. *London* :
Macmillan & Co. 8vo. xii, 473 pp.

1888. The Theory of Political Economy. Third edition ; a
reprint, with continuation of the Bibliography of Mathematico-
Economic Writings to date. *London* : Macmillan & Co.
8vo. lvi, 296 pp.

1894. The State in Relation to Labour. Second edition (and
third impression), edited with notes and an introduction by
Michael Cababé. (The English Citizen Series.) *London* :
Macmillan & Co. Cr. 8vo. xxix, 171 pp.

1905. The Principles of Economics. A Fragment of a Treatise
on the Industrial Mechanism of Society, and other papers.
(Cantillon, the Future of Political Economy, Match Tax,
Pressure of Taxation.) Edited, with a Preface, by Henry
Higgs. *London* : Macmillan & Co. 8vo. xxviii, 273 pp.

1906. The Coal Question. Third edition ; revised, with new
matter, notes, and preface, and a new chart, by A. W. Flux,
M.A. *London* : Macmillan & Co. 8vo. l, 467 pp.

1909. La Théorie d'économie politique, par W. Stanley Jevons,
traduit par H. E. Barrault et Maurice Alfassa, avec préface
de Paul Painlevé. (Bibliothèque Internationale d'Économie
Politique.) *Paris* : Giard & Brière. 8vo. xxiv, 405 pp.

1909. Investigations in Currency and Finance. Second edition,
abridged, issued at reduced price, with Preface by H. Stanley
Jevons, M.A., B.Sc. *London* : Macmillan & Co. 8vo.
xxxvi, 347 pp.

1910. The State in Relation to Labour. Third edition ; with
new introduction by F. W. Hirst, M.A. (The English
Citizen Series.) *London* : Macmillan & Co. Cr. 8vo. xviii,
175 pp.

1910. The Theory of Political Economy. Fourth edition ;
edited with notes, preface, and new appendixes by H. Stanley
Jevons, M.A., B.Sc. *London* : Macmillan & Co. 8vo. lxiv,
339 pp.

APPENDIX V

LIST OF MATHEMATICO-ECONOMIC BOOKS, MEMOIRS, AND OTHER PUBLISHED WRITINGS

Remarks upon the purpose and some of the contents of this list will be found in the preface to the second edition of this book.

Works unknown to the Author are placed in square brackets.

The criticisms and summaries in small type are by the author unless the contrary is indicated, thus [Ed.]. At the pages indicated will be found notices of the particular works to which the references are attached.

1711. CEVA (Joanne). De re nummaria quoad fieri potuit geometrice actata. *Mantua.* 4to. 60 pp.

1717. MARIOTTE (Esme). Essaie de logique. Second edition. In collected works. *Leide.* See Principe 97 and 11me Partie, Article III.

1720. HUTCHESON (Francis). An Inquiry into the Original of our Ideas of Beauty and Virtue. *London.* 8vo. (3rd edition, 1729, xxii, 304 pp.)

> In his "Inquiry" Hutcheson makes a bold attempt to employ mathematical expressions in computing the morality of actions. It is naturally a somewhat crude attempt, but I am unable to see that there is anything absurd in it. I think Hutcheson's views have not received the attention they deserve.
> See Preface, pp. xxv-xxvi.

1728. HUTCHESON (Francis). An Essay on the Nature and

Conduct of the Passions and Affections, with illustrations on
the Moral Sense. *London.* 8vo. xxiv, 333 pp.

This second moral work does not contain an explicit employment of
mathematical method, but there is throughout a marked tendency
towards mathematical ideas. In Section 2, Article IV., he lays
down in the clearest manner the foundation of a quantitative theory
of pleasure and pain, almost as it was afterwards repeated by
Jeremy Bentham.

[1738. BERNOUILLI (Daniel). Specimen theoriae novae de
mensura sortis. Commentarii academiae scientiarum im-
perialis Petropolitanae, vol. v., pp. 175-92. German translation, 1896, by A. Pringsheim: Die Grundlage der modernen
Wertlehre. Versuch einer neuen Theorie der Wertbestim-
mung von Glücksfällen (Einleitung von Ludwig Fick).
Leipzig. (Duncker & Humblot.) 60 pp.]

[1754. ANONYMOUS (F. Forbonnais). Élémens du commerce,
2nd edition, vol. ii. chap. ix. *et passim. Leyde* and *Paris.*
12mo.]

1765. BECCARIA (Cesare). Tentativo analitico sui contrabbandi.
Estratto dal foglio periodico intitolato : Il Caffè (vol. i.
Brescia). Reprinted in Custodi's Scrittori classici italiani di
Economia politica. Parte moderna, vol. xii., pp. 235-41.
Milano, 1804.

See Preface, p. xli.

1771. ANONYMOUS. An Essay on the Theory of Money.
London. 8vo. 161 pp. (attributed to Major-General
Henry Lloyd).

See Preface, p. xlii.

1776. CONDILLAC (Étienne Bonnot de). Le Commerce et le
gouvernement. *Paris.*

See Preface, p. xxviii.

1781. ANONYMOUS (A. N. Isnard). Traité des richesses.
Londres et *Lausanne.* 2 vols. 8vo. xxiv, 344, 327 pp.

1786. CONDORCET (M. J. A. N. Caritat de). Vie de M. Turgot.
Two editions, same year, both *London.* pp. 246 and 299
respectively.

Slightly mathematical, pp. 162-9.

1787. CONDORCET (C. de). Life of Turgot. Translation of above. *London.*

Slightly mathematical, pp. 403-9.

1792. SILIO (Guglielmo). Saggio sull' influenza dell' analisi nelle scienze politiche ed economiche. (In vol. v. of the collection Nuova Raccolta d' opuscoli di autori siciliani. *Palermo.*)

1793. LANG. Historische Entwickelung der deutschen Steuerverfassung. *Riga.*

1801. CANARD (Nicolas François). Principes d'économie politique : ouvrage couronné par l'Institut. *Paris.* 8vo. 384 pp.

Reviewed by Francis Horner, *Edinburgh Review*, vol. i. p. 431.

1801. CANARD (Nicolas François). Mémoire sur la question s'il est vrai que, dans un pays agricole, toute espèce d'impôt retombe sur les propriétaires fonciers. *Paris.*

1802. BRISSON (B.). Essai sur la navigation. *Paris.*

Brisson was a profound mathematician as well as an eminent engineer. He appears to have presented to the Institut in this year, in conjunction with his friend Dupuis de Torcy, an Essai, part of which has been printed in the *14ᵉ Cahier du Journal de l'École Polytechnique.* Other portions of the memoir, however, are stated never to have been published, including the first part, which contained "des considerations d'économie publique appliquée aux projets de communications nouvelles." See "Essai sur le système général de navigation intérieure de la France," by B. Brisson, *Paris*, 1829, p. ii.

Some indications of the nature of Brisson's financial theory are found at pp. xiv, 160-61.

1802. KRÖNCKE (Claus). Versuch einer Theorie des Fuhrwerks mit Anwendung auf dem Strassenbau. *Giessen.* 8vo.

[1803. SISMONDI (J. C. L. Simonde de). De la richesse commerciale. 2 vols.

Slightly mathematical, vol. i. pp. 105-9.]

1804. KRÖNCKE (Claus). Das Steuerwesen nach seiner Natur und seinen Wirkungen untersucht. *Darmstadt* und *Giessen* (Heyer). 8vo. xxxii, 440 pp.

1809. LANG (Joseph). Ueber den obersten Grundsatz der politischen Oekonomie. *Riga.* 8vo.

[1810. KRÖNCKE (Claus). Anleitung zur Regulirung der Steuer.]

[1811. LANG (Joseph). Grundlinien der politischen Arithmetik. *Kursk* (Langner). xxii, 216 pp.]

1815. BUQUOY (Georg von). Die Theorie der Nationalwirthschaft, nach einen neuen Plane und nach mehreren eigenen Ansichten dargestellt. *Leipzig*. 4to. 3 Nachträge: 1816, 1817 (524 pp.), 1818.

[1816. ANONYMOUS (L. M. Valeriani). Apologia della formola $p = \dfrac{i}{o}$, trattandosi del come si determini il prezzo delle cose tutte mercatabili, contro ciò che ne dice il celebre autore del "Nuova Prospetto delle scienze economiche." *Bologna* (Marsigli). 62 pp.]

[1817. ANONYMOUS (L. M. Valeriani). Discorso apologetico in cui si sostiene recarsi invano pel celebre autore del "Nuovo Prospetto delle scienze economiche" contro l' Apologia della formola $p = \dfrac{i}{o}$, trattandosi del come si determini il prezzo delle cose tutte mercatabili, ciò che il medisimo ha scritto nel tomo II, il pag. 114-17, 141-6, e nel IV, pag. 214 9, 244-63, dell' opera suddetta. *Bologna* (Marsigli). 114 pp.]

1824. ANONYMOUS (T. Perronet Thompson). On the Instrument of Exchange. Westminster Review, vol. i., pp. 171-205. Reprinted separately, 1830, 27 pp., and later, see 1842. Postscript to same, see 1830.

An able and remarkable article reviewing a tract of Sir John Sinclair and Huskisson's "Question concerning the Depreciation of our Currency."

1825. CAZAUT. Élémens d'économie privée et publique. *Paris* and *Toulouse*. 251 pp.

1825. FUOCO (Francesco). Saggi economici. Prima serie. 2 tomes. 8vo. *Pisa*, 1825-27.

1826. RAU (K. H.). Grundsätze der Volkswirtschaftslehre. *Leipzig* and *Heidelberg*. Subsequent editions: 1833, 1837, 1841, 1863, 1868.

Very slightly mathematical [I. F.].

1826. THOMPSON (T. Perronet). On Rent.

1826. THÜNEN (Johann Heinrich von). Der isolirte Staat in Beziehung auf Landwirthschaft und Nationalökonomie, oder Untersuchungen über den Einfluss, den die Getreidepreise, der Reichthum des Bodens und die Abgaben auf den Ackerbau ausüben. Erster Thiel. *Hamburg.* 8vo. viii, 290 pp. [See also 1842, 1850, 1851, 1857, and 1863.]

1829. WHEWELL (William). Mathematical Exposition of some Doctrines of Political Economy. Cambridge Philosophical Transactions, vol. iii., pp. 191-230. *Cambridge.* 4to. [See also 1831, 1850, and 1875.]

1830. Westminster Review. Postscript to article "On the Instrument of Exchange." Vol. xii., pp. 525-33.

1831. WALRAS (Auguste). De la nature de la richesse et de l'origine de la valeur. *Paris.* 8vo. xxiv, 334 pp.

See Preface, p. xxxix.

1831. WHEWELL (William). Mathematical Exposition of the Leading Doctrines of Mr. Ricardo's "Principles of Political Economy and Taxation." Cambridge Philosophical Transactions, vol. iv., pp. 155-98. *Cambridge.* 4to.

1832. LUBÉ (D. G.). Argument against the Gold Standard. *London.* 8vo. iv., 192 pp.

1832. HERMANN (F. B. W.). Staatswirthschaftliche Untersuchungen.

1838. COURNOT (Augustin). Recherches sur les principes mathématiques de la théorie des richesses. *Paris.* 8vo. xi, 198 pp. [Translated into Italian (1875), and English (1897), *q.v.*]

See Preface, pp. xxix.-xxxii.

1838. TOZER (John). Mathematical Investigation of the Effect of Machinery on the Wealth of a Community in which it is employed, and on the Fund for the Payment of Wages. Cambridge Philosophical Transactions, vol. vi., pp. 507-22. *Cambridge.* 4to.

1839. HAGEN (Karl Heinrich). Von der Staatslehre und von der Vorbereitung zum Dienste in der Staatsverwaltung. Aufsätze gerichtet an angehende Cameralisten, zunächst an seine Herren Zuhörer, von K. H. H. *Koenigsberg.* 8vo. 477 pp.

[1839. ELLET (Chas., Jr.). An Essay on the Laws of Trade in reference to the Works of Internal Improvement in the United States. viii, 248 pp. Plate. 8vo.]

1840. ANONYMOUS (J. W. Lubbock). On Currency. *London* (Charles Knight and Co.). 8vo. viii, 43, xxi pp.

1840. TOZER (John). On the Effect of the Non-Residence of Landlords, etc., on the Wealth of a Community. Cambridge Philosophical Transactions, vol. vii. pp. 189-96. *Cambridge.* 4to.

1842. THÜNEN (J. H. von). Der isolirte Staat, etc. Erster Theil, zweite Ausgabe. *Rostock.* 8vo. xv, 391 pp.

1842. THOMPSON (T. Perronet). Exercises, Political and others. Vol. iii., pp. 295-343. On the Instrument of Exchange. See 1824, THOMPSON.

1844. DUPUIT (Étienne Juvenal). De la mesure de l'utilité des travaux publics. Annales des Ponts et Chaussées. 2me série. Tome viii., pp. 332-75. *Paris.* 8vo.

See Preface, pp. xxviii-xxix.

1844. HAGEN (Karl Heinrich). Die Nothwendigkeit der Handelsfreiheit für das Nationaleinkommen, mathematisch nachgewiesen. *Königsberg.* (Cräte u. Unger.) 8vo. 32 pp.

A curious mathematical investigation into the relation of prices and quantities of commodity in trade, and the results of importation and exportation upon the wealth of a country. In p. 30 the author acknowledges his indebtedness to COURNOT.

1844. HAGEN (K. H.). System of Political Economy. Translated from the German by John Prince Smith. *London.* 8vo. viii, 88 pp.

Clear statement of the principles of the Science as then understood. Mathematical footnotes.—[ED.]

1844. DE QUINCEY (Thomas). Logic of Political Economy. *Edinburgh* and *London.* 8vo. 260 pp.

1847. BORDAS. De la mesure de l'utilité des travaux publics. Annales des Ponts et Chaussées, 1847. 1er semestre. 2me série. Tome xiii., p. 249.

1848. MILL (John Stuart). Principles of Political Economy, with some of their applications to Social Philosophy. *London.* 2 vols. 8vo. Book iii, chapters xvii, xviii. See especially sec. 7 (3rd edition, 1852, vol. ii., pp. 143-44).

See Preface, pp. xxiv-xxv.

1849. ESMENARD DU MAZET (Camille). Nouveaux principes d'économie politique. *Paris.* 8vo. ix, 456 pp.

A work going over the greater part of the field of political economy and touching points here and there in a novel and interesting way. The general tenor of the author is to the effect that Political Economy is a science of calculation.

The author assumes the relations of economic quantities to be much more simple than they really are. Then he holds that (p. 22) "la richesse d'une nation est en raison directe du travail et de l'industrie." He takes labour and industry to be invariables in their nature, at least that we may consider them to be so since the most distant historical ages.

It is not requisite to trace out the contents of the book, as it is plain that Esmenard du Mazet, although viewing intelligently the use of mathematical methods, had no real comprehension of the complexity of the relations with which he was dealing. His work is far inferior to the memoirs of Dupuit, or to the *Recherches* of Cournot to which he refers (p. 176).

1849. DUPUIT (J.). De l'influence des péages sur l'utilité des voies de communication. Annales des Ponts et Chaussées, No. 207 ; 2me série, 1849, 1er semestre, pp. 170-248.

This extensive and valuable memoir is described by Dupuit as a sequel to 1844 DUPUIT, and as an answer to 1847 BORDAS, the explanation of the theory of utility which he gave before having been found insufficient to convince certain readers. In treating of the definition of utility, he reviews the correspondence on this subject between Say and Ricardo. Taking an example of J. B. Say of a workman who buys meat to the extent of 30 sous a day, Dupuit proceeds to show most clearly (p. 186), that as the price of meat rises the workman buys less and less, and therefore desires more strongly what he buys at a greater proportional sacrifice. Hence, when he buys, say, three pounds, each pound must be desired with a different degree of urgency. "A 10 sous on consomme trois livres ; à 15 sous on n'en consomme plus que deux ; le ménage qui se prive de cette troisième livre parce qu'elle vaut 15 sous, n'y attache donc pas la même utilité qu'aux deux autres. Les deux premières ont satisfait un besoin plus pressant, la troisième est encore désirée, puisque dans certaines circonstances on l'achète ; mais le désir qu'on épreuve n'est pas tel qu'on veuille faire un sacrifice de 15 sous pour l'obtenir. Élevons encore le prix de la viande par degrés insensibles, et évidemment nous arriverons à réduire la consommation à une livre. . . . Je n'ai voulu que faire comprendre les divers degrés d'utilité que le même produit avait pour le même consommateur." Manufacturers and merchants, he continues, often take advantage of this gradation of utility to make more profit, by offering goods at various prices. Thus, a publisher brings out a book perhaps in a costly form at 100 francs, and when the sale of this costly edition stops, he makes a great sacrifice, as is said, and discovers that he can sell a second edition at half the price. Subsequently he discovers that there are still a few copies on hand which he can sell at 30 francs each for a time. Afterwards follow cheaper editions still, adapted to the purses of every class (pp. 188-9).

1849. WOLKOFF (Mathieu). Prémisses philosophiques de l'économie rationnelle des sociétés. *Paris*. (Guillaumin.) See also 1861 and 1868.

See Preface, pp. xxviii-xxix.

1850. MINARD. De l'usage gratuit des constructions établies aux frais de l'État. Annales des Ponts et Chaussées, 2me série, 1er semestre. p. 27.

See text, p. 240.

1850. LARDNER (Dionysius). Railway Economy. *London*. 8vo. (Chapter xiii.)

See Preface, p. xviii. Treats the theory of maximum monopoly revenue graphically.—[ED.]

1850. THÜNEN (J. H. von). Der isolirte Staat, etc. Zweiter Theil; erste Abtheilung. Der naturgemässe Arbeitslohn und dessen Verhaltniss zum Zinsfuss und zur Landrente. *Rostock*. 8vo. vi, 285 pp.

1850. WHEWELL (William). Mathematical Exposition of Certain Doctrines of Political Economy. Second and Third Memoirs, Cambridge Philosophical Transactions. Vol. ix., pp. 128-49, and Part ii, pp. 1-7. *Cambridge*. 4to.

1851. ESMENARD DU MAZET (C.). De la valeur : lettre à M. J. Garnier. *Paris*. (Joubert.) 8vo. 23 pp.

1851. DE THÜNEN. Recherches sur l'influence que le prix des grains, la richesse du sol, et les impôts exercent sur les systèmes de culture. Traduit par Laverrière. *Paris*. (Guillaumin). 8vo. viii, 340 pp.

1852. JELLICOE (Charles). On the Contrivances required to render Contingent Reversionary Interests marketable Securities. Assurance Magazine, vol. ii., pp. 159-66.

[1853. FARR (William). Income and Property Tax. Jour. Royal Statist. Soc., vol. xvi., pp. 3-44.]

1853. HARDY (Peter). An exposé of the fallacy "that it is just to tax temporary annuities at the same rate as perpetual annuities." Assur. Mag. and Jour. Inst. Actuaries, vol. iii., pp. 195-204.]

[1853. JELLICOE (Charles). On the true Measure of Liability in a System of Direct Taxation. Assur. Mag. and Jour. Inst. Actuaries, vol. iii., pp. 1-7.]

1854. WOLKOFF (Mathieu). Opuscules sur la rente foncière. *Paris.* 8vo. 231 pp.

1854. GOSSEN (Hermann Heinrich). Entwickelung der Gesetze des menschlichen Verkehrs, und der daraus fliessenden Regeln für menschliches Handeln. *Braunschweig,* (now Prager, *Berlin,* holds original edition). 8vo. 278 pp.

> See Preface, pp. xxxii-xxxix ; also Article on Gossen by Hooper, Journal of the Statistical Society, September 1879, pp. 727-33 ; review by Walras, Journal des économistes, 1885, 4e série, t. xxx. pp. 68-90 ; Pantaleoni's Pure Economics, 1898, pp. 28-38 ; and Palgrave's Dictionary.—[ED.]

1855. JENNINGS (Richard, M.A.). Natural Elements of Political Economy. *London.* 8vo. 275 pp.

> Deals with fundamental psychological principles and applies them generally to economic actions. Not symbolic or graphical in method. For quotations see text, pp. 55-7.—[ED.]

1856. BENNER. Théorie mathématique de l'économie politique.

1856. WOLKOFF (M.). Le Salaire naturel d'après M. de Thünen. Journal des économistes, 2me série, tome x., pp. 263-70.

1857. DE THÜNEN. Le Salaire naturel, et son rapport au taux de l'intérêt. Traduit de l'Allemand par M. Wolkoff. *Paris.*

[1857. WOLKOFF (M.). Nouvelles Observations au sujet de l'ouvrage de M. de Thünen sur le salaire naturel. Jour. des écon., 2me série, tome xvi.]

1857. MACLEOD (Henry Dunning). The Elements of Political Economy. *London.* 8vo.

1857. BOCCARDO (Gerolamo). Dizionario dell' Economia politica e del commercio, etc. *Torino.* 4to.

The article *Lavori pubblici* treats excellently of the utility, profit, cost, etc., of public works (vol. ii. pp. 653-9). In pp. 652-3 the relations of first cost, interest, cost of maintenance, and return are investigated mathematically.

1858. COURCELLE-SENEUIL (J. G.). Traité théorique et pratique d'économie politique. *Paris* (Amyot).

[1859. VAN HOUTEN (S.). Verhandeling over de Waarde.]

1860. DU MESNIL-MARIGNY. Les Libre-échangistes et les protectionnistes conciliés. 8vo. *Paris.* (2nd ed., 1860, ii, 413 pp.). See also 1878.

1861. WOLKOFF (M.). Lectures d'économie politique rationnelle. *Paris.* 12mo.

A revised edition of 1849 WOLKOFF.—[ED.]

1862. DE MORGAN (Augustus). Athenaeum, 15th November, p. 632.

1862. JEVONS (William Stanley). Notice of a General Mathematical Theory of Political Economy. Report of the 32nd meeting of the British Association for the Advancement of Science, held at Cambridge in October, 1862. Reports of Sections, p. 158. *London* : 1863.

Printed in full later, see 1866 JEVONS.—[ED.]

1862. MACLEOD (H. D.). On the Definition and Nature of the Science of Political Economy. Report of the 32nd meeting of the British Association, etc. Reports of Sections, pp. 159-61. Also separately printed, *Cambridge and London.* 16 pp.

1863. COURNOT (Augustin). Principes de la théorie des richesses. *Paris.* 8vo. iv, 527 pp.

See Preface, p. xxxi.

1863. MACLEOD (H. D.). A Dictionary of Political Economy : Biographical, Bibliographical, Historical, and Practical. Vol. i. *London.* 8vo.

The article *Credit*, pp. 567-617, contains a discussion of the subject from the mathematical point of view. On pp. 573 *et seq.* we find sections " on the application of the Theory of Algebraical signs, and of the separation of the signs of position and operation in Political Economy."

1863. DU MESNIL-MARIGNY. Catéchisme de l'économie politique basée sur des principes rationnels. *Paris.* 18mo. 355 pp.

1863. MANGOLDT (H. von). Grundriss der Volkswirtschaftslehre. *Stuttgart* (Engelhorn). xvi, 224 pp.

1863. THÜNEN (J. H. von). Der isolirte Staat. Zweiter Theil ; zweite Abtheilung. Der naturgemässe Arbeitslohn, etc. *Rostock.* 8vo. ix, 444 pp.

1864. FAUVEAU (G.). Considérations mathématiques sur la théorie de l'impôt. *Paris.* 8vo. 64 pp.

1865. KNAPP (Georg Friedrich). Zur Prüfung der Untersuchungen Thünen's über Lohn und Zinsfuss im isolirten Staate. *Braunschweig.* 8vo. 35 pp.

1866. JEVONS (William Stanley). Brief Account of a General Mathematical Theory of Political Economy. Journal of the Statistical Society of London, June 1866. vol. xxix., pp. 282-7.

Abstract previously published, see 1862 JEVONS.—[ED.]

1867. COURCELLE - SENEUIL (J. G.). Traité théorique et pratique d'économie politique. 2me éd. 2 vols. *Paris.* 8vo. viii, 495, 538 pp.

Mathematical in vol. i. livre i. chap. 2.

1867. FAUVEAU (G.). Considérations mathématiques sur la théorie de la valeur. Journal des économistes. 3me série, 2me année, tome v. pp. 31-40.

1867. BRENTANO (L. J.) Über J. H. von Thünen's Naturgemässen Lohn und Zinsfuss. *Göttingen.* 61 pp.

1868. RAU (Karl Heinrich). Grundsätze der Volkswirthschaftslehre. Achte Ausgabe. Erste Abtheilung, p. 368. *Leipzig und Heidelberg.* 8vo.

1868. JENKIN (Fleeming). Trades Unions. How far Legitimate. North British Review, March 1858. 8vo. (Footnote.)

1868. WOLKOFF (Mathieu). Précis d'économie politique rationnelle. *Paris.* 329 pp. Revised edition of 1849 and 1861 WOLKOFF.

1869. FAUVEAU (G.) Étude sur la théorie de l'impôt. Journal des économistes, 3me série, 4me année, tome xiii. pp. 391-403.

1869. FAUVEAU (G.) L'Impôt sur le revenu du capital et sur le revenu du travail. Journal des économistes, 3me série, 4me année, tome xvi., pp. 466-468.

1869. SCHUMACHER (H.) Über J. H. von Thünen's Gesetz vom naturgemässen Arbeitslohne. *Rostock.* 84 pp.

1870. JENKIN (Fleeming). The Graphic Representation of the Laws of Supply and Demand, and their application to Labour. Recess Studies, edited by Sir Alexander Grant, pp. 151-185. *Edinburgh.* 8vo.

> Professor Jenkin represents the action of the laws of supply and demand by intersecting curves, the market price being determined by the point of intersection of the curve of demand with that of supply. Variation of supply or of demand is shown by additional dotted line curves. . . . The essay is ingenious and instructive, and probably correct at almost all points ; but I may add that from about the year 1863 I regularly employed intersecting curves to illustrate the determination of the market price in my lectures at Owens College.

1870. LEFÈVRE (H.). Traité théorique et pratique des valeurs mobilières et des opérations de bourse. *Paris.* (Lachaud.)

1870. LEFÈVRE (H.). Théorie élémentaire des opérations de bourse.

1871. JEVONS (W. S.) The Theory of Political Economy. 8vo. *London.* xvi, 267 pp.

1871. JENKIN (Fleeming). On the Principles which regulate the incidence of Taxes. Proceedings of the Royal Society of Edinburgh ; Session 1871-72 ; pp. 618-31.

1871. FAUVEAU (G.) Rendement maximum de l'impôt indirect. Journal des économistes. 3me série, 6me année, tome xxiv., pp. 445-48.

[1871. MENGER (Carl). Grundsätze der Volkswirthschaftslehre. *Wien.*]

[1872. LAUNHARDT (Wilhelm). Kommerzielle Trassirung der Verkehrswege. *Hannover.*]

1872. MARCHAND (J.) Recherche sur la méthode à adopter pour la discussion des éléments de la statistique. Journal des actuaires français. Tome i., pp. 267-73 and 393-409 ; tome ii. (1873), pp. 58-78 et 254-63 ; and tome iii. (1874), pp. 307-25.

1873. BING OG PETERSEN. Bestemmelse af den rationelle Arbeidslön samt nogle Bemærkninger om Œkonomiens Methode. Nationaløkonomisk Tidsskrift. Förste Bind, p. 296. Copenhagen.

1873. PETERSEN, FREDERIKSEN, etc. Nationaløkonomisk Forening. Diskussion om Œkonomiens Methode. Nationaløkonomisk Tidsskrift, Maanedsskrift for Œkonomie, etc. Andet Bind, p. 248. Copenhagen.

1873. POCHET (Léon). Géométrie des jeux de bourse. Journal des actuaires français. Tome ii. pp. 153-60.

1873. LEFÈVRE (H.). Physiologie et mécanique sociales. Journal des actuaires français. Tome ii., pp. 211-50 and 351-88.

1874. WALRAS (Léon). Principe d'une théorie mathématique de l'échange. Mémoire lu à l'Académie des sciences morale et politique (Séances des 16 et 23 août 1873). Orléans. 8vo. 24 pp.

See Preface, pp. xxxix-xl.

1874. JEVONS et WALRAS. Correspondance. Extrait du Journal des économistes (numéro du 15 juin 1874). Paris. 8vo. 8 pp.

1874. BOCCARDO (Gerolamo). Dizionario universale dell' economia politica e del commercio. Milano. 8vo.

1874. LEFÈVRE (H.). Principe de la science de la bourse. Méthode approuvée par la chambre syndicale des agents de change de Paris. Paris. 8vo. 113 pp.

1874. WALRAS (Léon). Éléments d'économie politique pure, ou théorie de la richesse sociale. Premier fascicule. Lausanne, Paris, et Bâle. 8vo. viii, 208 pp.

1874. ZANON (Giovanni Antonio). Sulla teoria matematica dello scambio del professore M. L. Walras, lettera al professore Alberto Errera. Estratto dalla Rassegna di agricoltura, industria e commercio. Padova. 8vo. 7 pp.

1874. LETORT (Charles). De l'application des mathématiques à l'étude de l'économie politique. L'Économiste français, 31 octobre 1874, p. 540.

1874. D'AULNIS DE BOUROUILL (Johan). Het Inkomen der Maatschappij. Eene Proeve van theoretische Staathuishoudkunde. *Leiden.* 8vo. xiii, 215 pp.

1874. LEFÈVRE (H.) Physiologie et mécanique sociales. Journal des actuaires français. Tome iii., pp. 93-118.

1874. DORMOY (Emile). Les Matières premières. Établissement des coefficients d'élaboration. Journal des actuaires français. Tome iii., pp. 142-162.

1874. AVIGDOR (Septime N.) Question d'économie sociale. Journal des actuaires français. Tome iii. pp. 300-306.

1875. JEVONS (W. Stanley). The progress of the mathematical theory of Political Economy, with an explanation of the principles of the theory. Transactions of the Manchester Statistical Society ; pp. 1-19. 8vo. (Read Nov. 11, 1874.)

1875. DARWIN (George H.) The Theory of Exchange Value. Fortnightly Review. New series. Vol. xvii., pp. 243-53.

A review of "Some Leading Principles of Political Economy Newly Expounded" by J. E. Cairnes, so far as relates to the mathematical theory of economics. The article resolves itself into a defence of this work [*The Theory of Political Economy*] against Cairnes' unfortunate misapprehensions, and is of great importance as coming from the pen of an accomplished mathematician. Mr. Darwin points out, moreover, that some of the more original and important doctrines of Cairnes are really consistent with the results of the mathematical theory.

1875. BOCCARDO (Gerolamo). Del metodo in economia politica. Estratto dal Giornale degli economisti. *Padova.* 8vo. 23 pp.

1875. BOCCARDO (Gerolamo). L' Economia politica odierna come scienza e come ordinamento sociale. Introduzione generale alla Biblioteca dell' Economista. 3ª série, pp. 1-43.

1875. ERRERA (Alberto). Appunto bibliografico. Éléments d'économie politique pure par Léon Walras. Estratto dal giornale La Perseveranza. *Milano.* 18mo. 16 pp.

1875. BOCCARDO (Gerolamo). Dell' applicazione dei metodi

quantitativi alle scienze economiche, statistiche e sociali. Saggio di logica economica. Prefazione al 2° volume della Biblioteca dell' Economista, pp. i-lxxii.

1875. WHEWELL (W.) Esposizione matematica di alcune dottrine di economia politica. Due memorie. Biblioteca dell' Economista. 3ª serie. Vol. ii., pp. 1-65.

1875. COURNOT (Agostino). Ricerche intorno ai principii matematici della teorica delle ricchezze. Biblioteca dell' Economista. 3ª serie. Vol. ii., pp. 67-170.

1875. JEVONS (W. Stanley). La Teorica dell' economia politica. Biblioteca dell' Economista. 3ª serie. Vol. ii., pp. 173-311.

1875. NEWCOMB (Simon). North American Review, No. ccxlix. Review of Cairnes' Logical Method of Political Economy.

1875. PIERSON (N. G.) Grondbeginselen der Staatthuishoudkunde. Harlem. 1875-6. 2 vols.

1875. ACHARD (M. A.) Influence des taxes qui frappent les obligations sur leur prix d'après un taux déterminé. Journal des actuaires français. Tome iv. pp. 70-4.

1875. FONTANEAU (E.). Principes de chrématistique. Journal des actuaires français. Tome iv. pp. 75-83 et 151-72.

The problems resolved by M. Avigdor, having attracted the attention of those who believe in the possibility of applying calculation to political economy, M. Fontaneau, without at present undertaking a theoretical examination of the principles of political economy, shows how certain problems of various difficulty are susceptible of mathematical treatment.

His first is an ingenious and elegant problem, but it is quite evident that it rests purely upon assumed premises, which in all probability will not correspond with the conditions of any particular market, except by accident.

In his second problem, M. Fontaneau treats a society composed of four groups of persons, each of whom applies himself to the production respectively of four commodities. He comes to the conclusion that the price of each unit of commodity is directly proportional to the *total monetary sum*, and to the number of labourers who equally co-operate in its production ; it is inversely proportional to the square of the total number of consumers. The mathematics of M. Fontaneau is good, but the political economy is purely arbitrary or hypothetical.

His second paper (pp. 151-72) contains some much more complicated, and, if anything, less real problems.

1875. LAURENT (H.). Démonstration simple du principe de M. Menier. Journal des actuaires français. Tome iv. pp. 84-7. (Also printed in Menier's Théorie et application de l'impôt sur le capital. 2me éd. *Paris.* 1875. 12mo. Appendice, pp. 607-12.)

1875. FONTANEAU (E.). De la valeur. Journal des actuaires français. Tome iv., pp. 175-99, 267-77.

These two papers form a continuation of those on Chrematistics already described. The author starts from the mathematical expression of value $V_q = \dfrac{Q\omega}{s}$, and works out the result at considerable length. I regret to come to the conclusion that his essays cannot compare in value with those of Cournot with which he manifests acquaintance. M. Fontaneau appears to be not conversant with other recent works on the mathematical theory of political economy.

1875. FALCK (G. von). Die Thünensche Lehre vom Bildungsgesetz des Zinsfusses und vom naturgemässen Arbeitslohn. *Leipzig.* 55 pp.

1876. WALRAS (Leone). Un Nuovo Ramo della matematica. Dell' applicazione delle matematiche all' economia politica. Estratto dal Giornale degli economisti. *Padova.* 8vo. vol. iii. Fascicolo N.I. Aprile 1876. 40 pp.

1876. WALRAS (Léon). Équations de l'échange. Équations de la production. Mémoires lus à la Société vaudoise des sciences naturelles. (Séances des 1er et 15 décembre 1875, 19 janvier et 16 février 1876.) *Lausanne.* 8vo. 66 pp.

1876. ZAMBELLI (Andrea). La Teoria matematica dello scambio del signor Leone Walras. Lettera diretta al prof. Errera dott. Alberto. *Padova.* 8vo. 28 pp.

1876. JEVONS (W. Stanley). The Future of Political Economy. Fortnightly Review, November 1, 1876. Vol. xx., pp. 617-31.

1876. WALRAS (Léon). Équations de la capitalisation. Mémoire lu à la Société vaudoise des sciences naturelles (Séance du 5 juillet 1876). 8vo. 40 pp.

1876. FONTANEAU (E.) Chrématistique — développements et applications. Journal des actuaires français. Tome v., pp. 70-96, 341-65.

Here again we have much ingenious analysis, but with certain exceptions, as, for instance, the theory of foreign exchanges, treated much in the manner of Cournot. Fontaneau's doctrines are arbitrary and speculative.

1876. MADSEN (C. L.) Den Sandsynlige Lov for den internationale Telegraftrafik. *Copenhagen.* 8vo.

[1876. WESTERGAARD (Harald). Den moralske Formue og det moralske Haab. Tidsskrift for Mathematik.]

1877. MADSEN (C. L.) Nye Undersögelser om Loven for den internationale Trafik. Geografisk Tidskrift. 1ste Bind, pp. 192-201.

1877. MADSEN (C. L.) Recherches sur la loi du mouvement télégraphique internationale. *Copenhagen, Paris.* 8vo. ix, 68 pp., avec 10 tableaux.

1877. JEVONS (W. Stanley). Le Passé et l'avenir de l'économie politique. Les méthodes. Les économistes contemporains. Le Political Economy club. Journal des économistes, Mars 1877. 3e série. Tome xlv., pp. 325-42.

1877. WALRAS (Léon). Éléments d'économie politique pure, ou théorie de la richesse sociale. Deuxième fascicule, pp. 209-407. *Lausanne, Paris, et Bâle.* 8vo.

1877. MOLL (L. A.) Der Werth. Eine neue Theorie desselben. *Leipzig.* 48 pp.

1878. WESTERGAARD (Harald). Den Sandsynlige Lov for den internationale Telegraftrafik. Anmeldt af H. W. Nationaloekonomisk Tidsskrift. Bind xi. *Copenhagen.* 8vo.

1878. DU MESNIL-MARIGNY. L'Économie politique devenue science exacte ou les libre-échangistes et les protectionnistes conciliés. 3e édition. *Paris.* 8vo. 413 pp.

1878. WALRAS (Leone). Teoria matematica della richezza sociale. Quattro memorie lette all' Accademia delle science morali e politiche, a Parigi, ed alla Società Valdese delle scienze naturali, a Losanna. Biblioteca dell' Economista. 3a serie. Vol. ii., pp. 1289-1388.

1878. WEISZ (Dr. Bela, of Budapesth, Hungary). Die mathematische Methode in der Nationalökonomie. Hildebrandt's Jahrbücher für Nationalökonomie und Statistik ; vol. xxxi., pp. 295-316. *Jena.*

1878 NICOLINI. Un antico Economista matematico (Ceva).

Giornale degli economisti ; vol. viii. fasc. 1. Oct. *Padova.*
8vo.

[1878. MADSEN (C. L.), and Westergaard (H.) Correspondence
Nationaloekonomisk Tidsskrift.]

[1878. MADSEN (C. L.). Den Sandsynlige Lov og den internationale Telegraftrafik. Nationaloekonomisk Tidsskrift ;
Bind xi., pp. 171-83.]

[1878. MADSEN (C. L.). On the Law of International Telegraph
Traffic. Journal of the Society of Telegraph Engineers.
London.]

1879. MADSEN (C. L.) Danmarks, Sveriges og Norges
Samkvem med Udlandet. *Copenhagen.* 1871-7. xxiv, 26
pp. 4to.

1879. VAN DEN BERG (C. P. J.) De Theorie van het arbeids-
loon. *Utrecht.* 35 pp. 8vo.

[1879. S. De la mesure de l'utilité des chemins de fer.
Journal des économistes.]

1879. MARSHALL (Alfred). The Pure Theory of Foreign Trade.
The Pure Theory of Domestic Values. *Cambridge.* 8vo.
Privately printed.

1879. MARSHALL (Alfred, and Mary Paley). The Economics
of Industry. *London.* 18mo. xiv, 231 pp.

1879. WALRAS (Léon). Théorie mathématique du billet de
banque. Bull. Soc. Vaud. Sci. Nat. ; vol. xvi., 83 pp.
8vo.

APPENDIX VI

Extension of List of Mathematico-Economic Writings

1880. WALRAS (Léon). Théorie Mathématique du Prix des
Terres et de Leur Rachat par l'État. *Bull. Soc. Vaud.
Sc. Nat.* xxii, 85, 8vo.

[1880. SCHAFFLER (Hermann). Ueber die Normirung der
Einkommensteuer. *Vierteljahrsschrift für Volkswirth-
schaft und Culturgeschichte.*]

1880. BERG (C. P. J. van den). The Theory of Wages.
Translated from the Dutch. 25 pp. 8vo. *London.*

1881. EDGEWORTH (F. Y.) Mathematical Psychics. An
Essay on the Application of Mathematics to the Moral
Sciences 8vo. *London.* viii, 150 pp.

1881. GIDE (Charles). La Théorie de l'économie politique
de M. Stanley Jevons. *Journal des Economistes.* Nov.
Pp. 179-191.

[1881. SACHER (Eduard). Grundzüge einer Mechanik des
Gesellschaft. I. Theoretischer Theil. *Jena.* 246 pp. 8vo.]

1881. WALRAS (Léon). Théorie Mathématique du Bimé-
tallisme. *Paris.* 8vo.

1881. WALRAS (Léon). Mathematische Theorie de Preis-
bestimmung der Wirthschaftlichen Güter, Vier Denk-
schriften, etc. Translated by Ludwig von Winterfeld.
Stuttgart.

1882. LAUNHARDT (Wilhelm). Der zweckmässigste Standort
einer gewerblichen Anlage. Zeitschrift des Vereins
deutscher Ingenieure.

1882. WALRAS (Léon). De la Fixité de Valeur de l'Etalon
Monétaire. *Journal des Economistes.* October. 8vo.

1883. EDGEWORTH (F. Y.) The Method of Ascertaining a Change in the Value of Gold. *Journ. Statistical Society, London,* vol. xlvi, pp. 714-718.

1883. LAUNHARDT (Wilhelm). Wirthschaftliche Fragen des Eisenbahnwesens. Centralblatt der Bauverwaltung.

1883. WALRAS (Léon). Théorie mathematique de la Richesse sociale. 253 pp. 4to. *Lausanne.*

1884. EDGEWORTH (F. Y.) The Rationale of Exchange. *Journ. Statistical Society, London,* vol. xlvii, pp. 164-166.

1884. POYNTING (J. H.) A Comparison of the Fluctuations in the Price of Wheat, and in Cotton and Silk Imports into Great Britain. *Jour. Statistical Society, London,* vol. xlvii, pp. 34-64.

1884. WALRAS (Léon). Monnaie d'Or avec Billon d'Argent Regulateur. *Bruxelles.* 8vo.

1884. PIERSON (N. G.) Leerboek der Staathuishoudkunde. Erste deel. *Haarlem.*

1884. WIESER (F. von). Ueber den Ursprung und die Hauptgesetze des wirthschaftlichen Werthes. *Wien.*

1884. HOUDARD (Adolphe). Théorie générale de la valeur. Journal des Economistes.

1884. WICKSTEED (Philip H.) Das Kapital. A Criticism. Today, Oct. *London.*

1884. GIDE (Charles). Principes d'economie politique. *Paris.*

1885. WALRAS (Léon). D'une Methode de Régularisation de la Variation de Valeur de la Monnaie. *Bull. Soc. Vaud. Sc. Nat.* 22 pp. 8vo.

1885. SIMON (Alfred) and WALRAS (Léon). Contribution à l'étude des variations des prix. *Bull. Soc. Vaud. Sc. Nat.* 11 pp. 8vo.

1885. LAUNHARDT (Wilhelm). Mathematische Begründung der Volkswirthschaftslehre. *Leipsig.* viii, 216 pp. 8vo.

1885. LAUNHARDT (Wilhelm). Das Wesen des Geldes. *Leipsig.* vi. 75 pp. 8vo.

1886. GROSSMAN. Die Mathematik im Dienste der Nationalökonomie. 1ste Lieferung. 80 pp. 4to. *Vienna.*

1886. NEWCOMB (Simon). Principles of Political Economy. 8vo. *New York.* xvi, 543 pp.

1886. BOEHM-BAWERK. Grundzüge der Theorie des Wirtschaftlichen Güterwerts. *Jahrbücher für Nationalökonomie und Statistik* N. F. Band xiii. *Jena.*

1886. PIERSON (N. G.) Grondbeginselen der Staathuishoudkunde Tweede Druk. *Haarlem.*

1886. FEAUVEAU (G.) Études sur les Premiers Principes de la Science Économique. *Journal des Economistes.*

1886. ANTONELLI (G. B.) Sulla Teoria Mathematica della economica politica. *Pisa.*

1886. WALRAS (Léon). Théorie de la Monnaie. 8vo. xii, 120 pp. *Lausanne.*

1886. GROSSMANN (Ludwig). Die Mathematik im Dienste der Nationalökonomie. II Lieferung. *Vienna.*

1887. EDGEWORTH (F. Y.) On the Method of ascertaining and measuring Variations in the Value of the Monetary Standard. Report of the British Association for the Advancement of Science.

1887. EDGEWORTH (F. Y.) Metritike, or the Method of measuring Probability and Utility. *London:* Temple Co.

1887. AIKIN-KAROLY. Solutions nouvelles de deux Questions Fondamentales d'Économie Sociale. *Revue d'Economic Politique.*

1887. LAUNHARDT (Wilhelm). Theorie des Trassirens. Heft I. Die kommerzielle Trassirung. Second Edition. iv, 112 pp. *Hannover.*

1887. HELM (G.) Die Bisherigen Versuche Mathematik auf Volkswirthschaftliche Fragen anzuwenden. *Ges. Isis. in Dresden.* Abh. I. 13 pp.

1887. VAN DORSTEN (Dr. R. K.) Mathematische onderzoekingen op het gebied der Staathuishoudkunde. Ar chief voor politieke en sociale rekenkunde, 1ste deel, 3de en 4de aflevering.

1887. WESTERGAARD (H.) Mathematiken i Nationalökomiens Tjeneste. In the volume Smaaskrifter Tilegnede A. F. Krieger. *Copenhagen.*

1887. PANTALEONI (Maffeo). Teoria della pressione tributaria e metodi per misurarla. Parte prima Teoria della pressione tributaria. 78 pp. *Roma.*

1888. EDGEWORTH (F. Y.) The Mathematical Theory of Banking. *Jour. Statistical Society, London,* March 1888.

1888. WICKSTEED (Philip H.) The Alphabet of Economic Science. I. Elements of the Theory of Value or Worth. *London.*

THE END